Seasons of Wisdom

– Selected Talks from the Annual Sufi Conferences –

Shaykh Fadhlalla Haeri

Zahra Publications

Zahra Publications

ISBN-13 (Printed Version): 978-1-92-832945-9

First Edition Published by Zahra Publications
Distributed and Published by Zahra Publications
PO Box 50764
Wierda Park 0149 Centurion
South Africa
www.zahrapublications.pub

Designed and typeset in South Africa by Quintessence Publishing
Cover Design by Quintessence Publishing
Project Management by Quintessence Publishing

Set in 12 point on 17 point, Adobe Garamond Pro

Seasons of Wisdom

– Selected Talks from the Annual Sufi Conferences –

Shaykh Fadhlalla Haeri

Zahra Publications

TABLE OF CONTENTS

8. THE QUR'AN'S UNIVERSAL MESSAGE: A MERCY FOR ALL THE WORLDS

9. THE ORIGINAL MEANING OF SACRED MESSAGES I..........209

10. THE ORIGINAL MEANING OF SACRED MESSAGES II........221

PUBLISHER'S NOTE

Seasons of Wisdom is mostly collated from the closing unscripted talks given by Shaykh Fadhlalla Haeri to seal the annual conferences held by the Academy of Self Knowledge in South Africa. Two talks from one year have been included, one from the closing talk, but the other given after the main *dhikr* event at the gathering, while another was the opening address. The transcripts have been edited for the purpose of print, with sub-headings added for ease of navigation or locating specific topics, and reflect the rich array of spiritual themes anchoring each gathering.

Established by Shaykh Fadhlalla Haeri in 2003, the Academy offered online courses, resource materials and workshops in self-knowledge, focusing on the cosmology of the human being by laying out the mapping of the self and soul according to the wisdom heritage of Islam and Sufism. For over 17 years annual gatherings were also held with participants joining in from all over the world, to explore themes, such as: Living Islam, Voices of Wisdom from our Past, Global Spirituality Today, Gnostics and Politics, the Power of Prayer, Devotion and Worship of the Unseen, Celebrating Life through Sacred Expressions, Celebrating the Universal Message of the Qur'an, Humanity and Divinity, and From Darkness to Light.

PREFACE

Some three decades ago I visited South Africa and realized it might be right destination for me to move to from England, as I was not interested in the Western state of culture or development. My natural attraction has always been for emerging countries, without denying the rise in human consciousness and the inevitable complexities that evolving life brings about.

It was my love for Qur'an that brought about a situation of regularly sharing commentaries and delights in the eternal Truth that whatever is known and unknown emanates from one Cosmic Source that is not subject to space or time. A few friends and students I had from the past and new ones in South Africa began to visit and that led to an annual gathering at the centre outside Pretoria, covering different aspects of human concern. The various themes of these gatherings emanate from the Eternal Light and lead to it. They are presented here with some minor editing and rearrangements.

Shaykh Fadhlalla Haeri

CHAPTER ONE

Living Islam

Given in 2002

Living Islam has many dimensions. You use your '*aql* (reason), you use your tongue, your heart, your state and your light. It is light upon light. If you do not do that, you are not alive. It is as simple as that.

Living Islam means living its full dimensionality. You have multi-faceted attentions - directions, objectives, needs, wants. However, 'living' implies being with the Ever-Living—*al-Hayy*. How do you delineate, how do you put bounds on, how do you define the Ever-Living? He has de-signed and created the definitions and boundaries. He is *al-Kāmil* —the Complete and Perfect. That is why all of us are desperately impassioned by the love of that perfection.

The great Moroccan *Walī*, Abu Madyan (1126-1198CE), whose influence has been most profound, says that to reach perfection we must use what is understandable by ordinary people. You will never be able to reach that perfection, for that perfection has already reached you. You will never be able to see Him, for He has seen you already. Stop seeing, and see *by* Him. He says, 'My servant gets closer to Me by his deeds, his obligations, his service, his correct actions until I become the eye by which he sees.'

Sight is a minuscule aspect of the divine quality of seeing. Hearing is the same. Knowing is the same. Knowledge is a tiny aspect of His unfathomable knowing—which is beyond time and space. It is an immense affair. That is why we feel completely pulverised by the call of '*Allahu Akbar*' (God is most great). Allah is greater than we can ever perceive, conceive, or imagine. So that is why the true living Muslim is humbled. Through that humility, Allah elevates your inner state such that it is illuminated.

THE STORY OF ZAM ZAM

It is said that Hajar was desperate for water. By Allah's mercy a bit of wet-ness at the foot of Ismail became a gushing stream of water. Rather than relief, Hajar's anxiety as a mother surfaced even more. First she was Allah's creation, Allah's manifestation in a human situation, then suddenly she became a mother and cried out, 'Stop! Stop! *Zamzami!* Gather! Gather!'

Our Prophet said were it not for that, Zam Zam would have become a river running from Makkah to the Red Sea. We too experience the same anxiety. We too become overwhelmed; we stop the flow. Do not stop the *rahma*, the mercy or blessing, which comes to you because you want to tell somebody or want to be acknowledged. Allah has already acknowledged you. You have been created! What more is it that you are trying to prove and to whom?

Relax and let the main project take its course. The birds do it. The trees do it. The insects do it. Let the river take its course. Its fruit is the knowledge that though you do not know, you will come to know. So, relax! The work is already done. Enter that abode of inner sanctity, of eternal silence. Living Islam is to live beyond time and space and yet acknowledge time and space.

Do not deny physicality either. Do not deny that you are a human being in need of this shell. Do not deny the outer. If you deny the outer, you will be, by definition, denying the inner. There cannot be anything in this existence unless it contains both. Allah says in the Qur'an that of everything He has created a pair; therefore, there cannot be in this existence any experience or any aspect without its opposite.

ENTANGLEMENT WITH *DUNYA*

It is Allah's *rahma* (mercy) upon us that in this age people can take the time and trouble to get away from the enslavement and strangulation of the day-to-day demands of physical and material existence. It will become rarer and more infrequent because of the monolithic monoculture of *dunya* (the entangling material world). All of it is about this world, your education, your home. The sooner you get something, the more immediately you need something else, and this is how the spiral spins into its conclusion of self-destructiveness.

So, it is a big gift for us to be able to meet people who question the totality of this existence. What is death? Why do we want harmony? Why do we want well-beingness? From where do we get this desire?

What are desires? What are good desires? What are not? How does one deal with one's inner confusion? How does one deal with other human beings? What is this 'thing' that is beyond us? Why did He create us like this? Where is perfection? Where is imperfection? Who am I? Who are you? What is the difference between us?

WE ARE ESSENTIALLY LIGHT

As Muslims, we have been gifted with all these answers. However, the answer must transform, not end up simply informing and creating more religious divisions. For centuries we Muslims have benefited from this discernment: that you are light. From that light emanates multiple, transformed and different versions of light (including even metals)—nothing other than light. What are these solids but electrons streaming around with enormous spaces in them?

We have been given all this. We have been shown this by the way and life of the great ones, by the Prophet and his followers, family, and the great enlightened beings. Before the glorious Prophet, thousands had discovered that they were essentially manifested in this realm of existence as Adamic beings, as a grace, a gift from this infinite, unfathomable, pure light called God, or Allah, or the Divine, manifesting and cascading into infinite creations. This has been so from time immemorial.

Why are we then under these tyrannical shadows of misconceptions, deceptions, illusions and delusions? It is because we have not 'read.' Allah commands us to read: '*Iqra!*' To read the truth. The truth never changes. Every reality has in it an aspect of truth. It is real that we are sitting here, but in two hours' time, it will not be true anymore as we will have moved. It is true that you are listening now, but close your ears, and you will *not* hear. Do not deny this reality. Do not deny the reality of the moment, but these realities change with time.

IDENTITY AND *RŪH*

You and I, he and she, and every creation on this earth, is driven towards the ultimate truth that does not change in time. Truth is beyond time and space and has brought about this basket of time and space that we are now experiencing. We are prisoners, and the prison is the divine precinct, and the master of prisoners is also the liberator and is called Allah. However, once you identify with the so-called I—I have an identity, I was born, I have a beginning, I have an end, I am this fellow, I am the father, I am the teacher—then you are veiled by that identity.

So the path of Living Islam is to see that identity, embrace these so-called blockages and go *through* them. Do not let them become stumbling blocks. Step on them and go higher. Do not let the body be your final miserable destination. It is already dead! The cell is on its way to recycling and change. Indeed, no cell ever remains in the body for more than few years. Most cells renew themselves every few hours or every few days. Accept who you are, where you are now, and move according to Allah's programme.

Allah's programme says: 'I was a hidden treasure and I loved to be known, and thus I created' *(hadīth qudsī)*. The programme is to know Allah. It is to start where you are, with the knowledge or the experience of your own state, and yearn for that inner awakening in you that is beyond description. This is what we call joy or bliss. It is the kind of happiness that is perpetually available to you. Allah's *rahma* is to avoid misery. So, avoid it!

This programme means you are already sitting within the precinct of the inner garden. If you do not practice the gardenic state now, then you will be in turmoil after you leave the body, because you are not the body. So we have this incredible cosmology which reveals that essentially all human beings are *rūh*, which is an energy or aspect of light which we cannot define or delineate. It is by grace, mercy, and the command of Allah that there is this *rūh* .

Rūh is related to the Arabic root of 'perfume' *(rā'iha)*. It also shares the same root for 'breeze' *(rīh)*, and the verb meaning 'to depart'. In other words, it is pure spirit or light activating mud to create this full entity of the human being which contains within it multi-faceted forms (or paradigms, or holograms) of the entire cosmos. You would never be able to understand the bird diving down onto a worm for its breakfast, unless that model is in you. You would never be able to understand the cry of a mother who has lost her child, the grief of separation, unless that flavour is in you. You would never be able to see colours, never be able to hear, if all was not within you. However, because you have constantly been preoccupied with other things, this most important priority—understanding who you really are—has not been given attention.

TRADITIONAL EDUCATION

A hundred years ago in the Muslim world, any decent, wholesome being from a self-respecting God-fearing family would have by the age of eight or nine known the Qur'an. By the age of twelve, they would have known the *shari'a* and the way of the Prophet. By the age of sixteen, they would have moved onto other things, other skills, whatever they may have been. Amongst our greatest saints were carpenters, cloth-makers, perfumers. Their names give clues to their professions: Al-Hallaj (d.922 CE), for example, was none other than the man who beat cotton to puff up the fibres. They were equipped with the cosmology of being-ness and therefore 'living Islam' for them was not talked about: it was lived.

Now we are in the most unfortunate situation where we have to dig everywhere to find the gems amongst the debris of disinformation, misinformation and a lot of other half-baked, half-regurgitated stuff. It is for this reason that so many of the young generation of Muslims are angry and disappointed. That is why so many of them want to believe in the hegemony of this *kufr* (denial of reality) system: there is only this life so go for it – more pleasure, yet more pleasure, and by the age of 24, if you haven't made your millions, you are not cool. Burning hot inside, but cool outside. You need connectivity every second so you don't miss something. Once you get it, you lose something else.

Look at people's lives; look at people you or your parents may have known, those who have gained wealth. You will find that they are never better off. Invariably they are worse off. Why? Where is Allah's mercy? Why is it people start off simple and generous? If you were to visit their village, you would see how generously they share. However, if you give the fellow a small house in Lahore you'll then see a different side. Suddenly he wants a bigger house, two cars; then the children have to go to private schools, then he needs three cars. It never ends, until he ends up being the prime minister.

FLASHES OF LIGHT FROM THE *RŪH*

What causes this sliding scale whose end is burning inside and outside? The answer is already in our heritage. Allah says: *'To me belongs all that you are seeking, all of the great attributes are mine and I have created you in my image to yearn for these.'* [see e.g. 7:180, 17:110]

A flash of that light is already within us. Those flashes are in your *rūh (soul/ spirit)*. Your *rūh* knows what glory, wealth, and beyond wealth are. It knows what contentment is and what is beyond contentment. These are attributes of Allah. Allah has no needs. You and I have needs, so He hooks us into the zone of inner contentment. All of those great attributes have their flashes or reflections in our heart. I say the 'heart' because the heart is the home of the *rūh*. That is why the heart has to be clear and clean. Otherwise your *rūh* will not rule over your *nafs* (ego-self).

All of these cosmologies are available to us. What you and I need is to spend a bit of time, to reflect upon them, digest them, and be transformed by them. The human makeup has light beyond description as well as attitudes, emotions or possibilities that are at the same time the lowest of the low. What an incredible entity this thing called 'self' is! It is a cosmic jelly that can contain all the infinite varieties of possibilities of emanations.

If you tune in to that waveband, it will come back to you. If you tune in to the ultimate waveband of light in you, you will be in delight!

You will not even be able to talk about it, and that is the correct nourishment of the heart. If you do not produce that constant nourishment of the heart that goes beyond description, then you are sick. Otherwise, you will yearn for some outer pleasure to replace it.

We all love a bit more pleasure. We crave beautiful scenery but the air is now so polluted and the horizon filled with concrete that you can no longer see any 'nice' scenery! Now you have to look to the inner garden, because the outer is artificial. Several years ago on a beautiful Hawaiian island they had to remove all the coconuts because everybody was suing the municipality—they would drop on peoples' heads! So they replaced them all with plastic coconuts. By now they may have replaced the human beings with plastic versions because the real ones can be so troublesome.

DUNYA: MIMICRY OF THE DIVINE

The reason we all run after *dunya* (this world) is that it mimics the divine. You love wealth because you love the Rich beyond need (*al-Ghani*). You love power because you love the most Strong (*al-Qawi*, or *al-Qadir*). So, it is a bit perverted: you've taken a wrong turn on the map, that's all. Stop your vehicle, think, look back, reverse, and return. Allah is Ever-forgiving, Allah is Ever-there, but are *you* present? Are you aware of what you are doing? Why are you doing it? Blame yourself. Take responsibility. Stop blaming others.

Everyone seems to have a list of complaints. It shows that they are disappointed. Why are you disappointed? Why aren't you re-appointed? You are seeking the right thing: bliss, constant access to joy, unconditional pure beingness—living Islam. It is because you are looking for the right thing in the wrong place. You are looking to your wife to save you from your own tyranny. You are looking to your boss to give you whatever you think you deserve.

The reason there is so much anger now amongst Muslims is because we have mixed up the Divine Pattern with a tradition, a culture, or with other religious inheritances.

ISLAM AND MUSLIMS

Separate Islam, and the perfection it offers to all the Adamic beings, from the conduct of Muslims, and you will then understand. We have collectively inherited a lot of past preconceptions, misconceptions, and all sorts of things that were appropriate at a certain time, but no longer. So, you can forgive your parents and the past generations and move on. If we do not forgive and move on, we will have millions of gatherings just condemning the past people, their atrocities, the dreadful leadership of Muslims, the tyranny they have brought about and how they have deviated from the way of the Prophet.

That may have been so, but what can we do about it now? We are only responsible for delivering ourselves to our Maker. First deliver yourself to Him Who has created you. Deliver yourself to Him Who is ever-present, Who will remain after we have gone to Him, Who is before us and is uncontaminated, Who is the carrier of all perfections that we are passionate about. That is what you should care about. That is why, throughout the history of humankind, people took to the mountains and hills, to isolation, so that they could rekindle this original light that was already there.

SUFI TEACHINGS

The most important qualification for gnosis, arrival, enlightenment, and awakening is sincerity and honesty. Once you read some of the books written by the great ones, you'll be confused at best. The great ones include Abu Madyan (d.1198 CE) and Ibn 'Arabi (d.1240 CE) because they have been truly, fully, and ultimately freed from illusions. They speak in the voice of *haqq* (truth), and *haqq* addresses everyone. It addresses the starter on the path and the one who is almost at its peak. Take what is appropriate for you. Do not get confused.

To share an example. So many of our great masters say, '*Do not be a beloved, be a lover.*' Equally, you find the reverse injunction: '*Be a beloved, do not be a lover*'. So what do you do? Both are true. If you are starting, you must love. You must love those who are ahead of you in the knowledge of truth. You must love them, adore them, die for them because you cannot yet die for Allah. Die for that which you can perceive as a means, an example, and a possible lighter of your candle.

One of the great aspects of the Chishti *tariqa* is the practice of *fanā' fi'l-Shaykh,* or 'dying in your Shaykh'. Until 100 years ago, it was fully meaningful but not anymore. It is now comparable to replacing political or economical tyranny, or the bank's tyranny, with the Shaykh's tyranny, be-cause our time is different. Therefore, you have to start as a lover of that which is higher than you, until you begin to have flashes of the knowledge that you are His beloved.

You are already loved by Allah, otherwise why would you be like this? He could have created you as a worm. You could have been a wasp. Why not? Instead, He has created you as Adam, and Adam contains all the different forms of knowledge that angels do not know. The angels nearly went on strike, but there were no unions then. They said, 'What is this that you have created? This entity is going to cause havoc.' They knew what was going to happen. Everywhere you go, half of this world are people who can barely subsist. Then you have 5% who are barely able to deal with the luxuries they have.

MAP OF OUR TIMES

How can there be justice in the world when there is such divergence between humanity? So we as Muslims have to read the appropriate map of the day. I have some old maps of Africa which are more than 300 years old. The only roads you can find in them are elephant trails. These major elephant trails have now become the main highways because at that time the elephants made the road much straighter than people could. However, nowadays those maps are no good for me if I want to go to Lusaka.

You need a map that gives you the right direction, appropriate to the time that you are living in. The values, needs and desires do not change. The way to fulfil them changes. The Prophet used to have the best of mounts because he was the servant of Allah. He wanted to get from point A to point B with the least disturbance, so Allah made it possible for him to have the best of mounts. Now I would be foolish if I come to you every morning riding a horse. With traffic fumes, the poor horse will die. It is not about the horse or the car. It is about getting there. It is about using a vehicle that is going to cause the least disruption or trouble.

The values and objectives are the same. Clothes are there to cover us from the changing outer elements, so the inner remains more constant and steadier. The material may change. Unfortunately, all of us are now clad in these dreadful electric-shocking synthetics. The time we are living in is different to any other time before. There are a few radical changes that did not exist before.

Amongst these radical changes is the discontinuation of accountability to family and society. 50-60 years ago, members of Parliament and people who were elected to public office in Europe were held accountable by the people in their locality. They were accountable for the quality of their behaviour and conduct, charity, and goodness. However, once it became party politics, then this dynamic changed. You might be from the North-West of Britain but could be elected in Kent because your Parliamentary party wants you there; they have spotted you as a good politician. You can hide more lies without being caught by the law.

We are living in a time consisting of unique change. Parents have no more influence on children. There is no extended family to reflect human values. The grooming of the self and reforming of character is no longer important. The overwhelming *kufr* system now teaches the entire globe that you deserve the best, pamper yourself, love yourself. The bank is there to serve you: come and borrow and then be buried by your borrowing.

We are living in a different time. I consider it a time of emergency. The most important priority is to save yourself. But once you have taken that as a programme, you realise that you cannot do it alone. You must have other mirrors, ones that are a bit clearer, to enhance the spark in your heart, that original aspect of pure beingness. You need to have periods of loneliness or quietude to let your scorpions out. Don't become superstitious about whatever comes out of you. It is you! Whatever you perceive or conceive is from you. It is from your cosmology.

THE DREAM WORLD

It is for that reason the world of dreams has always been very important. Dreams are free from this illusion of physicality and materialism. They are less solid. You think that the dream world is less real but, as far as the truth is concerned, it is far more real than this one. We think it less real because it is a little bit removed from this so-called concrete reality. That 'concrete reality' is only electrons whizzing around. It is all light. The dream is more real: if you look at your dreams, you'll learn more about your state.

If you see the Prophet in your dream, it could just mean that your state is such that you want to have the companionship of people who are perfect mirrors and perfect beings. If you have seen dreadful creatures, they are also from you: it is you who have become that creature. So do not make something big out of it—I've just had *such* a dream! Does it mean everybody has to bow down before you because your 'Excellency' had some dream?

Everyone has their world. The entire perception of the outer is because of your inner. It is as simple as that. There is no outer cosmology without your inner, personal cosmology. What is needed is balance between these two. Then go beyond both because you are already beyond but you do not realise it.

READING THE CONTEXT

In the age we live in, distances have diminished—through communication or physical accessibility. As a result of this phenomenon, this is also the era of presence. Presence is now! Your contact with reality and truth is now! When we say Allah is All-Forgiving, it means not to go to the past. Looking to the past will only be useful in a simple utilitarian sense, for example, to determine which day did we travel, or which day did I plant these seeds because I want to make sure of the season.

If you look at the past emotionally, you are doomed—they did this to me, they didn't respect me, and I was kind to them, but they didn't acknowledge my kindness. There are only so many streets that can be named after politicians. How many streets can you have in a town? How many airports can you have? It is not possible to be given this acknowledgement all the time.

I have a friend in Tangier. He is a very fine man who, for about three years, helped us tremendously with Ibn 'Ajība's work. Many of my letters to him received no reply, then it turned out that the name of his street had changed from an Arabic name to 'Washington'. Some representative from America had visited Tangier and they changed the street name because it was a main street. So I was writing these letters which never went to 'Washington'. When my friend later explained how the street changed names, I asked, 'But didn't the people object?' He replied, 'Yes, since this Arabic name cannot be a street so it will be a Mosque. So now they have given the name to a Mosque.'

HUMILITY

The path of Islam is based on humility, realising your nothingness. If you truly and fully realise your nothingness, then the light of everything-ness, which is in you, will beam. This is the secret to the door of the eternal garden. Shaykh Abdul-Qadir Jilani once said (paraphrasing), 'When I approached the doors that people were knocking on to enter into Allah's *rahma*, (such as) the door of worship *('ibāda)*, there were so many people perfecting their worship, I couldn't get near that door. The same happened at the door of sacrifice and abandonment, as well as at giving and generosity. I couldn't get anywhere near those doors. Eventually I came near the door of humility and humbleness, and nobody was there, so I entered.'

How do you humble yourself? Remember death. Take heed. Do not be pompous, or seek more books, more of this, more of that. Allah sent the ultimate tyrannical man of the day, Hulagu Khan, grandson of Genghis Khan, in 1258 to Baghdad and at that time there was no place on earth as endowed with books as Baghdad. They made a whole bridge of about 2 km of books across the river Tigris. It is said that for 2 to 3 years the river still bled blood (ink) from the books.

READ YOUR INNER BOOK

Read His book: *Iqra*! Read, do not accumulate books. There are many books and Islamic studies, but Islam is buried amongst the real people of Allah. I'm not saying you may not need a book to remind you of the 'book' that is in you. It is useful, but do not be infatuated by how you produced one book, or two books. Are you free from your own tyranny? Are you free from your own illusions and insecurities? Are you free to let go of this world? Do you belong to another world? These are the key questions!

So this gathering, if Allah wills, will give you some nourishment for the state you are in. Be free from this illusion that you are this or that. These are roles. Like every other role, they get consumed too. You are acting as a talker, as a speaker, as a father, as a friend, as a mover. This is fine, but who are you? If you are not a reflector of the ultimate Divine, all these other roles are lies upon lies because they change. A lie is that which does not last whereas the truth lasts. We need presence because presence lasts forever. Presence is the moment. If you truly enter into the moment, you have entered into the timeless zone of boundless realities, and that is the purpose of all of our *'ibāda* (worship). What is the ultimate meaning of *sajda* (prostration) other than disappearing from that which appears to your sight.

Disappearing to sight means you are in the zone of insight. Then you are perfecting your *'ibāda* (worship) in what gives you that nourishment, that recharge of your batteries. Allah has given us a self-charging battery which is called the *rūh* or soul, but we consume it all the time by demands of the *nafs* (ego-self)— I want more of this and yet more. Realise that the *nafs* will constantly make its demands until it yields to the *rūh*. The *nafs* must still recognize its animal side, that in it there are these lowest of the low tendencies. Laugh at it. Do not make a big thing of it.

Stop your illusion and you'll see wonder upon wonder. Stop blaming and criticizing others. Do you want to be content and read the present-day situation? Look at the misconduct of most of us amongst humanity. Whether so-called believers or unbelievers, look at our misconduct and infatuation with the world—ever-increasing worldliness, until we are choked with excess. It is all about abstention: abstention of the heart, of your inner zest, and inner appetite.

Feed the body, *bismillah* – in the name of Allah. Allah has given you this donkey, you have to look after it. It's all about awakening to the higher in you so that the lower is put in its proper place and you can move along the map of existence in perfection, which is reflective of His Perfection. You must then learn some of the basic laws, some of Allah's rules from the Qur'an, from the way of the Prophet, so that you know that everything is in its opposite, so that you realise that you are in between, caught between the ultimate and the very limited. Learn to read the situation.

HUMAN CRISES

What is going on in the world is atrocious—the hypocrisy, the dreadful massacres—because people are not accountable in the moment. Look at what is happening in Palestine or anywhere else. *We* are doing it. Allah is allowing us to create all of these fires so we call upon His *rahma* to get us out. It is very easy to blame somebody and label them but it is not going to change them. I've known so many Muslim countries where people had a simple life, a basic, decent family life, but from among these same families quarrels and killings arose.

This is a human dilemma. This is a basic dilemma due to lack of enlightenment. So, go to the highest and you will understand the lower and then you can deal with it. If you feel you can save some people's lives, do it. Then move on until you find that you know you are seeing it all because all is within you. There is nothing in the world that you can experience or think unless a reflection of it is within you.

REAL *TAWAKKUL* AND LIVING ISLAM

So if Allah wills, each one of you will take what is appropriate for your state and station, until such time as you truly and utterly trust in Allah's ways so that you don't even talk about it. There is a big difference between talking about *tawakkul* (total reliance) and being in a state of *tawakkul*. There is a big difference between talking about inner freedom and being free. Talking about it is an expression of yearning, which is good. Allah says that those of us who are most honoured by Allah are those of us who are most in awareness of Allah's presence. Everything you do or think is recorded in you. To where then do you escape?

It is about beingness. It is about living Islam, not discussing it. Living Islam means living *fitra* (original pattern). The *fitra* of Allah is the original crack: that there is none other than the eternal light, none other than eternal light *now*. So bask in it. And there will be major changes globally because the way we have gone now is like the father who allows his children to play in the house, but once a few of the rooms are ruined the house will collapse. We are at the edge of that now. Beingness, inner human beingness, has collapsed. If the inner fortress has been completely eradicated there is no outer safety and security.

PRESCRIPTIONS

I can only thank Allah for His mercy upon us at this time and age, to be here together, not looking at colour, nationality, and background, but looking only at that which is ever-present with love and trust between us, with trust that Allah will give us more than we deserve so that we are always put to shame. When he was put on the pedestal and admired for his incredible prophetic qualities, Imam 'Ali would always say, 'O Allah make me feel humble in my heart as much as they have exalted me and lifted me up.' So that is the balance.

These are the rules of the wayfarer and I pray to Allah that all of us be given these qualities. The giver is one and the takers are many, so be courteous. Let your inner be quiet and absorb. Remind the *nafs* (lower self) of its place because the *nafs* is very treacherous and clever. Remind yourself of death and place it in front of you. One of the biggest reminders is the willingness to die. If we could have collapsible coffins it would be a great thing. In an instant you could press a button, and this thing opens and you go and lie in it. You must trick the mind, you must trick the self, for it is very tricky.

So have a good time through self-awareness. Be ashamed of yourself, if you've been childish and reacted stupidly and then regretted it. Stop that. But instantly be aware now. A gathering of people of love and light is like a room full of mirrors: even a small spark will get magnified.

POEM: OCEAN OF LIGHT

The hidden treasure is safe from intruders
The jewels reflect His perfection
and countless glorious manifestations,
dazzling sights and nourishing insights,
contained yet boundless.
Sharī'a perfecting Haqīqa,
Haqīqa manifesting as Sharīa,
apparent and hidden, timeless and in time —
two facets of one face.
Sharī'a is rational, dutiful and honest performance
following the pen of acceptance,

yielding and reading all changes in perception,

then transcends self-protective resistance

and imaginal independent existence

to realise His glorious eternal presence.

Now to enter that zone,

ever true and effulgent,

we need to cross the dark ocean

of imaginal illusions, of dusks and dawns,

and flickering images adrift

in endless space by His grace,

reading His book phrase by phrase

with no reference to veils of the past

or the reed bed that saved Moses,

disclosed by his cry.

Every entity is endowed with its path of ease

and causal growth and flow,

reason, intellect and cognition of His Light and its glow.

The bush of Moses

with countless forms, sounds, and worshippers,

reflecting His will and cascading lights,

exuding timeless love and affection,

embracing with beauty and grace

Anyone who enters the abode of His perfection.

So please, O lover of the Real,

Give up and give in with joy and contentment,

for exhaustion is the door to relief

and the price of the eternal fruit is unconditional surrender,

accompanied by joyful knowledge

in the One Who is behind all,

the Hidden, the Evident, the First and the Last,

Encompassing and permeating all.

Drown in His infinite ocean

and re-live your foreverness

in this land of His boundlessness.

LIVING BARZAKH

Every part of the glorious Qur'an presents *haqq* (truth) in its appropriate way, moving it higher and higher. It takes us away from the lower side of existence, which has its nature and reality, as it deals with physicality and form, cause and effect. Allah says everything in existence is *barzakh*. Cosmos is none other than *barzakh*. *Barzakh* is a barrier or a bridge, an entity or a reality with one part in a certain state and the other part in another state.

Like a bridge, we human beings are living the *barzakh*: *in* this world and not *of* this world. Part of you knows what gatheredness is: when your heart is gathered and content, when your mind is gathered, and you can think clearly. And then the other side is dispersed. No aspect of life exists unless it is one of two, and the human being is the *barzakh* (barrier/bridge), able to understand both, with one leading to the other.

If you seek beauty, you will come to realise that the origin of beauty is in majesty. Beauty has to do with *zāhir* (that which is manifest), majesty has to do with the *bātin* (that which is hidden). Majesty is before the creational manifestation of Allah's *kun* (God's command 'Be!'). And you understand both: you have within you both majesty *and* beauty. The more you grow in knowledge and wisdom, the more you'll find that you will have majesty inwardly and beauty outwardly. Other aspects and states will reverse it for you. So, when there is chaos, you will exhibit majesty outwardly while your inner exhibits beauty. And it moves from one to the other, but one will not overcome the other.

Knowledge and ignorance are the same. Ignorance is majesty and knowledge is beauty because it is the outer. Allah says: '

$$\text{أَلَّا تَطْغَوْا فِى ٱلْمِيزَانِ} \; (٨)$$

How can you transgress [all these dualities of] the balance (mizan)?' [55:8]

You are both. One aspect of you is beyond time and space; another aspect of you can understand all the animals and all the insects. If you deny one, you'll deny the other.

This is the ultimate gift that can be given by the Ultimate and the Most Generous Creator: all of that is encapsulated within us, in our heart. We must first remove all of these veils, which are essential earlier on, until such time as we are rendered with nothing, clear and simple. Then we see things as they are. Then we are truly *'abd Allah* (servant of Allah), a true *shāhid* (witnesser) and able to see.

For years while in Makka, the Prophet saw all the miseries and terrible discourtesies by his own family and everyone around him. He witnessed the truth. Those around him were ignorant. Once the woman who used to throw rubbish at the Prophet did not appear. The Prophet asked, 'Where is this woman?' They said she was sick, and the Prophet went to visit her. She was surprised and said, 'You've come to visit me because I'm not throwing rubbish at you?' Her astonishment made her realise the Prophet's behaviour was noble. Because he was *'abd Allah* (servant of Allah), meaning the witnesser of Allah's creation, so he was free from all of these trivialities.

ONLY ALLAH

Give them good news: there was only Allah and nothing else, and it is the same now. Allah is not contaminated by the ups and the downs. These are cascading lights from the *nūr al-anwār (light of lights)*. Everything you witness is *nūr* and is connected by the eternal thread of Allah's unique One-ness. Give them the good news: you are eternal, here for a short while, returning to that in which you are already.

You are not travelling *to* Allah: there is only Allah and that is why we say Allah is All-Forgiving. Allah is now! The only contact you have is now. The past is your own fantasy, and the future is your own anxiety. This is the good news. Give them the good news and then equally the warning that if you don't do it now, it will be too late. Don't delay it. Don't think that some other time will be easier. It will not be. The urgency is now! Corner yourself in the *mihrāb* (prayer niche). And then it all begins to come out from you.

NO *DA'WA* WITHOUT *IDHN*

Call people to Allah only if it overflows from you. These miserable people flogging *da'wa, da'wa, da'wa*. For what? If you are not content with everything that is happening and has happened, and you know the reason of it and origin of it, how can you invite others? This is the *idhn* of Allah, when your self is not there. When your *nafs* is not in the formula then Allah has given you *idhn*. When you are in it, then it is your own interference, your own project—another miserable project. If there is no one you just sing away. It does not matter. Dance your eternal dance for Allah, by Allah. Be in your *salāt*. The bird sings because it was programmed to acknowledge its Creator even if somebody was trying to shoot it. It does not matter. What matters is *you*. So, deliver yourself to the Creator and then you are in the company of the Ultimate.

We are most blessed in having openings or flashes of this journey to and in truth. Once you have flashes of this truth, you become hooked because it is in you, until these flashes and moods become nothing other than stations (*maqāms*). And then you move on and on.

THE FOUR JOURNEYS

The first facet is the journey from creation: running away from creation into the Creator. The next opening is being in the presence of the Ever-Present Creator. Then the next flash is the journey by the power of the Creator towards creation. Lastly, being amongst creation connected entirely and utterly to the Creator, without denying creation. These are the great four journeys and they do not necessarily happen in such a simplistic sequence.

Every one of us gets a glimpse of it every now and then. You suddenly see the map and realize that map is already in you. We are indeed blessed to be true 'Muhammadis' on the path of the one and only way of saving ourselves, our little planet and everything else worthy of being treasured. We are indeed blessed and should be in constant thanks and gratitude to Allah.

THIS IS A GRAND AFFAIR

It is always said that the end is as good as the beginning. If the beginning is made with the right intention, with the right foothold or direction, then doubtless the end will be as good. Our beginning and our end are encapsulated by Allah's light, by Allah's designs, by Allah's order to Be (*kun*)! If we believe that we are His creation, that we have been brought about to adore, worship, and know Him, then we truly know *lā ilāha illā'llah* —meaning there is no source other than Him. No primal entity energizes the cosmos other than the Maker of the Cosmos.

We have a wonderful tradition from our glorious Prophet who says that all of the seven heavens and the earth and what is between them, and what is beyond them—as far as Allah's immensity, the unfathomable truth of *Allahu Akbar* is concerned—are like little rings at the edge of a desert that has no end. So, the affair is a grand one. And you, I, and everyone else will absorb it according to our ability and readiness.

We human beings have the potential of knowing the ultimate, knowing the truth of *Allahu Akbar*—which is mind-boggling, heart-blowing, illuminating, and flying beyond flying. The potential is in everyone, but the key issue is readiness. A two-year-old girl is a potential grandmother, but she will have to wait for another 60 years before that potential becomes evident. A whole set of teeth will have to change, hormones will alter, and many other things will need to change for the grandmother to be realised. The potential is there but not the readiness.

It is the same with each one of us. There is the potential in us to know that our Creator is the purpose of our creation, but the readiness is not there. We need to groom the self, we need to reform character. The entire business is based on changing the traits of our character, replacing the lower qualities with Allah's ever-shining, glorious, higher qualities; recognizing our meanness and constantly visualising Allah's immense generosity that covers it.

ALLEGORY OF THE MAP OF TRUTH

The path of arrival to Allah is like the terrain on this earth: it differs from one country to another. There are valleys, rivers, canyons, deserts, oceans and so on. As a result, you find there are as many ways to Allah as there are creations, as many ways as there are breaths, according to the actual tradition. *Nafas* is breath or breathing and also means the self or soul. We come from Him, we are journeying to Him, by Him, by His mercy. The blockages are only part of His mercy for us to work at them to remove them, so that the readiness is there.

It isn't that any person has been given more potential than the other. Rather, we are given more readiness than another according to our *himma*. *Himma* is yearning to get to the point, which is already in us, which is that of truth, not changing realities. Reality, with capital R, is that which never ever changes. Therefore, no matter how high the winds are blowing around you, you have access to that central pole in you that never ever changes, because you know that this is not the end.

STRUGGLE AS A MERCY

You die. It's not a big deal. As long as you don't cause a lot of trouble for people at an inconvenient time. Each one of us must struggle in a natural way, the same way as the moth or any other creature struggles to move into another phase of their lives. It is not 'struggle' in the way of being afflicted or tested for the sake of some punishing deity—there is no such thing. Allah does not want us to be punished. He wants us to have joy upon joy. After all, according to the Prophet (S) Allah said that 'He created us for eternal happiness'.

The reason we are unhappy is part of His mercy because we have deviated. There is also an element in us that causes that unhappiness. You feel guilty. Guilt is a simple measure of the distance between your action and what could have been an appropriate action. That's guilt, no more, no less. You've done something very stupid, you could have done better, but you didn't, so now you feel guilty. It is a distance between these two points. You feel greater guilt if the distance is greater, you feel less guilt if the distance is smaller.

All of these are His perfect creational patterns. The birds obey them, the trees obey them; and the seeds dissolve their outside shell so that the inner starts its chemical changes and a part of it grows up above the soil and a part of it grows down beneath. In no more than 2-3 years it starts fruiting and the birds will come to help perpetuate it. They are all worshiping *al-Bāqī*, the Everlasting, which we also worship because we love eternity.

There was One, there is One, there will only be One, and the apparent two is only to return to the knowledge of the essence that has emanated from the One. Our path is a path of *tawhīd*.

LOVE THE HIGHER SELF

My advice to you is to love the higher self in you and despise the lower self in you. You hear many people say, 'Love yourself', while the Sufis say 'Hate [renounce] yourself'. Both are correct, but you should distinguish *which* self! The higher self in you is the generous, forgiving, patient, and selfless one. The lower self is the reverse. So love the higher in you and let that be a true reflector of the highest of all heights, Allah, and despise the lower, and see other people as better than you. And yet, do not look at others, just care for yourself. Care for the higher self in you and be respectful to others. There is room for every creation in this existence.

The only required urgency in this exercise is for you to be honest and realise that you have nothing of your own. That is why many of our great masters say, 'The garden is full of simpletons,' or, in other words, full of people who are simple at heart. They trust in Allah, they follow Allah, and that's it. But people like us who have been subjected to a bit of education, a bit of sophistication, a bit of this and that, have to re-work our thinking to realise that the higher agenda is the knowledge of the divine zone within us. And that this will come about by removing the lower zone in us.

GROOMING THE SELF

The most important step to take is reforming the self, refining it and improving our character. Spirituality is not possible if you do not work on getting rid of, or become increasingly in charge of, the lower aspect, which is in all of us. This is our duty. Allah will fulfil His part of the bargain, or of His contract, for His *nūr* is ever effulgent, but you and I must take care of the darkness.

Stop all the anger, rancour, and blame. Every difficult situation is an opportunity for us to blame *ourselves*. It's very easy to blame everybody else. But where does that leave you? You remain an older ego which is more difficult to get rid of. That is why those who have been fortunate enough in their youth to have someone to follow, to have a teacher, a master, or an enlightened father, are quite blessed.

I have seen the atrocious conditions of people in their middle age behaving worse than children. They talk about dignity but behave without it—no teaching, no *adab* (etiquette), no *tarbiya* (upbringing). Put that right first. Do not talk about your fancy dreams and visions of having talked with the prophets and so on. It is not interesting. These are mostly hallucinations. That is why Ibn 'Ata'ullah, our great master, says:

The source of every disobedience, indifference, and passion is self-satisfaction. The source of every obedience, vigilance, and virtue is dissatisfaction with one's self. It is better for you to keep company with an ignorant man dissatisfied with himself than to keep company with a learned man satisfied with himself. For what knowledge is there in a self-satisfied scholar? And what ignorance is there in an unlearned man dissatisfied with himself?

When you are in the company of someone who is considered to be the greatest '*ālim* (person of knowledge) and yet still fancies himself, run away. Whoever is supposed to be ignorant but despises the lower self knows —his knowledge is real. Our duty is to recognise our own meanness, our humbleness; and then we will see that His glory is there already.

AN UNFOLDING PROCESS

We are all at different levels. Some have only begun with half a step. Some are almost at the edge of total enlightenment. If Allah wills, as time goes by, if there are more people who desire to know their Creator before it's too late, then we can stream it. In previous times there were so many great *walis* (friends of God) among whom were many hierarchies of people who could train others. Today, however, we are living in times of emergency. That is why we must leave the doors open and say *bismillah*: whoever comes, everybody will get something. So if you have noticed discourtesies, difficulties, or certain incongruities, it is because of that. The intention, however, is good.

We try to discover our Creator. What is life, what is death, why is there confusion, where is the fusion behind confusion, where is the order in chaos? This is what we want to know. We should also realise our own position and be respectful of those who know more than us.

IMAM 'ALI'S UNVEILING

Let me give you a small gift before parting. These eight lines are from Imam 'Ali (AS), in which he says:

'Your illness is caused by yourself,
And the remedy is within yourself.
You think that you are a tiny entity,
But within you is folded the entire Cosmos.
You are the evident book
By your alphabet, by the basic patterns in you
The entire Cosmos has been constructed
So you have no need for anything outside of you
Because everything is already there, by Allah's rahma.'

CHAPTER TWO

Enlightened Islam

Given in 2003

- Islam Original
- Human Cosmology and its Relation to Truth
- Society Today
- Purpose of Existence
- Consciousness and Revealed Knowledge
- Matter and Control
- The Heritage of Divine Attributes
- The Love of Longevity
- All *Rūh* but Differentiated
- Inhabited versus the Habit
- Be One to Know Oneness
- Love is the Foundation
- The Confused Muslim
- Know Truth by Exclusion
- *Shari'a* and *Haqiqa*
- The Place of Discrimination
- The Vice of Structuralism
- No Otherness
- Die Before You Die
- Maps of the Inner and Outer
- The Onus is on You
- Courtesies of the Maps
- Signs on the Horizon and Within
- Destiny
- The Ultimate Recollection
- Apparent Loss and Inner Success
- Stress & Refining the Self
- Appropriateness or *Adab*
- Inner Attainment
- Poem: Inner Sight
- Stillness and Awareness
- Poem: Effulgent Treasure
- A Prescription: The Ease after Difficulty

ISLAM ORIGINAL

I thank the One and Only Creator, and Maker of all that we know, and do not know. I thank the One Who has made it possible for us to be together so we realise that separateness and individuality are only an aspect of the One-ness and gathered-ness.

It is very important for every one of us to have a reflector, to be able to reflect upon another layer of consciousness. We all go through this life seeking perfection. We seek perfection until we realise that perfection has been seeking us. Allah has created us in order to know Him, to worship and adore Him. That is where so many people throughout ages have been amazed by this situation where the seeker and the sought meet or inter-change as in a union.

In reality there is only One-ness, one Source, one Light from which other lights emanate, manifest, and cascade. That is why all those who truly sought this knowledge were considered to be in submission and in Islam. We have been taught, therefore—by our teachers and people of our heritage, by all the prophets, all messengers of Islam—to accept, submit, and be truthful and honest at all levels. You submit to your pain and yet you want to get out of it; you recognise it, but you want to reach a point of equilibrium, balance, and homoeostasis, because you are programmed to want to transcend the consciousness of the body.

HUMAN COSMOLOGY AND ITS RELATION TO TRUTH

We all have these amazing 'bandages' without which we would not have realised what life is about. You have a body, all the senses, a mind, emotions, but at the end of the day, all of this is activated and energized by another entity which is called your soul.

I use 'soul' for the equivalent of what some other people might call 'spirit'. In Arabic, this most profound language which can convey both the material as well as the immaterial (or the unseen), it is called *rūh* (spirit/ soul). The root of it is from the same root for 'breeze' and also 'perfume', 'fragrance'. All of these *arwāh* (plural of *rūh*), our souls, emanate from One Source.

The Prophetic unveiling is that all souls are the same. No soul is better, higher, or greater than another. Do not fall prey to the linguistic barriers when you say, 'he is a good soul'. The soul is always good. The soul is always pure. It is its shadow that can be dreadful, nasty, or criminal, and that shadow is the so-called 'you', the ego-self. This is what we call the *nafs* (ego), which is 'breathing' because *nafs* is from the root of breath—*nafas*.

Breath is only one of two, which are also movements: either in or out. Like every phenomenon in this world, it is always one of two things. You cannot see, perceive, or touch anything unless its opposite is also there. You taste sweetness, so there is also sourness. You experience goodness, so there is also badness. You experience heat, so there is cold. You experience love, so there is hate. Everything we experience in this life is balanced between these apparent opposites. In reality, they are complementary: you cannot have one without the other.

As beings, our situation is based on a very simple cosmology of a *rūh* that contains the entire patterning or operating system of the governing principle of existence from the Creator. Nowadays our technology is moving more towards the smaller, the micro, or the ever smaller 'nano', until we reach a point where it cannot be described or handled anymore. It goes beyond measurement of size.

Our openings and successes in quantum mechanics and the sub-atomic world, are really at the beginning of another shore of vastness. It is for that reason that the realization of the One, the worship of the One, love of the One, or the science of *tawhīd* (unity), is coming far more from the areas of scientific endeavours and technological break-throughs than from the humanities or religious studies. There are scientists who are beginning to be far more *muwahhid*, far more unified, and more connected to the unseen. Many scientists are in pursuit of this zone of uncertainty.

SOCIETY TODAY

Today it is the politician who thumps the table about certainty. The politician must appear to have all the answers. If he goes to visit the townspeople without a plan for employment they will ask, 'What do we do? We are unemployed!' The idea of employment or unemployment is relatively new. 100 years ago these terms hardly existed. It's all these economists who want to create more jobs for themselves. They have structured everything in life and turned it into a prison. The only escape is through illicit activities—or through drink, sex, or anything else.

When a politician wants to be elected they will say, 'I know exactly what we are going to do: we are going to get a Japanese firm and we are going to get IMF funding and there will be employment.' A state governor may have been found to be a liar and a cheater, but after being knocked down, he writes a biography which rewards him with money, or he ends up as a director of a bank.

You will rarely, if ever, find a politician who comes and asks, 'What shall we do about this unemployment?' It would be unimaginable if he or she were to say, 'I really don't know, let's talk about it, let's find out who are the unemployed and what is the right thing for this country, or this town. I am not talking of short-term measures but something that will last longer. Maybe we should scrap the whole thing and do something more organic.' If they talked like this nobody would ever talk to them anymore. If they express doubt or equivocation it is not considered good.

This just shows how our measures, judgements and thinking have become distorted. We want immediate gratification. It's all about the shorter term. However, when I studied economics, most of the corporate world was not accountable to the public other than every quarter when they showed their trial balance sheets or at the annual general meeting. Now that accountability is instantaneous.

PURPOSE OF EXISTENCE

Like everything in life, there is a downside and an upside. You must take it upon yourself to be, as we are described by the Creator, in the middle. An aspect of you seeks certainty and an aspect of you can never be certain. An aspect of you is in this life and another aspect belongs to the forever boundless life. The reason we treasure life and respect it is simply a reflection of the truth that life is forever. Allah is forever, God is forever, your *rūh* (soul/spirit) is forever. You are only brought here in order to finish the process of realising this by the mercy of the Creator of it. All the other activities that you undertake are peripheral to this major task of discovering who you are. What are you looking for?

Why is it that you constantly yearn for perfection and yet you know that the moment you reach it, it starts to decay? So much work has gone into making this hall attractive, for example. Fresh flowers, for instance, are on their way to their death the moment you cut them to put in a vase. Just because this is so, it does not mean that we would not stop this constancy of being pulled by perfection, for perfection, unto perfection, whilst realising that perfection is surrounded by natural time-related imperfections. There are momentary perfections which we seek and nature herself makes us constantly yearn for those moments where we are no longer self-conscious.

What is this business of self-consciousness? It's a disaster if a mother with a 2-3 month old baby realises that the baby doesn't respond quite normally or naturally to the rattle. She will be distressed that the child is not responding to her agitation, or that the child is not agitating *her* when he or she grows to be 1 or 2 years by running around causing havoc. So we are always looking for movement, change and agitation, and yet as we grow in our consciousness we yearn for peace and tranquillity which is not punctuated by time.

How do we put this together? How do we reconcile that an aspect of us is dying, decaying, never perfect, always experiencing chaos, difficulty, turmoil, agitation, conflict, and yet another aspect is yearning for harmony, love, reliance, peace and all the other higher qualities? How do we reconcile these apparent opposite powers within us? From time immemorial we find individuals of that orientation—prophets, messengers, great philosophers, enlightened people, saints—who have access to another zone of consciousness that is not definable in physical or material terms. It is a subtler knowledge that we call 'revealed knowledge'.

CONSCIOUSNESS AND REVEALED KNOWLEDGE

Revealed knowledge starts with the rise of Adamic consciousness. In a sense, God's mercy in creating Adam and sending him to earth is part of His plan to complete the evolution of our reality, of our consciousness. It is part of His plan; it is not haphazard. It isn't suddenly that *shaytān* (Satan) appeared from nowhere and the *Rahmān* immediately had to change His script and produce another loop in His film. It is perfection, upon perfection.

The Adamic consciousness belongs to the infinite garden where there is no beginning or end. But that consciousness was not aware of the downside, that there is also hell, change, uncertainty. The Adamic consciousness—my *rūh*, yours, his, hers—belongs to the infinite garden, to total tranquillity. But it did not 'know' that it is tranquil, just as a baby does not know how dependent its limited consciousness is.

The intellect grows and grows until such time you practice silence by stopping every movement, physically, mentally and in your heart. Then you can tap into the highest zone of consciousness, pure consciousness.

The ongoing purpose is to constantly tap into a zone in you that gives you unconditional bliss. It is not mysterious nor is it mystical. It is natural. We only consider a part, or an aspect of this nature—it's *my* family I have to work for, I have my children, their schooling, I need a new car, I need to cheat the income tax man. When we say we are pre-occupied that means we are now occupied by some other energy; we are not allowing our normal growth to move from the physical, material, to the mind, beyond the emotions, into light—layer after layer.

Allah says in the Qur'an that there are infinite layers of yourself. One minute you are a bit mean, the next you are confused. You can move from being certain, hungry, generous, scared, hateful and a multitude of other feelings in a short amount of time. So who are you? That is why those who are more confused than we are try to make some order out of this disorder. They are called psychologists, psychotherapists or their allies, counsellors. There is nothing wrong with that because we are all seekers, but in truth we are also sought. This is what we need to realise.

The realised being knows it is not a question of discussion or argument, or forcefulness, or of imposing your will upon others. He or she just knows. Allah has brought us that unknown power that encompasses all powers for us to subtly move a step at a time easily, not by enormous jolts or by huge catastrophic shake-ups. It is a natural process. You've come from the unseen and now you are beginning to see and make some sense of the cause and effect; and you then return to the unseen with insight.

Allah refers to '*al-nafs al-mutma'inna*' or the *nafs* that has submitted and is reassured. Isn't this Islam? 'Islam Original' is the only way to allow yourself to progress along this operating system by reaching yourself, *by* yourself, to the higher self. It is very simple. It does not require a great deal of scholarship. Islamic studies and all the other approaches are only an aspect of Islam. It is about outer conduct and how to optimally perform your outer duties, how to optimally perform your disappearance in *salāt*, how to optimally perform *zakāt*, to purify, to give that which is not yours.

MATTER AND CONTROL

What do we know about matter? When I first studied physics it was a bit simpler. Back in the 50's it was still influenced by 1930/1940 physics: there was still this hope and belief that there is some sort of building block. Although we knew that Newtonian theory was over, we knew that the more you look, the more you would encounter other subtler things that are actually immeasurable. That's why every time you think you've reached a point of discovery, a final point from which everything is evolved or built or dependent upon, it is not there. It is so elusive!

A lot of spiritual disease comes from the arrogance of thinking that one knows absolutely or can control everything. Our current environment is full of human beings, mainly men, who love to control. Illusions of money and power enhance this fantasy that man is in control. He wants to buy everything because he is control. But what are you really in control of?

You might be in control of minor things. But even that control gives you no freedom. Whoever thinks he is free is ignorant, stupid, and even mad. Free of what? You are not free insofar as you know that the One functions through you and has brought you for Him and you have no option other than to yield to Him. There is no freedom in that! There is a natural appropriateness and progression in that, but there is no freedom. Islam 'Original' has to do with appropriateness: doing the right thing, at the right time, in the right way. Or do nothing and wait.

THE HERITAGE OF DIVINE ATTRIBUTES

As Muslims we are endowed with such a sublime heritage, but do we deserve it? Are we worthy heirs? We have these incredible healing packages: Allah's Divine Names and Attributes are not only in calligraphies to be hung on walls but are in your heart. Who is it that does not long for the quality of forever-ness? That quality belongs only to the Creator—only He is forever. The so-called you and I have been caught in this prison of the body so as to realise its limitations and then turn away from its shadow and dust to the Limitless. The light that shines upon this shadow is limitless. It is the Light of lights.

It is by Allah, Who is forever, that you know your scenario or biography in this world is short-lived; yet your *reality* is forever. The short bubble of experience in this life simply shows you what is behind it, which frightens you. We fear death. But how can you fear death if you believe in the All-Merciful? Where is His mercy if you fear death? That fear will take you to another zone in which you'll realise that it is only a tiny phase, a changing chapter in your life. It is not an end; it is a beginning.

This does not mean that you become suicidal or that you look forward to death. You must go through the phases that are appropriate. If you are faced with a difficulty in the outer world, it is due to your consciousness and the level of that consciousness that picks or elicits that difficulty. The proof of this is that *his* difficulty is not the same as *mine* and your difficulty *now* is not the same as your difficulty *tomorrow*. It changes from moment to moment, from person to person, but yet we know we are constantly challenged by an outer experience that is either desirable or undesirable. There is no third: you either desire something or you want to avoid something else, at all times.

That is why as Muslims and people who are on the prophetic path we have no option other than to groom our lower self by recognizing these two powers underlying it. We like wealth and power, because the Ever-Wealthy, the Ever-Powerful is in the soul, in the *rūh,* is beaming those pulses. His pattern is already in my heart, so I have no option other than to yield to these patterns.

The rocks in front of us are probably 200, 300 or 500 million years old, and yet we don't have patience for two, three days, one month, or two months. Why? Because our consciousness has been dwarfed into seeking immediate pleasure. Immediate pleasure implies my mind is ticking away wanting something and I want to keep it still by bringing in that thing which is called pleasure. You are constantly enticed through this world of reflection and distraction called entertainment.

Yet it is inner attainment that we seek, not entertainment. We all want to be able, at no cost, at any moment, to switch into a zone of perfect harmony in our hearts. If you haven't done that then you are not ready to depart from this world. So you had better prolong your life and hope that you succeed. That is the only justification for prolonging life.

THE LOVE OF LONGEVITY

Why do people look for longevity? Think ahead: if you end up being 150 years old, none of your childhood friends or many family members will be around anymore. The whole longevity game is one global casino, with everybody at their slot machines completely plugged into this frenzy. Do you really want to be there?

It is acceptable if you have arrived at where you have started, which is your *rūh*. Then it is justifiable. Otherwise what is the justification? In this pursuit of longevity, new markets have developed and are geared up for this new generation of geriatrics who are past their 80s. Give them some pills so they can live a bit longer, so that he or she can have their independent life in their miserable one-room apartments, without neighbours to talk to. When they die they are discovered 3 days later. This *cul de sac* of destructive materialism and control will implode upon itself.

But the impulse to seek longevity is because we are both: we are *rūh* which has no beginning or end, as well as an individual self or *nafs*, which is finite. Everyone is different in a superficial way—different eyes, parents, different genetic advantages or disadvantages. Soon children will start suing their parents for their genetic disadvantages! Let me assure you there are already lawyers for this.

ALL *RŪH* BUT DIFFERENTIATED

Once you are certain that you cannot do anything by yourself, you will realise that you only exist by courtesy of the One and Only Self, for Allah says, 'I created you from one self,' meaning, from one *rūh* (soul/spirit). The *nafs*, or the ego, differs from one person to another. We have to respect that we are different from each other. In fact, from this moment to the next you will be different. At the same time, we must not forget to ultimately respect and prioritise the truth that we are essentially one, seeking constant joy, contentment, and happiness. We are the same *and* different. The differences change all the time, the sameness remains constant. This is the foundation of humanity.

People speak about human rights, but nobody talks about human duty. Your duty is to your higher self. Are you performing your duty to the higher self? Stop the shadow by moving away from it. Confusion happens because the shadow has its own cybernetic system geared towards self-destruct or self-construct. All of this is courtesy of the ever-recharging battery called the *rūh* or soul. Our duty is to be *in* it, to be *with* it and to also realise that there is this donkey, this monkey, and all the other animals living in the self's zoo. If you do not realise this then you will never be able to understand all the animals.

Each of us comprises the entire patterning of creation, discernible and indiscernible. It must be there, for otherwise how? do you match it or recognize it? How do you realise *this* is right and *that* is not? That cosmic totality must be lodged within us so that we can comprehend the ever-changing reflections outside in the world, which remind us of the eternal Reality behind the changing reality.

INHABITED VERSUS THE HABIT

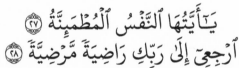

O tranquil content soul, return to your Lord pleased and well-pleasing.

(89:27-28)

In other words, you have come to know now that there is no way for you other than by submitting to this truth, to return now to your Lord who is Ever-Present.

In fact, you are always there, able to access this state, but you do not know it because you are looking somewhere else. It is like the old stories where we are looking for the right thing but in the wrong way, in the wrong place. Why? Because it is more convenient, and it is by force of habit.

How do these habits arise? How do you become habitual unless you have already been *inhabited* by an everlasting permanent reality called *rūh* (spirit/soul). The real 'habit' is your *rūh*, so be habitual and refer to *it*, rather than habitually referring to your physical customs. 'I always have my tea at 9 o'clock in the morning.' Then if it's two minutes late, it proves that his wife doesn't love him as much as she loves the monster (the child) who'll come to ruin his life. Children often end up being used as an excuse for this constant conflict: 'She loved me much more before, but now that Johnny is there...!' The poor woman is overtaken by hormones; it's natural. But this idiot still sits there thinking he is the everlasting pharaoh or the patriarch. That is why we have gangsters ruling the world, and everybody is looking at them wanting to be like them. Allah in His *rahma* every week shows us how they tumble and mumble, and yet everybody wants to be the ruler, nobody wants to be ruled.

BE ONE TO KNOW ONENESS

The true spiritual path has very few people, for it is about adherence. Allah says in the Qur'an:

$$وَمَا يُؤْمِنُ أَكْثَرُهُم بِٱللَّهِ إِلَّا وَهُم مُّشْرِكُونَ ۝$$

'and most of those who profess faith and belief, they are in shirk (associating with god).' (12:106)

They do not see the One. Your access to the One is through your oneness. That is why you should be wary of a person who tells you about 'on the one hand and on the other hand'. They are usually successful lawyers who know how to juggle. Also avoid people who say, 'I'll be honest with you'!

Be One! You have no access to Allah except through your oneness —the integration of all your elements and facets. How can you allude to, discuss, or even have a feel or a touch of the light of the *Ahad* (One) unless you are *wāhid* (one)? *Wahdānīyah* (Unity) is the door of *Ahadiyyah* (Singularity) so be one, don't be two. You don't have to remember what you said if you are fully integrated. You go back to Source. Original means Source, which in turn means the start: Islam Original is the only path. This is not dogma about us Muslims. There is no other path other than admitting our inadequacy, our love for control, and our love for eternal love.

LOVE IS THE FOUNDATION

The entire business of existence is founded on layer after layer of love, until you find the whole thing is glued by divine love that holds the Cosmos together. Divine love is unconditional; it is reflected best in the love of the mother for her child. Every other love is conditional, with varying degrees of mobility or independent factors at play. Whatever you love you praise, as Allah declares in the Qur'an. When you say *al-hamdu li'llah* (praise be to Allah), you are expressing your being in love with praise-worthy qualities. We love all the divine qualities of Allah — infinite power, infinite generosity, constant wellness, utter peace. We love a state in our heart that never changes, which is based on *as-Salam*, the Ever-Well, the Ever-Peaceful.

We love all these qualities and so we praise them, and that is the *nafs al-mutma'innah* (the self that is certain) (89:27); from uncertainty the self will return to the certainty that was already there. If it was not already there then it is not true. Truth is always 'there'. It is through different realities that we experience change, and they change by courtesy of the Ever-Present Truth. Hence we realise that change will happen quite quickly. We also soon grasp that there is a hierarchy of change—some are small and inconsequential, but others can cause a great deal of emotional upheaval and insecurity, which are far more difficult to deal with.

How do you know? You know because of the zone in you of permanent, un-changing absoluteness. The relativity of this world becomes wonderful when you refer it to the Absolute. This is what Allah is showing you. Allah is teaching us reflections of different higher Attributes, qualities that we all praise. This is the state of *nafs al-mutma'inna* (the self that is tranquil and content): I know that I don't know; but I know there is a zone of knowledge that knows everything and knows what I need to know, and it will be given to me at the time I need to know. So it is not me controlling *it*, it is me allowing *myself* to be controlled. The question of decree and destiny gets resolved if you dissolve into this state.

Allah's decrees are His infinite laws, known and unknown, physical, material, subtle, emotional, and all of the other, far greater, unseen laws. This tiny world of ours is floating in an enormous Cosmos, with its own material, physical, subtle, unseen, and multi-layered dimensions within. They are its decrees and we are its witnesses. The soul contains His ultimate generosity of patterning, the highest possible, encompassing all, so that it witnesses Him, within it. Adoration, love, worship is what we have already been programmed with.

THE CONFUSED MUSLIM

So the *nafs al-mutma'inna* is the self that is completely insecure in one aspect and completely secure in another. That is where the confusion arises with many sincere religious people. They do their best but suddenly they undermine the whole foundation by saying, 'Never mind, Allah knows best.' But what do *you* know? You know Allah knows best but do not use that as an excuse to hide your ignorance. 'I wanted this and that, but Allah didn't want it for me.' What do you mean Allah didn't want it? Is Allah quarrelling with you? What sort of deity or a divine creator is He who does not love you all the time?

We are selective. We believe that when we make more money, it is Allah's sign that He loves us. Does that mean next year when we don't make more money, Allah hates us? What a miserable relationship! What a confused, materialistic spirituality. That is our doom—more houses, more centres, more Muslims, more *da'wa*. 1.6 billion people, but look at us! Look at the Arabs. We entered Jerusalem as true followers and *sahābas* of *Rasūl Allah* and we were kicked out as Arab nationalists. Shame upon us!

This example is on the macro, social level, but society reflects the individual. 'As you are thus you will be ruled.' It is not haphazard; it is not by chance that suddenly we have one despotic ruler after another. Each one thinks he can do better than the other. It reflects the individuals. The Arabs of the Gulf used to hope that they would one day catch a lizard to eat. Now suddenly they own casinos and they say *al-hamdu li'llah* and *bismillah* and have imported a few reciters of the Qur'an. It is a lie upon a lie.

Allah will act such that if we collectively do not rebuild our immune systems, in a spiritual sense, we will catch a new virus, like those we currently have. Wherever you turn, the danger is there. Look at Allah's *rahma*: we have brought this situation upon ourselves collectively.

The Ottoman Empire started in a glorious way, imitating the early days of Islam, and ended up being an over-structured, imperialist state. How did it end up like that? Because by the years 1400–1500, whatever we had as a Muslim community was far superior to whatever they had in the West. So it filled in the gap. Granada fell in 1492 and the last Muslims there were promised that they would not be persecuted. They would be given land and there was a whole agreement with Ferdinand and Isabella. Yet within 20-30 years there was an inquisition.

The inquisition was directed at the Muslims, the Jews, or anyone who objected to that high-handed Christian attitude that they were God's people. They killed anybody who was not willing to convert to Christianity. A few minor families ended up isolated in the Sierra mountains of Andalusia, forgotten. All that remained was some architectural heritage and names. There are still so many wonderful Spanish names with their roots in their Muslim past—names like Alvarez which means the horseman, or the ultimate man of honour and dignity.

At that time around when these atrocities were taking place upon this minority people, the Ottomans were taking over Istanbul and look what they did: they maintained and allowed the Eastern church to have its headquarters there and honoured them. Look at the tolerance, acceptance, and how the minorities in the Muslim world had a greater voice than the Muslims. A small Jewish community somewhere would have a direct representative with the ruler; they were listened to and cared for.

But look at us now. It has to be a totalitarian cultural thrashing: if you are not with us you are our enemy. What a disastrous situation we have brought about. Why? Because we wanted to live in Disneyland. That's what the Gulf has had to become—a full Disneyland. Water is now more expensive than oil! Look at Allah's *Rahma*. If I had told you this 30 years ago, you would have said I was crazy, but go and buy any water you want from any miserable petrol station and you will see it is more expensive than oil. Allah is showing us that wherever you turn, there is a lesson. We have to look for the meaning behind events, otherwise we will end up like the corporate world where they are always jittery about the performance of world's markets.

Here we are, constantly yearning for a community. There are many people who have been searching for a place to go in this world. The truth is, it doesn't matter much where you go. What matters is that you are appropriate to your inner state. You could be in the middle of an orchard but producing hell. I have been to many wealthy homes with lush gardens but the quarrels between the couple are so intense that you long to leave. The house is nice, the garden is nice, the servants, the cars, but stay for a few days and you'll see. Hardly any sharing or caring is left. In Sweden we had a movement called CASH! It started with the idea of caring and it occurred to me that the world understands cash, so we called it CASH (Caring and Sharing).

The dominant nexus in this existence is now the cash nexus. Nothing else matters. It doesn't matter who you are, what you are, if you can pay for it, you can be scrutinized, you are accepted, you can get away with it—until you die lonely. The children yearn for your departure, because they want to have a new sports car, which you wisely told them to postpone to later. Is that what you want?

Ultimately what matters is your sincerity about what you want in your life. If you want knowledge, knowledge is already there. But you are living in ignorance, and you are reading the book of ignorance, which ultimately will lead to self-destruction. If you read the book of knowledge it will open up to self-construction.

KNOW TRUTH BY EXCLUSION

Ultimately Allah knows all, and I know that He is here. I know that He is with me by exclusion. I know that I am nowhere else other than with Him by a process of exclusion. When you say, 'I'm with Allah', how do you know you are with Allah? Only when you know that you have no other way to turn.

You are not dependent upon any particular entity, and you do not deny (contingent) entities. The Prophet says, 'Do not forget to thank, or acknowledge creation, because they are Allah's messengers.' The ultimate messenger is your *rūh*: the messenger of Allah to you is your soul. But are you listening to that messenger? That messenger has total courtesy towards existence because it is representative of the creation of all existence.

SHARI'A AND HAQIQA

Do not deny the outer just because your priority is the inner. Different maps require different courtesies. What time is it? Is it time for *salat*? Where is the *qibla*? Am I properly on *wudu*? Did I seal myself from interaction or imposition of the outer world? Is it the right time to call others for it? Where am I? Where am I pointing? What is my intention? Correct that! Change your vices into virtues, your meanness into an evaluation of appropriateness. Become mean against your lower self and generous to others. Be generous to yourself, meaning to your *Rūh* and be mean and watchful towards the ego. These are the outer laws.

'Islam Original' is not just a random set of laws made to turn you upside down and quarrel about which *madhhab* is the correct one. This is boring! If you were born in a particular *madhhab*, carry on. But if that *madhhab* doesn't take you to the abode of inner tranquillity, then it has not been a flying carpet. You may then be worshipping your *madhhab*, not Allah. Are you worshipping what you are used to or are you worshipping

Him Who has brought you about for Him, unto Him, for eternal joy? Big difference!

People are not tolerant because they have not attained that inner joy. How can you be tolerant of others if you have not discovered that there is no other? You should be frightened of 'you' because there are two of you. You are confused. If you are confused you'll also seek confusion all around you and therefore discord, because you have not attained your inner accord.

THE PLACE OF DISCRIMINATION

They say the worst catastrophe is the one which makes us laugh. That is why there is wisdom in every instant. The *nafs al-mutma'inna* is the self which knows that it will never come to know itself by controlling mechanisms or through outer discrimination (89:27). It is certainly vital to have outer discrimination (discernment). It is vital to control the minimal things that are under your control—your house, the doors, your windows. These are minor insignificant things that you can control.

I am reminded of a husband-and-wife relationship that worked very smoothly and everybody wondered why. The man said, 'It is very easy. We agreed from day one that I make the decisions for major things in life. My wife would make the decisions for the minor things in life. The major things are whether you should continue with the moon mission or not, or whether America should make democracy universal all over the world or should they stop only at the Equator. But minor decisions like where we live and what job I should do are hers.' The same thing applies to existence—minor decisions such as whether you should wash your hands or not, stop talking or whether it is time to eat or not.

THE VICE OF STRUCTURALISM

The Prophet was not this rigid figure; he was a dynamic being, living in the moment, perfectly appropriate in every moment. But we have become straight-jacketed by *hadīth* (verbal tradition). Ironically, the word *hadīth* is from *hadatha*, to happen, as in an event. A *hadīth* is an incident, event, or a happening. It is 'live' so you cannot take it out of its context—it is a living situation.

When rigidity set in Islam this movement called *Tasawwuf* (Sufism) emerged. Sufism arose because of the excessive rigid structuralism that was also repeatedly replicated on the macro scale within different Islamic states, cultures and so on. I alluded earlier to the Ottoman Empire. At its peak, it was the best ever. But by the time 1800 arrived, they were clients of Europe — they were known as the 'Sick Man of Europe'. Huge amounts of money were loaned to them because of their desperation. In 1810, Sultan Mahmud changed the whole thing and called it *Tanzimat*[1], the new order. The Empire started mimicking the West without the foundation of a Western culture or Western education, which, by that time, was a fully evolved heir of the modified Greco-Roman and Judaeo-Christian versions of it, after the reformation and industrial revolution. Europeans appeared to have it all while the Ottomans saw themselves as behind or backward. Everybody wanted to jump on the wealth wagon, first the Uthmani sultans, then soon after Muhammad Ali in Egypt. Everybody tried to mimic them.

We can regain our spiritual heritage by going to the root of it all, admit how horrible we were, and move much faster by regaining meaning and being worthy of regaining it. We can either move ahead or we can continue to deny our faults, accuse others, and end up being defiant and defensive. If we choose denial, we will have to maintain a point of reference from which to deny, but that; point of reference is now more local and transient than durable. So we have to invent a centre. That is what happens.

As far as I can discern, this has happened repeatedly in our history — at least 38 times in the last 200 years. Modern Muslims have a choice: either they admit the depth of their deviation from their true spiritual heritage, or they deny it. If they admit it, they will be able to regain this heritage, but if they deny their faults, their defiance will make them refuse to see where they have gone wrong. Since the original centre has been destroyed, they create false ones.

---

1. The Tanzimât, literally meaning reorganization of the Ottoman Empire, was a period of reformation that began in 1839 and ended with the First Constitutional Era in 1876.

In 1798, when the Mamluks ruled in Egypt, they were so arrogant that they kept the peasants at the very lowest level while 200-300 elite families lived very comfortably. They took great pride in their military prowess. When Napoleon came, when he was at Cairo's gates, they said, 'We will slaughter him before he enters the gates of Cairo. We will bury him outside the gate.'

This is almost what Saddam said during the Gulf war. It took Napoleon's forces one day to enter Cairo. In the Sinai war, Nasser deployed 600 tanks but because the soldiers could not drive them well in sand, they annihilated each other. 300 tanks bombed the other 300. They buried each other. A true Muslim state cannot be powerful militarily by oppressing its people.

NO OTHERNESS

There is no quick fix globally but individually you can save yourself, from yourself, by yourself by unifying your intention and carrying it out with appropriate action. Learn how to do the right thing in the right courteous way, not by hanging onto somebody else, or having some sort of nonsensical illusion about 'other-ness'. There is no other-ness. There is One Creator and from *It* have come infinite varieties in the outward appearances of creation. In truth, everything is connected, controlled, energized, and owned by *One* Creator.

The cell knows when to divide, the plant knows when to drop a leaf, by grace of the One Unifying Force. Our Prophet (S) says there are 7 angels, meaning 7 pulses of energy that decide when the leaf drops. Yet here we do not know how to treat each other, or how to look into the cosmos which is within us. Shame on us! If we do not start with self-reproach, we will not arrive at the glory of the ultimate gift of the Adamic-Consciousness that Allah in His mercy has given us. We have to know when to stop before we know how to move on. Therefore, the whole business is 'Islam Original'. Everybody is 'original', everybody is authentic, every movement is original, every instant is original. Allah says: 'O self who is content with my presence, content with my Light...'—so you are content in the knowledge that outwardly you can only do a small amount: where you are going to wash your hands, or rest your head?

Look at the wars in the world: millions of people don't even get a burial. So consider yourself most fortunate. Be in gratitude. Allah says that the more you are in gratitude, the more your heart is content and the more your *rūh* shines and the more your lower *nafs* and shadows become insignificant. You acknowledge this and you say to yourself, 'I know you *nafs*, who is always there barking at me, keep quiet now!' Give it a bit of food and shut it up. Feed it and then tell it, 'Now you are going to sleep', because you are a *rūh* (soul/spirit).

DIE BEFORE YOU DIE

This is the outer map based on the inner map. The rules of the inner map are not in anybody's hands. It is according to Allah's timing, and this is the prophetic teaching of 'die and you'll live forever'. You die in the sense of learning how to reflect, how to meditate, how to perfect your *salāt* in *sajda*, so that you know what appears are only minor aberrations, flashes of what is eternal, permanent in you. You become 'alive'. By the time death comes it is not a big deal. But if you created chaos then it will be a permanent nightmare.

The best example is that your life is like an eternal perfect light covered by the casing which is your so-called ego. If the ego has been rarefied, purified, cleansed, then it allows light to beam, and this is what will carry over into the next phase of existence.

MAPS OF THE INNER AND OUTER

There are two maps: the outer map is the Prophetic and the inner map is beyond us. The outer map is one of courtesy, accountability, responsibility —where are you, who are you, what are you doing, why are you doing it?

The inner map is 'light upon light'. Without that 'light upon light,' this map will not become multi-dimensional, only materially dimensional.

Many of us are still trapped in 'baby' consciousness. In the womb you had no consciousness, but there was an autonomic, innate consciousness. For 9 months you were using all this food from your mother. You will probably end up having to pay a lifetime of obedience to her as rent for those 9 months. It is unfortunate that some men marry their mothers. They marry a wife that reflects the mother, who pampers them like she once did. Then they ask why the marriage failed. It was doomed from the beginning! There was no compatibility, there was no proper contract. If their marriage is based on helping each other to come to know themselves instead of idealizing a notion of 'perfect' spouse, then it has a chance.

Every pleasure also has displeasure. These are parts of the laws of Allah. There cannot be anything in this life unless it is one of two—except for the light in you, which is one of One, one from One, one by One, one returning to One, one witnessing the One. That is why these two maps are described by Allah as 'two oceans meeting in you, one of them is not overcome by the other' (25:53). You are an outer animal and an inner beyond and above the angels. So which one of you is talking? Which one of you is the 'I'? People rarely ever stop for a second to question this. When you were 4 years old and pinched the chocolate from the other fellow, you said, 'I pinched it'. How come now you are saying, 'I'm giving', 'I'm loving'? Who is 'I'? How can it change every instant, unless there is something in you that never changes? This is the map, the atlas that has these two oceans.

THE ONUS IS ON YOU

We are the beneficiaries, and the giver is Allah. We acknowledge the Source, and we thank the means and the manifestation of it, at the same time. I would like to remind you that you have no excuse for not reaching—through the constant Self, through the ever-present Light—to your own soul within. If you are not getting in touch with it, then it is because you have gone into such a wilderness that it will take you longer to stop your past habits. We are all prisoners of habits, prisoners of our minds. The mind is such a wonderful gift of Allah that can take you higher and higher into the zone of the intellect (*'aql*), and the intellect will indicate and show you the ever-present, permanent Light of the soul within you. Our experience in life is a journey towards higher consciousness, until it is consciousness without anything specific—pure consciousnesss.

You must do it, nobody else can do it. There is a fantasy that you can depend on this shaykh or that shaykh, or this teacher or this *wali* (friend of God). They are all mirrors. At best I can be a mirror to your higher self. If you run away because you are only used to your lower self, then good luck. But do it sooner so we are spared from wasting our time. Go to the wilderness where you have been because you are now worshipping your habits and that is the most difficult monument and idol to break. The worst habit is the repetition to yourself, 'I'm a religious person'. Everybody has to bow unto you because you have given a few things to the Mosque. If you don't move beyond these layers and levels of self-image, you will never be anywhere near the higher self.

We are not here as a little or big institute for information or Islamic studies. We are here as people who have reached a point in life where we want to know more before it's too late. Therefore, what we are engaged in is an adult, spiritual exercise in self-arrival. Everybody has to start somewhere. You may have started in a small way by being charitable and helping others. That is wonderful, but ultimately, what about you? Who are you? Whom do you love? How do you love the one you profess to love, and when?

We have had so many of these pep talks with executive gurus, which are finally now dying out. But over the last 10-15 years, there have been various attempts to bring about what they call self-esteem, loving yourself, trying to get you to see you have everything in you. But it has no mapping; it is a hodgepodge of loving the worst in you, the lowest, the ego—it's all mixed up. Because they don't have the cosmology, they cannot read the map and therefore cannot drive properly. Every now and then you find people perhaps in the political arena, or the corporate, who may be successful, but they are misguided. Because of this mix-up every week you find great monuments tumbling, destituted.

We do not know who we are, whom are we addressing, and who is addressing which one of you? Whatever the question is, the answer comes before it! This is your life. I cannot add an iota to *your* inner life unless you want it, *if* you want it. Allah says that *ihsān* is the station where you know that Allah is Ever-Present, though you may perceive it in-directly. You may be distracted, so you do not see the light behind the shadows, or the woods from the trees, but you consciously know and feel Allah's Ever-Presence.

It is your duty towards yourself to regain your higher self and deliver it from the lower self. It is as simple as that. All of the prophetic messages were about that. But they used the language that was familiar in those times. They dwelt a lot on obedience. Because they were closed communities people had this constant reflectiveness. The world of experiences is just mirrors interactively reflecting each other all the time. The world outside mirrors your world inside. If you are confused in your experience it is because you are not fused within your heart with your ultimate Maker. If an event happens, it is good or bad, just or unjust, healthy or otherwise. Through His decrees, Allah has allowed it to happen and if you do not see the perfection of the laws that govern what's happening, then you are not addressing the zone of perfection in you.

COURTESIES OF THE MAPS

There are different maps: one is a map of the outer and the other a map of the inner, and each has its courtesy, each has its own encoding. There are the following essential fundamental zones in life: the inner and the outer. The inner is to do with the vast unknown and unseen. The outer is the visible and discernible seen. At best we can discuss it using our *'aql* or intellect, so we can understand and share the foundations of the laws that govern the outer.

The outward world of the material and physical, complements the inward world of meaning and essence. If you start making sense of the outer—how cause and effect interact—and you continue your journey, you will reach the meaning behind it.

What does it mean for example when a husband feels depressed because his child is shouting and screaming and the mother is crying? It means he wants harmony and is unable to achieve it so he is depressed. Dep-ression is sorrow, and sorrow is regret for what happened in the past. Anxiety is the fear of what could happen in the future. Behind it all, encompassing it all, within it all, before it all, after it all, is the essential Light of Allah's Essence. Allah's *dhāt*, His Essence, encompasses all the *dhawāt* (essences). You also have an essence reflecting those qualities, which is why the Qur'an says your '*rūh* is from the command of your Lord' (17:85).

SIGNS ON THE HORIZON AND WITHIN

These are not preach-able religious matters; they are essential life-and-death matters. They are fundamental to your emancipation from the images, fantasies and fears that you have imposed upon yourself. So just as we have the inner and the outer, meaning and form, equally we have aspects that are heavenly and earthly. Many of the things around us are earthly, but those that are beyond us we deem heavenly.

If you are religious and have read the Qur'an, then you translate these terms into what is meaningful. When we say that there are hundreds, thousands, millions or countless angels for every event, we must understand them as impulses. 50-60 years ago, there were no cell phones. Now the signal comes and the thing starts shaking in your pocket. Angels are equivalent to the electromagnetic pulses, though there may be thousands of other related types, but we only understand the chemical, mechanical, physiological, and biological. There are, however, subtler elements. These are what we call the heavenly aspects. It is much easier nowadays for us to understand our cosmology because we can use these examples.

What, for example, is *Azra'il*, the angel of death? Consider this scenario: the *rūh* has multiple operating systems governing other things. When a woman is pregnant suddenly a new system takes over. The hormones begin the orchestration, she is taken over, perhaps even ending up with post-natal depression. We are subject to multitudes of signals operating from our *rūh*. Eventually our *rūh* is subjected to *Azra'il*, another system, beyond all these detectable ones, which emanates from the heavenly domain. When *Azra'il* comes and dislodges the *rūh* and the self which have been moving together, another system kicks in. As people, we try to understand by mind or by intellect and by heart—multiple levels of consciousness.

DESTINY

Everyone wonders about destiny. Imam 'Ali (AS) says, 'Leave it, do not dive into it, because it is an ocean in which many people have drowned'. But we take licence and permission from our greatest beings and guides because the age we are living in is very different. We have become very complex and sophisticated in our intellect, so I will give you a window into this, and the rest is up to you.

Ustadh 'Ali 'Allawi talked about the *Qādiriyya* and *Jābiriya*, the two schools of thought about free will and predestination. Both are true within the limitations of what is discussable, and both are false. As Imam 'Ali (AS) said the truth was between the two, it is *barzakhiya* (interspatial). Everything in life is a *barzakh* (interspace), the quality of being 'in-between'. It is the Heisenberg uncertainty principle: if you can discern the position of the electron, you will not be able to ascertain its mass, and if you measure its mass, you will not be sure of its orbit. Or Schrödinger's cat, which came to the same conclusion that you are both dead and alive. You have both an aspect of it in your hand and, in reality, nothing is in your hand.

It is *you* who sets the train in motion. When we think of a certain thing together, the destiny has already been pre-determined in Allah's knowledge, not in our knowledge. It is pre-determined in the non-time zone that we will reach somewhere according to our plot. It's as simple as that. You will set the whole thing moving, collectively and nationally. That is why Allah warns us to watch out for trouble that comes to us not because of our personal doing but because we are subjected to other doings.

وَٱتَّقُواْ فِتْنَةً لَّا تُصِيبَنَّ ٱلَّذِينَ ظَلَمُواْ مِنكُمْ خَاصَّةً وَٱعْلَمُوٓاْ أَنَّ ٱللَّهَ شَدِيدُ ٱلْعِقَابِ ۝

And beware of discord which does not afflict the wrongdoers among you exclusively; and know that God is severe in retribution (8:25)

There are various levels and layers of these influences. So in a sense your future, your destiny, is in your hands, according to your intention.

If your intention is *ikhlās* – sincerity – and being and seeing the One, you are already on the perfect destiny. If it is not that—'no, first I want to do *this*, second my career, third my husband, and fourth this' etc—what unfolds will also be according to that intention. The rest you have to work out for yourself. That working it out will bring you to the constancy of *taqwā* (awareness)—'Oh Allah I don't know if that is the right thing for me, because the right thing for me is when my heart is consistently filled up with your light'. That is the destiny we all want. Everybody wants happiness; it will never be attained except with this final, constant situation in which your heart is overflowing with the knowledge and joy of the Creator's principle of the Essence.

THE ULTIMATE RECOLLECTION

I'd like to introduce a new concept I call the 'ultimate recollection'. We are all caught by this thing called mind and memory. Without it you are a cabbage, but with a strong mind and memory you are imprisoned in the mind. As a baby grows he or she can only compare what they are experiencing with past experiences—the smell of milk, the feel of the breast, or the sound of the rattle. Babies only have that and that's why it is very important for them to have both containment—being tightly wrapped with a cloth—as well as gentleness.

No sensible mother would want her baby to be subjected to fireworks and loud noises because the baby will be startled. That pure consciousness, that pure slate or mirror, gets fractured. That's why it is very important that the baby is subjected to the right sounds as he or she grows in the womb. The first 2-3 years of the baby's life are critical. As you start life and grow with age, you develop a memory bank to relate to, making memory relative.

This relativeness grows wider. When you are 40 years old, you may remember a time when you broke your foot, but because it healed after a month or two, you now know that if you were to break your finger now, it would also heal given enough time. However, if you were to tell a 3-year-old child that his injured finger would take 3 to 5 months to heal, he would despair because 5 months is a sixth of his whole life. When you are 60, 5 months does not sound like much time and is therefore not as significant. As you grow older, your relative comparison becomes longer until such time that you reach a point of remembering that which was pre-memory.

Allah, 'azza wa jalla (mighty and powerful), says in the Qur'an there was a time when you could not be remembered (76:1). If you have awakened to your Essence, you know that the Essence was there before any inscription of memory. This is the zone of the rūh. So, you recollect not yesterday, nor last year, but instead, you recollect when you were collected, when you were gathered with only the Divine Source. This life is a life of dispersion, of calling for, yearning for, not only human gatheredness, but the original state of gatheredness, of Oneness.

There are small samples of the original blueprint in your heart for whatever you desire or would like to avoid in this world. If you read that then you are with the original map and will not be confused.

In this life you grow according to many cycles of several years. Let's say there are 5 cycles, starting with one when you were in the womb, where you were not conscious of consciousness, but were in full abandonment and total innocent trust. It was like the Adamic situation when he was in the Garden, without knowing what the Garden was, what Hell was, or what long life or eternity was. He just was!

Then you are born. You start a journey of inter-dependence, of relying on others. First you begin to be conscious of the mother, then the father, perhaps an uncle, or others. Then at the age of 5 or 6 you realise that the old uncle will give you more chocolate than the mother, because she is more health conscious, so now there is inter-dependence. This increases until you reach full maturity, which is the prophetic age of 40. By now you've learnt all the tricks and how to cheat at different levels. You have become very clever.

From here on out, if you are not going to wake up to the 'ultimate recollection', to the inner dependence upon the *Nūr* (light) of Allah in you, then you are not being prepared for the full cycle of return. You start with utter reliance without knowing what reliance is. You move forward through 3 or 4 stages until you reach the point of knowing for sure that there is none other than the One Source permeating, encompassing, signalling, activating, and acting through every other means in this existence. You have now become truly awakened to *tawhīd*. You do not mix up the outer world with the inner world—you connect them and unify them within yourself. This is a matter of *furqān*, outer discrimination. The other one is a matter of *waslān* (arrival).

You can only have full *furqān* if you have full inner reliance and recollection that He, Who has already collected you under His *Rahma* (mercy), has brought you into this dispersion for you to understand and experience His *Rahma*. You experience this layer after layer until you see only His *Rahma* both in dispersion and in gatheredness, in both so-called failure *and* success.

APPARENT LOSS AND INNER SUCCESS

Whoever has reached that recollected state is always successful. In outer success, he sees both outer and inner success. In outer failure he sees only inner success and an outer experience which is simply balancing the opposites and that is the norm of outer life. You cannot have one with-out the other. Outer success is different from outer failure. However, it does not make a difference to your inner sense. It does not touch your heart. It is not going to overwhelm you or make you jump from the edge of a 60-storey building simply because you've lost your shares. When you confront outer failure, you consider that maybe this is the time to take a 10-year holiday, or to look for new employment, or see how the other side lives, or discern what gifts are behind it. You trust that Allah says that if there is goodness in your heart, He gives you better than that which you lost:

يَٰٓأَيُّهَا ٱلنَّبِىُّ قُل لِّمَن فِىٓ أَيْدِيكُم مِّنَ ٱلْأَسْرَىٰٓ إِن يَعْلَمِ ٱللَّهُ فِى قُلُوبِكُمْ خَيْرًا يُؤْتِكُمْ خَيْرًا مِّمَّآ أُخِذَ مِنكُمْ وَيَغْفِرْ لَكُمْ وَٱللَّهُ غَفُورٌ رَّحِيمٌ ٧٠

O prophet! Say to those you hold prisoners, "If God finds any good in your hearts, He will give you better than what was taken from you, and He will forgive you. God is Forgiving and Merciful." (8:70)

The specific purpose of this ayah was for the prisoners of war who were desperate and scared. Allah addresses them in the context of goodness or *khayr*. What is goodness? Goodness means living in faith and trust that there is only One who brought us here by His mercy, who will show us His mercy, and that we will return to His *absolute* mercy from what appears to be *relative* mercy. So when Allah knows there is goodness in your heart, He will give you better than that which you think has been taken away from you.

That is why He who knows the divine dominion, knows that when something has been swept off you, something better will come. By better, we do not mean in the way you have been habitually thinking. Most of the time less is better. Most of the suffering we experience is because of excess. If you were to go to the Gulf and see the *gulf* between humanity, you would realise that the women there are mostly suffering from excess and depression. They are distressed and stressed, but stress is part of Allah's basic foundation.

STRESS & REFINING THE SELF

Life is based on stress, but ideally, we should not be over-stressed or under-stressed. Stress is the fundamental stimulator of the two main driving factors attracting what you love and dispelling what you don't. When you begin to balance these two main drives, you will begin to groom and refine the self.

Our *dīn* (path) is grooming the lower self until it unifies with the soul. The main stages are simple. Initially we want to attract everything to us, anything that we feel and believe to be of benefit. But when the drive of attraction becomes relentless it becomes indulgence. The desire for instant gratification at all costs will eventually bring about negativity. However, when I begin to groom the self and examine this power and love for attraction, the same power will turn into the quality of modesty. When I observe the shamefulness of my excesses I quieten down. I begin to be benign and steadfast. All of these and other qualities stem from refining, modifying, and balancing this power of pull or attraction.

The power of push, or repulsion, is anger. Often in our Islamic literature it is symbolically equated with the dog, an animal that bites and barks. Once it is groomed, however, anger becomes courage. With it comes compassion for others, it becomes generosity and the desire to help others. It also becomes forbearance and all the other higher qualities which we ascribe as being virtuous. So *here* it was a vice and *there* it becomes a major virtue. When these two powers are balanced, then you can drive the car properly.

Between modesty and courage you begin to develop a third major quality called wisdom. Wisdom is the foundation of intelligence, of the intellect. Some people retain knowledge very quickly. It is because they are balanced between this power of pull and push. Not only do they become retentive, but they are also quick to absorb. All matters to do

71

with intellect, with *'aql*, will grow when these two forces are balanced. Only then can you talk about justice or fellowship, friendliness, fair-play, and piety. In 'Islam Original' piety is only meaningful as a by-product of being just, being in the middle, knowing the outer and inner maps and then acting appropriately.

APPROPRIATENESS OR *ADAB*

The entire business is about appropriateness at the individual level and on the collective level. The world is in such upheaval because the appropriateness of the collective level has gone completely askew. The only thing we can do is to start planting the seeds again from the beginning by grooming the self. Who are you? Which part of you is talking? Have you groomed the shadows? Have you gone past them and into the ever-present light in you? Are you using your intellect, your *'aql*, your reasoning? Are you always using the reference points that we have in our *dīn* (path), such as the willingness to die?

If you are willing to die at any minute, then you are closer to the point where greed no longer obsesses you. Greed can also manifest as imposing your views about what you consider to be goodness. When people consider themselves to be God's people they impose a new form of imperialism backed by this apparent religious fervour. Do not ever think that we cannot fall into the same categories. These are basic patterns and designs of consciousness: if we pick them up and resonate with them, we become them.

INNER ATTAINMENT

We need to constantly take counsel, give counsel, and reflect counsel. This reflection is vital. We need to be protected from poison that is not discernible. That is why our Islamic *adab* is to close the senses whenever they are likely to excite you. The modern *kufr* (truth covering) system is geared to excite you so you get interested in something that you never needed. The truth is that all you need is three feet of ground (for prostration) so that you can disappear into your nothingness. This is really the flying carpet of inner attainment; otherwise you are captured by the captains of entertainment.

If you have tasted this, nothing can touch it ever again. If you haven't, then you are a candidate for more abuse and you will end up being so angry that you accuse everybody else of misleading you. Why did they mislead you and not somebody else? Why don't you love your *real* self more than anything else? Be really selfish until you get to the real self and realise you are self-less. So counsel is vital, reflection of others is essential and unavoidable. Be in the right company. When you say somebody has got light, it means that they are less dependent or less afflicted by their shadow. There is *only* Light, modified and cascading through the multiple levels.

POEM: INNER SIGHT

Wisdom starts with hindsight,
which increases our insight,
leading subsequently
to greater foresight.
But all of these states
are mere reflections
of Divine Light,
visible and invisible,
energies and matter.

Illumined insights
and many more gifts
come with meanings hidden in forms,
transcending the norm.

When animal consciousness
is replaced by higher sights and lights,
then all of your past
becomes like a distant shadow
and the future promises
a state beyond description or aspiration.
In the beginning flashes of inner sight
and at the end
it is a cosmic treasure trove,
indescribable in its beauty and might.

STILLNESS AND AWARENESS

The grooming and refinement of the self continues throughout our lives. Nobody can say 'I'm safe now'. The battle, or the *jihād* (utmost striving), continues from the moment that agitation took place in the womb. Life only manifests when there is movement and heat, but the foundation of it is no movement and eternal peace. So if you practice having peace and no movement through your religious practices, then you are in this world but not of this world, and you are already aware of all the other consciousnesses. Do not deny the little pain or the little mental disturbance you occasionally have. Do not deny any of these.

Remember that the paramount effulgent presence that sheds light upon all of these is the Light of Light. Do not become this strange character, one moment not here, another moment aware. You *are* aware. You are fully *aware* but your awareness comes through different levels of a hierarchy, until you are aware of the lower *because* you are constantly in touch with pure awareness. Pure awareness is the state of the true *musalli* (one who prays), who is perpetually in the state of disappearance from the lower and constantly seeing the ever-present appearing from the eternal light within.

POEM: EFFULGENT TREASURE

Allah is a hidden treasure
Who loves to be known
and to that glorious station
the worthy shall surely be flown
experiencing aspects of the cosmic throne.

The journey of this ascension
born on wings of submission
fuelled by grace
of trust and realization.

You start with reason,
then go past the senses,
the good as well as nonsense!
You taste a new light from your soul,
which beckons you to move beyond your past.
This taste can then become a passion,
which ultimately burns out the old you,
yielding a new life with infinite delight.

A PRESCRIPTION: THE EASE AFTER DIFFICULTY

بِسْمِ ٱللَّهِ ٱلرَّحْمَٰنِ ٱلرَّحِيمِ

In the name of Allah, the beneficent, the merciful,

أَلَمْ نَشْرَحْ لَكَ صَدْرَكَ ﴿١﴾

Have We not expanded for you your breast,

وَوَضَعْنَا عَنكَ وِزْرَكَ ﴿٢﴾

And lifted off from you your burden,

ٱلَّذِىٓ أَنقَضَ ظَهْرَكَ ﴿٣﴾

Which pressed heavily upon your back

وَرَفَعْنَا لَكَ ذِكْرَكَ ﴿٤﴾

and granted you an exalted reputation?

فَإِنَّ مَعَ ٱلْعُسْرِ يُسْرًا ﴿٥﴾

So, verily, with every difficulty, there is ease

إِنَّ مَعَ ٱلْعُسْرِ يُسْرًا ﴿٦﴾

Certainly, after every difficulty there comes ease.

فَإِذَا فَرَغْتَ فَٱنصَبْ ﴿٧﴾

So when you are empty, be devout

وَإِلَىٰ رَبِّكَ فَٱرْغَب ﴿٨﴾

and let your Lord be your Quest.

During difficult times and episodes, we shrink. We want to disappear. We feel lifeless because we identify with the self that is being cornered. We feel depressed or oppressed or made small. Allah says to the Prophet, and by extension to us as followers of the prophetic path (paraphrasing): 'Haven't you had occasions where you suddenly felt your breast expanded? You felt illumined, delighted, happy.' Not because of some special event or scene. Simply because it has touched you. Those burdens or insecurities, fears, anxieties—gone!

That is what happens during sessions of *dhikr*. 'Always with difficulty, there is ease.' There is a double ease with every difficulty. One is when you discover the perfection of that difficulty and the other is the knowledge that it will pass. Then 'And your constancy, your awareness, your remembrance is being heightened, made more sublime.' You are aware that you may leave at any minute, so enjoy the present. See the immensity of the moment and the perfection in it, and you will see even more perfection. The more you see goodness, the more goodness you see.

Remember the times when your heart opened and you will find the heart is never closed. It is you who put up the barriers. The soul is ever there, throbbing, and it will continue after you leave the body. Remember more and it becomes a mental habit. Our *Dīn* (way) is the most positive path. You will become habitual in your mental processes. Think always of the best. Observe the difficulty and see how you can solve it. If not, leave it—it's not your problem. You've tried your best so get on with it! Move on! You must do this so that it becomes your norm to expect the best of Allah, so that you translate these so-called religious teachings into a lifestyle. So that you internalise it and are always positive.

You do not deny the negative, but you ensure that it does not touch you. These are the ways that we can internalise these wonderful *ayāt* (verses) and *surahs* (chapters). Celebrating Islam means celebrating the opportunities we are given constantly to turn from the lower to the higher!

CHAPTER THREE

Celebrating Islam

Given in 2004

- Living in the Moment
- Celebrating Gratitude
- Celebrating Oneness
- Needs Announce the Fulfiller of All Needs
- Consciousness and Childhood Development
- *Homo Economicus*
- The Muhammadi Package
- Turn Away from Self to Soul
- Outer Boundary Inner Boundlessness
- From Self-Confusion to Soul-Fusion
- The Worldview of *Homo Economicus*
- No Otherness
- Awareness of Perfection
- Needs—An Illusion?
- The Spiritual Responsibility of Parenthood
- Blaming Others
- Abundance Distracts
- Witnessing Opposites
- Different Selves, Same Soul
- On A.S.K
- Death is not the End
- Poem: The Ever-Present Peace
- Remaining in Gratitude
- Cardinal Points in the Compass
- Leadership of Muslims

All of us want to find a way to worship the Lord of the Worlds, Who oversees the *Day of Reckoning*. In the Qur'an it is asked (82:18-19):

$$\text{وَمَآ أَدْرَىٰكَ مَا يَوْمُ ٱلدِّينِ ۝}$$

Do you know what the Day of Reckoning is?

And the answer is:

$$\text{يَوْمَ لَا تَمْلِكُ نَفْسٌ لِّنَفْسٍ شَيْئًا ۖ وَٱلْأَمْرُ يَوْمَئِذٍ لِّلَّهِ ۝}$$

The Day when no soul will avail another soul anything; and the decision on that Day is God's.

That day is the period or state, when you have no possibility of doing anything for anyone, not even for yourself, for you will have been stripped of the apparent short-lived power that you had. We are empowered for a period of time in order to discover the All-Powerful behind everything, within it, before it and after it. This world is a tiny little glimmer or flash of the real and the true eternal state that has in it the Original Divine Light, modified as it cascades in creation to the present moment.

I thank Allah for the impeccable way He has designed this incredible cosmos into which we have tiny insights every now and then. If you do not acknowledge that great gift, then it will not open for you. First praise the Creator for His amazing qualities that have been made available for us to understand, to taste, and to participate. Then be in gratitude. Allah says (14:7):

$$\text{لَئِن شَكَرْتُمْ لَأَزِيدَنَّكُمْ}$$

If you are grateful I will grant you increase.

So we express gratitude for our ability to appreciate these great qualities.

LIVING IN THE MOMENT

Great qualities and attributes have always been there, but we were not present to appreciate them. So that appreciation cleans and opens the pipelines in the heart to see more of this infinite light manifesting in boundless and countless manifestations. The day of reckoning is now. The moment of reckoning is now. The period in which you can truly discover and uncover, is now. All of it is present in the moment. The moment is so dense that it contains all that had happened in the past, what is happening now, and the pattern that it is likely to move into and develop and unfold in the future. All of it is there in a single moment. Allah has bestowed upon human consciousness the ultimate gift.

CELEBRATING GRATITUDE

Now it is up to us to internalise it, reverberate with it, and live according to its perfections. I thank Allah for what we experience and for the depth that we cannot fully understand. Our thanks have no beginning or end. And the more you thank, the more you would like to thank. The more you are in gratitude, the more you find yourself unable to express your gratitude *ad infinitum*.

I also thank the means because we are a people of unity. We connect the essence and the output. If you don't thank those who have made what we experience, the health and the quality of life that we have, then you are not thankful to the Original Lord and Creator of it all.

So thank all the means and ways that Allah made our lives, growth, evolvement, and our spiritual development possible. We start by celebrating our ability to be in gratitude. I cannot fully express my gratitude. When I think of it, I just dissolve in the ocean that has no beginning or end. If you also look more towards the opportunities you've had, you enter an ocean of hope in which you do not see anything other than infinite clarities, layer upon layer of light. The immediate instant circumstance does not matter.

If you look at its cause, you will see perfection. So we are here celebrating our ability to truly express gratitude, which is the door to inner joy.

CELEBRATING ONENESS

If we say we are Muslims, or we are in submission, we are on the prophetic path. What is it we are celebrating? *Why* are we celebrating? How is it that we can celebrate? The life of the true believer and the transformation that comes from that light is an ongoing celebration, layer after layer. So we are celebrating the ability to experience this amazing miracle of both the physical and the meaning. There is nothing in this world that has no meaning. Most of the destitution in this world is because people are seeking the meaning of life, the purpose of life, but they are looking in the wrong place and therefore will not find it.

No one is separate from He Who has designed, created and is found within them. God is in you in the form of His messenger which is called your soul. Others call it spirit. It doesn't matter what name you give it. There is the representative of the Absolute Divine in you. If you yield to it, then you are in true submission. Then you do not talk about faith or belief. You know! It is no longer subject to discussion. Indeed, the Qur'an says, *Lā jadala fi'd-dīn*, 'There is no argument in the *Dīn*.' It is the truth of what you have been looking for because it has created you to know it. So, you have finished the circle and that is the beginning of your life. It is not the end of your life.

Enlightenment is the starting point of another birth, another awakening. Every day you are in a new state. If you are wise, alert, aware and able to see the meaning and subtle light behind the meaning *before* the meaning, so that every form immediately connects to its origin of creation, then you will encounter several more states. The foundation of all spiritual paths and all the prophetic messengers and unveilings is based on *tawḥīd*. There is only One, there has only been One, there will only be One. And the apparent two is only to re-discover the One.

NEEDS ANNOUNCE THE FULFILLER OF ALL NEEDS

Even in the human dilemma of trying to seek companionship, solace, marriage, or whatever, is a small step towards being self-contained and self-content. Now there are ways that Allah draws us to submission to His Ever-Presence, according to our needs. No human being ever has no needs and these needs change constantly. If they are towards the lower end of experience, the ego-self, then the more you satisfy these needs, newer needs arise. It is a never-ending cycle.

If those needs are oriented towards the higher, towards understanding the meaning and purpose of the situation, then it is part of a progression towards spiritual unfolding and the discovery of a zone of perfection in you—an absolute constancy to which you can refer no matter where you are, who you are, or how you are.

What we are celebrating is the journey towards that discovery. How are we celebrating? By turning away from that which is changing, from what is not going to last: the small pleasures, the small annoyances, and the difficulties. None of them are going to last. We have this incredible make up, as human beings—an amazing body which is like the replica of the cosmos with all the senses. It takes in messages from outside, relates them to your past, what you had in your mind which then gives you feedback, and then you refer to a higher part in your mind, which is called the intellect, to make sure that it is not an emotional response.

You then have the ever-present light of the enlightened heart, which is the house of the soul. It also gives you another reading that says, 'Never mind, be compassionate now, let go,' or 'No, these are good people. They deserve you acting to correct them.' So come with love and correct as required. Sometimes you turn the other cheek and ignore things and sometimes you give them one on their cheek out of love. If it is instigated or motivated by that wisdom and justice, then your actions will be appropriate. An appropriate action is the result of truly yielding to Islam. Islam is a way of life. Islam is life's transaction.

CONSCIOUSNESS AND CHILDHOOD DEVELOPMENT

Life begins in a most amazing way where matter and energy meet in the womb. Initially, there emerges this entity which is biologically and physiologically motivated. As the baby grows, it begins to take in more consciousnesses. It's not just the mother egging her on. As she begins to walk and grow, her consciousness grows more towards meaning, towards light and she wants to have joy in her heart and not just a bit of food in her mouth and belly. We are always in search of that which is behind what appears to be. We will never be content or secure with what we have immediately available to us.

HOMO ECONOMICUS

We have the birth of insurance companies to give us the assurance that the houses and cars we are used to in the outer world will remain. However, what is the use of a house or a car if there is no love, passion, or trust? What is the use of all this paraphernalia if the heart is not content? So, why not then go for the channel of resurrecting, developing, and enriching the contentment of the heart? Then you find the outer is perfectly alright and you can do with less. Our current world is the product of an era of a few generations having reduced the person to the economic man. Homo Sapiens has become Homo Economicus!

It's all about making more money, which ends reducing consciousness in every way. It starts with a simple matter of you and your little room, apartment or car, but it ends up becoming part of your personality. The car is no longer just a means of transport. We no longer say that my car doesn't suit me. We now say, 'I don't like the colour, the shape. The car just isn't me!' So, now it has become an extension of the person. This is the outcome of having reduced human beings to the economic animal. He is a producer. He has a salary.

We Muslims have also fallen into that trap. The word '*rātib*' until a few decades ago, meant 'litany', which is a prayer that you would have as your *wazīfa*, your regular duty. But nowadays it means a salary and *wazīfa* itself now also means an employment. When you say in colloquial Arabic '*Anā muwazzaf*', it doesn't mean 'I have an obligation towards a recitation to take me into higher consciousness.' It means 'I have a fixed job'! We lost this heritage in one or two generations. Due to this global advent of man being viewed as an economic animal everyone can be bought. Pay them more, appear more on television, and you will be elected.

We are now a product of at least 90 years of the scientific, technological era and the economic man who is motivated by their childhood sexuality and some other aberrations. We have taken away, inadvertently, that original nobility for which human beings were created, which is to recognise that you are the representative of your Creator on this earth.

THE MUHAMMADI PACKAGE

The path of Islam is a very clear, user-friendly, intact, and complete model of how to transact, grow, and deal with difficulties in this world. Islam is also a model of how to yield and enjoy the ever-present openings, insights, and bliss that is always available. It encourages us to say no to what is not conducive so that what is conducive will shine upon us. It teaches us to turn away from darkness to discover the light which was always there. The path of Islam is a prophetic path that encapsulates all the teachings that went before it. If you have been truly emancipated from the lower self and are thrilled by the transformation of Islam, you will understand all the paths that went before.

Buddhists renounce this world because it causes trouble. But as a Muslim you do not renounce it. You say instead, 'I deserve the affliction that has come to me, so I will stop being attached, engrossed, and in love with that which is not going to last.' How can any intelligent person love something which is going to disappear? This was the dilemma for our glorious, great Prophet Ibrahim (AS) who is the father of the great many Abrahamic unveilings and prophethoods. Hundreds of prophets came after him expounding, more or less, the same original teaching.

He observed the moon or the sun and thought that this was a wonderful object worthy of worship. But when he realized that it was not going to last he said: 'How can I worship that which is going to disappear?' If it is 'worship-able', if you adore something, if you are passionate about something, then that something must be eternal. It must transcend time. You don't want unreliability: one minute it is there and the next it is *not* there, like in our relationships. Before the fellow is fed, you can't approach the man. After he has eaten and is perhaps less angry, then you can come and say, 'We really want you to do something.'

We are moody, but we want a zone that is beyond moods, which is a permanent *mode*. This prophetic package of Islam, if we perform it, live it, listen to it, absorb it, and are transformed by it, then we are recreated in the manner that was intended—in this world but not of this world. We will then be fully accountable for what we are doing and thinking. You therefore have to protect your heart for it to always overflow with joy. It doesn't begin with joy and bliss. It begins with turning away from all the vices, from anything that is negative, not conducive.

In the path of Islam we have the most incredible, practical manual expressed to us and opened for us in the Qur'an and in the way of the Prophet and those who followed them. In whatever state you are in this can be the door of your salvation. You may have made the greediest error and if you discover that this was an erroneous move, then that too deserves gratitude to the Creator. How is it that you are programmed to recognise that this was a vice, that this was not a good thing to have done?

TURN AWAY FROM SELF TO SOUL

Indeed, all feelings of guilt are just the difference between what you did at the time and what you could have done at the time had you had your wits about you. Be grateful for feeling guilty, but don't do it again because you don't want to suffer. You love yourself. But which self do you love? If you truly love the higher self in you, then you begin by despising the lower self in you. If you look down at your meanness and greed, the tendency to lie and to hide, then you love the tendency in you of being open and straight, generous, correct, free from all those accumulations of the person behind the mask. Get rid of the mask and the persona. Be truly yourself. The self that never changes is your soul. That is your real self.

The self that can change is the self that plays different roles. I am in the role of the speaker but within me still lies that person, entity, light, or that soul that plays so many other roles. The key thing to realise is that this package is not there to be talked about. That is why so many Muslims have sunk into a situation of trying to worship their religion or trying to flog what they think is their religion to others. If it is a real path, then it is a flying carpet. We worship Allah, we worship God. We don't worship religion.

OUTER BOUNDARY INNER BOUNDLESSNESS

Celebrating Islam is to be grateful for this atlas, for this map. This map tells us that if you go in this direction, you will end up in the city. Indeed, there is only the 'city'. You are moving from one to another, but in reality, there is only the one and only One, who created otherness so that you are not satisfied with otherness. You are looking for Oneness by courtesy of the one and only One. The Qur'an says, 'And where do you run to?' You are running from Allah to Allah, disguised as different manifestations. There is only Allah.

There is only one God forever; one energy from which multitudes of different energies, lights, and forms have cascaded. The stone is light if you could only look inside the atoms and see how these incredible electrons are whizzing around in predetermined circuitry. Therefore, celebrating Islam is celebrating that we have come across a map which we know works. The map of the external world, which is that of *sharī'a*—the dos and the don'ts and the directions—is also echoed on the internal side. If I do not accept my outer limitations, I will not have access to my inner boundlessness. You cannot have one without the other. If I did not exist here for a short period of time, I would not have realised that my soul is forever.

Whatever is good, you want to keep forever. Whatever is bad, you want to run away from it. That which is forever, exuding and flashing the Divine Light, is your soul within you. It just takes you turning away from what is not agreeable to you, to find that the source of all agreeability is already there. It is by displacement we discover what is already in place.

FROM SELF-CONFUSION TO SOUL-FUSION

Nowadays, there are so many issues that constantly puzzle humankind. For instance, the matter of decree and destiny. Do we have any say in the matter? Or are we fatalists? What is good? What is bad? What is evil? What is the inner and the outer? Why do I often appear to be schizophrenic? Indeed, every one of us is made of two entities. One is constant, forever, elusive, an energy entity, and the other one is the ever-changing, so-called I. This is a big enigma, a huge paradox. You cannot solve it. It will dissolve in you.

I am a soul, I am a Divine Light caught in this prison for a while and I look at the outer world through my lens and that lens changes all the time. Sometimes it is cracked, sometimes it is murky. If I am healthy, well fed, and looked after, I find everything rosy. The moment everybody turns away and I am despised, the world becomes dreadful. What a drama! We all write our biographies and think we are victims.

Tell anybody that they are not really appreciated. They will say of course, you are right, I am not appreciated. This is especially the case between husbands and wives. Ask any wife, are you well appreciated, and they will say no. Then ask the husband if they are really looked up to, obeyed and loved, and they'll say no. This is just as well because if the poor woman followed this idiot all the time, the chaos would be greater. Look at the perfection behind the scenario and you will put up with apparent imperfection. You will laugh as we have laughed.

THE WORLDVIEW OF *HOMO ECONOMICUS*

The world is currently in a state where it promotes this illusion that you are an economic man or woman. You have to earn and do this and that, then you end up being indebted forever to this non-entity which is the financial services and then you end up paralysed.

You have no time. The cell phone is now with you even in the bathroom. There is no peace anymore. It is assumed that by having these connections, you are more secure, but it ends up being more damning and demanding. What a dilemma you are in! I am hopeful though that through this global suffering, people will increasingly search for the Ever-Present divine offering. Suffering and offering go together.

We have collectively arrived at a cul-de-sac. We think that by having better hygiene, food, and homes, or having more money, cars, and many other things, we are secure and content. In truth you may have some outer security if you like comfort and less pain, but who said less pain is better for you? If I take all the painkillers if I have had a serious ailment, a time will come when I can't live any longer. Whatever has been designed in nature, is correct and appropriate. If we feel guilty about having damaged other communities or other cultures, that is good, so that we don't repeat it.

NO OTHERNESS

In truth there is no otherness. Every country in the world, every flag, every politician now talks about the 'oneness' of humanity. But they don't mean it. They don't even see the oneness between them and their own families, wives, and children. So it is not true. There is dispersion, dispersion, dispersion. Allah's perfect way is that He created the entire cosmos from gatheredness, from that dot which was so dense that it contained everything—and then it exploded. We too 'explode' from the womb and we will also collapse, as the cosmos will collapse when we give up the body.

The individual human being echoes the cosmic story, from the beginning, to the intermediate and the end. The middle is all agitation and change. The beginning is an incredible situation where the known and the unknown meet; where the outer and the inner are the same; where light and matter are inseparable; and where the waveband and the photon are indistinguishable. To celebrate Islam is to celebrate the discovery of this map.

When you go to a city the first thing you ask for is either a guide or a map and then, even after having studied it, you make mistakes. This is what is meant by Allah being All-Forgiving. Allah has not created us for Him to laugh at our stupidities and our mistakes. Allah has created us to discover the light within our hearts, His eternal Presence every time, beyond time, and beyond space. This is our purpose. Therefore, the human being is potentially a most noble entity. It is for this reason that we respect other people.

The great ancient cultures in the East, the Far East, such as the Hindus, saw the Divine Presence in every speck of dust. There was this constant rule of 'Ahimsa'. Do not kill the ant, do not move anything. We as Muslims practise it during Hajj. Allah knows how damaging and destructive we are so He decreed that only during Hajj should we not kill animals, or hunt, or swat insects. The injunction asks us to be cautious. A Buddhist is not supposed to kill, but I assure you Buddhists have inadvertently killed thousands of ants under their feet. We don't know. What about the millions and billions of bacteria we kill in our guts and elsewhere? The story is about that which has no beginning and no end, that which is forever, perpetual, beyond time and space. If you don't honour that, then you have less care for other things, less concern for other things, like your food and all the other psychological factors.

AWARENESS OF PERFECTION

Our prophets and glorious messengers before us had no concern about self-image or self-worth. They knew the light in them is beyond calculation and worth because it was a flash of the eternal. They were not concerned about not getting enough respect from others. Be passionate about the light in your heart and your concern about other things will become appropriate. It does not mean that you don't have concern about your cleanliness or about your clothes, but this won't become your god. It simply means that it won't become the altar upon which you worship.

Instead, you will end up being at the altar of worshipping perfections, all the divine attributes, He whose mercy is beyond limitations, He who loves unconditionally even those who profess to be enemies of God. What compassion! If you take a little bit of that compassion, then as the Qur'an says, you are 'taking on the colour of Allah,' or *sibghat Allah*. Therefore, our *Dīn* contains all the channels that end up grooming the lower self. Who in this world does not want to have boundless wealth? Ask anybody what is enough for them, they will tell you, for the time being, treble my salary. But they will revise it after three days, because the more you have, the more you think you need.

NEEDS—AN ILLUSION?

There are no needs. They are all your fantasy. It is like a fire: the more wood you put on it, the more it burns. So, in our *Dīn*, the path of Islam and this map, we have all the warnings that once there is balance between the powers that propel us to attract things we want and repel things we don't want, this will eventually bring about modesty in us. They also bring about courage. Instead of repulsion being anger, it becomes courage. Instead of it being greed, it becomes modesty.

With balance and grooming comes wisdom. With that comes an awakening of a higher intellect. You will not forget what matters. You may be forgetful about material things such as what you ate six days ago. Imam 'Ali (AS) said that whoever is concerned about what goes in their stomach, derives their value from it. We have the package of grooming the self and of placing the boundaries.

This is where *sharīʿa* (outer law) comes in—I'm sorry I can't do that, this is *harām* (forbidden), it's not natural. *Halāl* (permitted) and *harām* had to do with perpetuating what is natural. A kitten knows how to lick itself. A human being on the other hand needs to struggle with his children for years until they learn how to cut their nails, let alone other things. It takes a long time for us to learn.

THE SPIRITUAL RESPONSIBILITY OF PARENTHOOD

This is why it is very dangerous to produce children. I am speaking to you from experience! You must have responsibility and compassion and realise that you are really doing it for a higher cause. Otherwise you end up oppressing your children, and the trust the children have in you will not get transferred into trusting God, trusting Allah, Whose light is in their hearts. You must, therefore, conduct yourself with your children, in a manner that delivers them to their Creator by Whose mercy and mystery they came about.

How much do we know about what goes on in the womb? How much do we know about what goes on in the mind? As for the heart, we don't even know what it is or how it works.

I am here to share with you, in celebration, my discovery of this incredible prophetic manual that never, ever fails. This prophetic manual is based on the Qur'an and the way of the Prophet, which is activated by you absorbing it, living it and thus being transformed by it. It is not by just preaching and talking.

If there is passion and love, then you love that which is in you more than anything else. Then He who is closest to you is more worthy of that love. What is closer to you than your own heart? So, love your heart by *not* loving all of the other things that bring about these illusions, delusions, and all the other confusions in the mind. It is indeed Allah's *Rahma* (Mercy) that brings you confusion. If you are confused now and you don't know where to turn, thank Allah. You are in a cul-de-sac. All you need to do is renew your *wudū'* (ritual ablution), ask yourself to forgive yourself and the Creator Who is Ever-Forgiving, then turn around and get out of the cul-de-sac. Otherwise you will be given other ways and means of maintaining what has now become a habit, which is blaming others.

BLAMING OTHERS

It is very easy to blame others. 'You don't know what kind of a husband, or perhaps brother, I have! You don't understand! Nobody understands!' You are creating your own world and Allah says in the Qur'an:

$$زَيَّنَّا لَهُمْ أَعْمَلَهُمْ فَهُمْ يَعْمَهُونَ$$

Their actions will be made attractive to them, so they wander aimlessly. (27:4)

The reason this is so is because you cannot remain without contentment, so it becomes pseudo-contentment. That is why many people love their sickness and live with it. Doctors realise this and increase the dosages of their medication. They are given more pills until they become the walking dead.

ABUNDANCE DISTRACTS

Allah reminds us that we are distracted by abundance that surrounds us and the desire for accumulation

$$أَلْهَىٰكُمُ ٱلتَّكَاثُرُ ۝$$

Abundance has distracted you

Allah revealed this when the Arabs were bragging about how big the tribe they belonged to was.

$$حَتَّىٰ زُرْتُمُ ٱلْمَقَابِرَ ۝$$

Until you visit the graves. (108:1-2)

When you proclaim pride about your tribe you place yourself in the grave-yards now. Most of us are walking graves, creating more pollution. Wake up before it is too late! Take the urgency seriously. Immediately realise that if this was your last day, what would you be doing? How do you know the breath that goes in may never come out? Bring about an urgency against yourself and against leisure as far as life is concerned. You will always be on 'holy-days'.

Every day is a holy day! Why can't we be thrilled all the time? The answer will come from within you: because you have been diverted and deflected in another direction. Allah is Ever-Forgiving. Allah does not want you to suffer. Allah has given you Himself as an offer. Himself meaning His qualities, all of His glorious Attributes such as the Ever-Present, the Ever Lasting, the Most Beautiful and the Most Majestic. Who doesn't want beauty?

WITNESSING OPPOSITES

As long as you don't fall into this cul-de-sac of just collecting beautiful objects, go for beauty itself, and then become subtler in your gaze so that you will see only beauty in what others see as ugly. I was taught in my youth to smell the fragrance of the ultimate flowers in the compost. I used to run away from the bad smell until one day somebody sat me down and said, 'Sit until you start smelling the rose from the compost.' See how the opposites meet? The great Shaykh Muhammad ibn Al-Habib said that you are destined to see both extremes instantly— '...the heart...gathered the two opposites in its vision...' . We have it in so many Quranic chapters such as :

$$ مَرَجَ ٱلۡبَحۡرَيۡنِ يَلۡتَقِيَانِ ۝ بَيۡنَهُمَا بَرۡزَخٌ لَّا يَبۡغِيَانِ ۝ $$

He merged the two seas, converging together. Between them is a barrier, which they do not overrun. (55:19-20)

The two oceans meet in you: the ocean of boundlessness and the ocean of limitation and in between the moment that passes. You are, in fact, the locus of the infinite and the finite, of both bliss and the apparent shadows which you interpret as difficulties or miseries. Give in to the difficulty. Surrender! But you have other agendas such as pleasing the wife or the husband. Don't please them. Go and tell them you are helpless. Why have you pretended to be God? Say, 'Look, I really tried but I can't do it anymore. Please excuse me. Goodbye.'

I remember being impressed by the philosopher Bertrand Russell when I read that in response to family issues he had realized while riding his bicycle that he could no longer maintain his relationship with his wife. The man was a mathematician to begin with and was driven by the love for knowledge. He had realized that his marriage could not be saved. In his time, however, divorce was socially taboo.

Try being honest and see. Be willing to give in and say, 'Yes, I made a mess of it, please excuse me. Help me if you can.' You will be amazed by how other people will rise by seeing you become humble. In my younger student days, as a foreigner I was so lonely that I would knock on a few doors and say, 'Please, I am lonely...' After a few days I just couldn't get out of all the invitations I was receiving. Be open and honest and admit you don't how to do it. Live in the moment and you will be at the edge of living forever. You will regain that inner sight; that higher sight of seeing infinity in the moment.

Accept time. Accept the clock, but as a tiny, ever-changing shadow which never changes. Discover the light of the Divine in you by turning away from all the ever-changing shadows and challenges. Respond to the challenge. Do not say it does not exist. It *does* exist. Admit the pain, but also admit that it is short-lived. Admit the difficulty but don't be swamped by it. This is the cause of my celebration. This is the cause of my courage to be amongst you and share that which is ordained, which has been given to us by the one and only Giver, where each one of us is a taker.

DIFFERENT SELVES, SAME SOUL

We are all essentially the same. We are all seeking constant and durable happiness and contentment. But each one of us is different. Isn't that wonderful? You are not the same. You don't have the same teeth as other people. You don't have the same eyes or the same body. It's difficult enough having this body, let alone if everybody were the same. Thank God for the apparent difference and for the sameness where it matters. We are different in every moment. My mind ticks differently in every moment, but if my heart is constantly reflecting that Ever-Present Light, then my being different and changing my mind is enjoyable. Otherwise I am confused.

If you come to ask, 'Have you changed your mind?' I will say, 'The mind is to be changed, but not the heart.' Because you have not read your atlas and map properly, you are mistaking your mind for your heart. Instead, what we should say is, 'I pray that my heart never ever changes, that it always reflects the light.' But my mind always changes! I now discover that this is not good enough for me, so I don't want it. Thank you! If you don't read the map, if you do not know your *dīn*, then you remain confused. When a person tells you that they are confused, know that they have either not read the map, or they are not willing to apply it, or they are not living it. If they were, then they would not be confused. They are fused by the one and only Creator of all lights and energy, inwardly and outwardly, out of His mercy.

Every challenge is wonderful. You don't know what to do? Wait! There's tomorrow. Say, 'I have absolutely no idea what to do.' Wonderful! Take a day's holiday. Let the rest of the world also be at peace from your agitation. You have no idea where to turn? Great! Don't turn. What's wrong with that? Take counsel and ask, and if there is no answer, shut up and enjoy it. Look at the bees, feel the wind. Let the breeze go through your hair. We are clumsy and Allah knows that. He says it repeatedly in the Qur'an that He created this entity and that is why the angels objected—they went on strike!

ON A.S.K.

I celebrate with you our intention, *my* intention, to discover that which is beyond, until there is no movement, no disturbance. I am grateful to Allah for making this opportunity for us to rediscover the path, the way, and for the possibility of being transformed by it. The software of the Academy (of Self Knowledge) is based on a new program wherein we are presenting the *Dīn* in a manner that is acceptable to the modern mind.

A hundred years ago, most Muslims considered it despicable to talk about the self. They would encourage you to give up your self, serve and help! Now, however, the self is paramount. Therefore, we will demolish that monument. The first part of the Academy's work is called Self Knowledge and the first module is about the self. That cosmology is most brilliantly produced for us in our *Dīn*, our path. Outwardly we are accountable for what we are doing: What is your intention? What have you done? Whom have you harmed? Why didn't you care for the elderly person or the child? Outwardly accountable, inwardly free. These are the maps which we are hoping to present as a model, an atlas called A.S.K.

Looking at the international scene nowadays, an aspect elevates mankind out of locality towards universality, while another aspect demeans it by making it more materialistic and corporatized. In all worldly endeavours, every human being is equally desperate. They may, therefore, discover the truth. We Muslims did not live our *Dīn* fully for it to overflow; it will be discovered despite us. This is cause for celebration.

DEATH IS NOT THE END

If you have become conscious of the Eternal Light in you, then it is easy to depart. If not, then you cause havoc and agony because you are scared of leaving the body. You find that some people are able to leave within just a few minutes. You must realise that you are not the body. This has only been your vehicle to get you back to the essence which has always been there.

POEM: THE EVER-PRESENT PEACE

Is permanent peace an illusion?
Is true contentment ever attainable?
If not, then why all of this yearning?
And life's search as to where, how, and when
But then look at life on earth
It begins and ends with agitation
When peace is invaded, and cells divided and then again sub-divided
To fulfil the original promise of birth and cosmic perfections
In regular unexpected rotations
And then man tills the earth
Creating dusty agitation
To help new growth, to survive, to interact and to learn
The first steps of inner and outer harmony
Whilst the womb is occupied, invaded, and colonized
To be challenged by the meanings and events of birth, death, weakness, and
strength
And to know that whatever appears will once again disappear
And to experience that whatever you see here, frivolous, or dear
Is indeed on its journey back to there
So where can you find peace? How and when?
Is it within change? And the battles of time and space?
Or is it before it all began? Or after the never-ending end
Or is that peace and love of joy are indeed the distorted responses of agitation
and heat
Whereas the cool breeze of peace is Ever Present Ever Lasting
Ever Beckoning to all who read and follow the illumined perfections of As-
Salaam.

REMAINING IN GRATITUDE

May your voice be carried by all the angels near and far so that the hearts remember what has already been put in them. That is called *fitra*. *Fitra* is the divine pattern that is transmitting through every soul via the encasement, or its harbour, which is every heart. Allah tells us repeatedly that creation is a blessing. It is a *baraka*, gift upon gifts, or *ni'ma* upon *wahba*. Where can you stop seeing the glorious, infinite layers of gifts? You think something was bad for you, change your mind! It was actually best for you. Once you see the 'bestness', you start recognising that repeatedly, until such time you become speechless. You can no longer say it. Allah says, 'It is He who has created seven heavens, one layer above the other. You can see no flaw in the creation of the Beneficent. Look again. Can you see faults?' (67:3) He says in the next *āya*, 'Then look again, and again, and your sight will return to you dazzled and exhausted.'

Nothing can happen unless it is part of the Divine laws. These laws come in multiple layers that are physical and discernible as well as subtler, non-discernible, and even sub-atomic. There are also the astrophysical laws and beyond. Allah describes it in the Qur'an as done by 'countless agents/angels/forces which you do not see' (*junudun lam tarawhā*) (33:9). The Prophet (S) said there are seven angels for every leaf that falls. This implies different energies or pulses. One of them has to do with heat, the other one is chemical, the other has to do with the cell's outer boundaries and so on. Others are to do with tiny changes in the ionic charges on the surface. The more you look into it, the more you find another ocean and another ocean and another. This is one part of the meaning of the seven layers.

We need to recognise the position we are in, which is a limited one, and use that as a launch-pad for our inner rockets. Our sight is limited, which is a blessing in itself. If you could see carpets microscopically then nobody would buy one, for they would be seeing billions of little mites! It is wonderful not to see too far and not to see too near, to be just in the middle. This is a *mithāl*. This is only a foundation which indicates many more subtle, wonderful, and glorious insights. Allah says, 'Look back, do you find any faults?' (67:3). In other words, if you look back *without* your emotions, or mental attachments, you will see only perfection.

As a human being, if I expect to be treated in a particular way, or to have a specific type of relationship, I am likely to be disappointed. We all fantasize – 'I want to look like so-and-so, my body to look like an athlete, my pocketbook to be like that of a millionaire, and the Maserati car that belongs to so-and-so'. Take away your expectations and fantasies about what you desire, then you will see the perfection of what is in front of you. See the meaning of it.

Read, read, read and apply and be transformed by that reading. Allah says:

ثُمَّ ٱرۡجِعِ ٱلۡبَصَرَ كَرَّتَيۡنِ يَنقَلِبۡ إِلَيۡكَ ٱلۡبَصَرُ خَاسِئًا وَهُوَ حَسِيرٌ ۝

Then look again, and again, and your sight will return to you dazzled and exhausted. (67:4)

Your eyesight will be humbled by seeing that perfection upon perfection upon perfection. That is why such intelligent people like yourselves have taken so much trouble to be here. All of you are, by Allah's Grace, from a background of study, discipline, education, scholarship, and other wonderful skills. By now, therefore, you will have already discovered that whatever is in front of you has perfection in it. Therefore, it must be a source of happiness.

So, do not ever come near me if you are unhappy. I cannot help you! If you are happy, you don't need me. Either way, we have the best companionship. If you have got the message, good luck to you. May you live well, and may others benefit from it. If you haven't got the message yet, I can't give it to you. It is that unconditional love and openness between us that is contagious. That's why some people come to us and find they can't leave. There is a natural attraction because of similarities and connectedness. And the reverse is also true. It has to do with polarisation. 'Birds of a feather flock together'. We also have some birds amongst us with very few feathers. That's fine! You will be amazed how healing takes place and wellness comes about from where we don't know. New strength and *resolve*, a new drive comes about. You need to be recharged.

One of our visitors tells me, 'When I come here, I am recharged'. I keep reminding him that I cannot recharge anybody. You reduce your own *dis*charge. We must get the language right, otherwise we won't get the cosmology. 'God' becomes a hotchpotch of ideas. Every now and then they note flippantly that 'Allah is generous' (*Karīm*), or 'Allah is Merciful' (*Rahīm*). Like all these Muslims they say '*Inshā'Allah*' when what they really mean is 'never-never'! Let us correct that. Let us put it right. Let us get back to correct habits.

CARDINAL POINTS IN THE COMPASS

Take care not to ever fall into this pitfall of accusing others, denouncing this or that *madhhab*. It is against the *sunna* of the Prophet (S) to do that. If people know, they know, and they will leave. If they don't know, then they will learn by companionship. Care for what *you* know, let that build and overflow then it will touch others. Care for yourself. If you are anorexic, spiritually speaking, you will not be able to feed others.

Take the Mickey out of yourself. Laugh at your lower self (*nafs*). The *nafs* tries to imitate the soul/spirit (*rūh*). The *nafs* cannot be the *rūh*. It is like the shadow of a person walking along a mountain ridge with ravines on both sides. At some points the shadow appears long and at other points it is short. At yet other times it is close and sometimes sharp. It is like that: the *nafs* mimics the *rūh*—the *rūh* is ever content while the *nafs* pretends to be content. The *rūh* is ever stable, while the *nafs* pretends to be stable. If you say to somebody, 'You change your mind all the time!' they'll probably say, 'I don't change my mind!' The fact is, the mind is made to be change—for the better. But don't change the direction (*qibla*) of love, of perfections in your soul. Change your mind! Freedom! But you are not free from the passion and love of perfections, of Allah's qualities, which are in your soul.

The values are the same. The path, the map, is the same. Sometimes it becomes corroded and the community falls into disarray. Sometimes rats and mice have nibbled at it and sometimes ink has splattered over it so they can't read it well. I believe we are heading towards a most magnificent global scene where human beings yearn to move towards the discovery of the higher in them. The movements of some of them are going to last longer, some of them not. Whether they are reborn or unborn, it does not matter. The signs are all indicating the yearning and thirst of humankind to discover their Creator.

Many times, however, this path becomes highly perverted, reactionary, and destructive. We are heading towards the worst part of that period and you must read the climate correctly. Read the map of the self and the soul/spirit (*rūh*) and the heart (*qalb*) and the relationship between them. If you want to maintain the *qibla* (direction), then you have to be on the path (*Dīn*). You must be constantly aware of whether you are in *wudū'* or not. What time is it? Where is *qibla*? That is the protection of the outer laws (*sharī'a*).

With the lower self groomed, you can then live as an individual with an identity, with a past, like anybody else. You realise that you are favoured by Allah Who did not create you as a frog. You are being honoured as an Adamic being, the representative (*khalīfa*) of Allah. You reflect an agent of goodness, the eternal goodness of the One and only Source of contentment.

LEADERSHIP OF MUSLIMS

Why have we not had a basic reformation of Muslim leadership? For centuries, we have not had leadership that reflects the Prophetic qualities. We have taken all these despots and authoritarian idiots in the place of prophetic beings. We have not had sufficient understanding of the conditions of leadership and the qualifications of that leadership. The first and most important qualification of anyone in leadership is to know the Absolute Leader. He would therefore not want to lead, because it is mischief and trouble. Leadership is exhausting!

I will never forget Sufi Barakat Ali during one of my last visits to him in the Punjab. He usually did not talk to people, having undertaken a vow of silence, but that day he did. There were some Swedish friends with me and he told them, 'I am the Shaykh of cows. Most people who come to me ask me about what supplication I can give them so their cows give more calves or milk. This is what I get asked.' True story!

So it is important to know the map of yourself. It is important to know your Path (*Dīn*). It is also important to know about timing. This blessed being, Sufi Barkat Ali, was living at a time and in a place where the only concern of the villagers and the people around him was the productivity of cows. This is where we have ended up, but it is changing. If you expect it to change right now, you are mistaken. Like any other human hallucination or illness, it has to reach its peak. It has not yet done so. So do not put the seeds in the soil thinking that it is early spring. Be patient. Do your part. Let your own inner finetuning and adjustments take place and be patient. If you do anything more than that, it will be destructive to others and also to yourself. You will burn out with expectations.

Allah orders us not to have sorrow for that which has passed. Can you do anything about it? No. Move on. Be *'abd al-waqt,* slave of the moment. It is critical to forgive all of those who came before us who could have done better, but did not. For years I stood in judgement of my own people. Why hadn't they done something in Iraq to preserve what was a most wonderful meeting place for many 'caravans'? As long as Iraq was in that position, people came from North, South, and East. It was alive. The word 'Iraq' means '*Irq*', which means origin, essence, or root. This is why Iraq was called that. But it has ended up mostly *'Araq. 'Araq* is a dreadful alcohol, exceptionally harsh.

Be patient and do your part. Don't ask why they didn't do it. They couldn't! People fall into their habits. They had a jolly good time and now they have gone. Times have changed. For the last three to four hundred years, we had no idea what was happening elsewhere in the world. So what is the use of me just sitting back, cursing, and blaming those poor people who went before me? They had a good time and are now probably having a better time. But what about poor me? We are now in a position where East and West meet at the level of the *dunyā* (world)—at the level of rationality, reason, materialism, and physics. Wonderful! Meet on that plane and if you can balance it by your inner values and the knowledge of who you are and who you can potentially be, then you are an example in every way, at least to yourself. Allah says:

$$إِنَّآ أَرْسَلْنَٰكَ شَٰهِدًا وَمُبَشِّرًا وَنَذِيرًا$$

We have sent you as a witness and a bringer of good tidings and a warner.
(33:45)

Look at the different stages which the Prophet goes through and, by extension, us too. Witness! Witness yourself. Witness before you and after you. Is it the right time? What season is it? Who is there? Who is not?

'And give them good news (tidings).' The good news is that you are eternal. You have been created to discover total happiness that is not contingent upon a person, a situation, a meal, or money. It is about eternal joy. And then 'the warning' that if they don't do it, they will die miserably, in darkness and in fear of death.

$$وَدَاعِيًا إِلَى ٱللَّهِ بِإِذْنِهِۦ وَسِرَاجًا مُّنِيرًا ۝$$

And as one who summons to God by His leave, and as a light-giving beacon.
(33:46)

And calling them to this knowledge, to this light when it is appropriate; if people are not going to listen, then who are you going to call?

'By His leave'—what does Allah's permission mean? It means all the elements are present, it means appropriateness. And finally, 'A light-giving beacon'. There is nothing around me except 'beaming light'! Sometimes when I hear somebody complaining, I show them the goodness I see in their complaint. Please see perfection and goodness in every situation. Don't react. You think it is bad? Wait! See the goodness behind badness and the benefit you can derive from that. Keep company with those who uplift you, who will remind you of your shortcomings and of the opportunity to give more and serve more. We have no option but to truly absorb our Path, living our *Dīn*—enjoy it and constantly be grateful. Allah says:

$$\text{لَئِن شَكَرْتُمْ لَأَزِيدَنَّكُمْ}$$

When you are in gratitude, I increase you. (14:7)

When you are in gratitude, your heart is tranquil; then you will see better and read better. If your heart is agitated, you are overtaken by the fire of anger. You must restore balance. We have the inner technologies to do so. There are dozens of ways of doing it: Renew your *wudū'* (ritual ablution), do a two *rak'a* (cycle) prayer. If you are standing, lie down. If you are lying down, stand. Change the outer in a manner that breaks that onslaught of your obsession and possession with your anger. We have the technology, but it has to be lived. All of us who have gone through youth and early life have messed up and did not have the right guidance. It doesn't matter! It's gone. Yesterday is finished. Do not bring back these memories that put you down. You will stop yourself.

We are always better at advising others than ourselves. We always know what the problem is with the neighbours but not in our own homes. We all want to play the healers and the *hakīms* to others, but not for ourselves because that implies certain rationing of our bad habits and diet—less chilli, less oil, less this or that. We are very clever!

This slipperiness is called *nifāq*, which originally means a hole with two entryways. Something can go into the tunnel and come out elsewhere. *Nafaq* in Arabic is a tunnel. *Nifāq* means hypocrisy. That is why I encourage you to read the Qur'an in Arabic, however little of it you can manage. You'll be amazed how many different facets it has. I am so delighted to hear that there are more people interested in the Qur'an. People are enjoying the publications and reprints. Make it easy for others. But you must be the first recipient. Think of your relatives and others close by. Have compassion for them. Do not constantly call back on your past memory of people. They change. Really! I have changed.

Yesterday morning I came eager to stay. Now I am eager to leave. A different mood. Times change, you change, your mind changes, and circumstances change. You change until you realise that in you there is something which has never changed, or never changes, and that is your anchor. Rumi says, 'The calls of the lovers echo in the valleys and the mountains. Answer back saying, I was waiting for you to call.' It is Allah who is waiting for us. He is the Ever Patient, *As-Sabūr*.

I would like to end by thanking Allah for having saved me from myself, by His Light, and brought me to Africa, and given me the best of the best of the best outwardly and inwardly. The best of companions and friends and an energetic crew to develop the Academy work and for us to put it in the breeze of *rahma*. So I am very optimistic about the new way of presenting our Path and our *Dīn*. There is nothing new in it in terms of teaching and essence, it is the presentation—I am following my great Imam, Ja'far As-Sadiq (AS), when he says, 'Do not expect your children to follow the same style that you did.' Our style fifty years ago was the *Madrasa* (religious school) which has become more obnoxious. Until about 20 years ago, it was used as a threat by parents as somewhere to send the naughty child for punishment: 'If you don't behave, I will send you to the *Madrasa*!' We have done ourselves in and now we must get ourselves out of it. So, it is the same original teaching but a new style.

We have a centre here for everyone [referring to the Academy of Self Knowledge, ASK]. Outsiders can come and enjoy and do their *'Ibāda* (worship) and *Salāt* (prayer), and insiders can come if they want to have more. Those who want to be drunk or sober will be in the company of those with whom you are now: inwardly beyond bounds but outwardly limited, bounded and accountable.

I thank Allah with no beginning and no end because the beginning is by Him and He has no end. This is your home, it is my home, and we have no doors. They are open, but only open for those who have the same taste (*dhawq*). So welcome, welcome, welcome and no goodbyes!

CHAPTER FOUR

Voices of Wisdom from Our Past

Given in 2005

- To Be Colonised by Allah
- Poem: Wisdom, Past, Present and Future
- Apparent Change, Timeless Patterns
- Three Key Balances
- Time and Space
- Evolving Socio-Cultural Contexts
- You Are the Project
- On Witnessing
- Perfect Conduct
- True Leadership

TO BE COLONISED BY ALLAH

Ultimately, all knowledge, everything that is in existence, is encapsulated in the dot of the letter *Bā'* (B) in *Bismillah* (by or in the name Allah). Ultimately, everything else is by the design of Allah and it has no end. If you take all the commands, you will never be able to count them. If you take all the trees and all the oceans to write down the commands, it will never be enough.

To all of you who have come a long way towards self-realisation, towards enlightenment, a few words will be more than enough. I have written a brief poem which I am going to share with you.

POEM: WISDOM, PAST, PRESENT AND FUTURE

Welcome to all present here
The past is a window closed
The future is a sight/ site not yet visited
The present conceals and reveals all
Its roots boundless and eternal
Its fruits defined by space time
Captured in flashes of frozen light
In ceaseless flight
Wisdom is sustained goodness and ease
Appropriateness leading to harmony and peace
Like time and space, it has no fixed face
The wise act of yesterday, could be the ultimate folly of today
But wisdom itself is the noble offspring
Brought about by modesty, courage and justice
Foundations for transformations that it can bring

The wise act of yesterday, could be the ultimate folly of today
But wisdom itself is the noble offspring
Brought about by modesty, courage and justice
Foundations for transformations that it can bring
The ecstasy and awesomeness of the present
Where no open or closed windows matter
Where the light of lights, rendered all shattered
And revealed the loving embrace of opposites
A threshold to the Divine treasury of His presence
Welcoming creation to the timeless present
The abode of beauty, majesty and eternity
Enhanced by earthly illusions, of absence, again

APPARENT CHANGE, TIMELESS PATTERNS

Everything appears to change and yet nothing changes. This is the foundation of worldly wisdom; in other words, do the right thing, at the right time, in the right way. The backdrop changes; today is different from yesterday. For example, today it rains, the temperature has changed, the venue has changed, some names have changed, a few new people have arrived, a few thousand have left this world, and a few thousand more have arrived. Essentially, we are looking for the same thing, but in the wrong place, with misconceptions and deceptions. We are looking for certainty in our hearts, and all human attempts to get security and certainty and knowledge of the outer world amount to little childish exercises that will lead the true seeker to the realisation of the ever-perfect inner security that has always been there.

What you have been looking for has actually been looking for you. Allah has created us to know his qualities. It is for this reason that we all love the Divine Qualities, the All-Powerful, the Holder of all Treasuries, the All-Knowing, the All-Hearing, the Ever-Present, He who has no beginning and no end—*Al-Awwal* (the First), *al-Ākhir* (The Last), *al-Zāhir* (The Manifest,) *al-Bātin* (The Hidden), as well as all of the other Attributes that we adore. Indeed, the clear heart *(fu'ād)* is where all of these qualities are etched. How do I know what generosity is unless its transmitted qualities, its frequency and cosmology, are not already in my heart?

So then what changes? What is generosity? Generosity could be when you give what you have to someone else. In some moments you give of your time, your wealth, or your attention. At another time, generosity would be to ignore something. For example, if someone is thriving on having captured your attention while blaming everything in existence and you listen, then you are actually perpetuating this person's illusion. As if they are separate from the rest of existence.

Generosity remains the same but the way it appears differs from minute to minute, from person to person, and from situation to situation. When a child is crying, it is generous of us to deflect the child's attention from the apparent cause of crying, but if a child has become too selfish and demanding, it is quite generous for the parents to reprimand them with love and affection.

All these values are forever etched in the human soul. Every soul has them. This is the Divine justice. We all know the meaning of mercy, the meaning of knowledge, and patience, but they differ according to the circumstance. Worldly wisdom is founded on doing the right thing at the right time in the right place in the right manner. It implies that you yourself have been reconciled. If you harbour a lot of anger, rancour, disappointments, and you have a very confused biography and are still concerned about that, then how can you truly and correctly reflect on what has come to you? If you are still heavily affected and influenced by your past, then you are not reconciled and you are not content.

Modesty is the foundation, and it is balanced upon courage. These are the two impetuses within every human being, based on the drive to attract and repel. We want to attract what we like, and we want to repel what we don't like. Love cannot exist unless its dark shadow, or its black hole, called hate, is also there. You cannot have any idea or possibility or manifestation in this life without its opposite. This is where the two opposites embrace. They are partners forever and are never separate. You can never separate good from bad, high from low, life from death, day from night. The root of each is in its opposite.

This is the fabric of existence and we are not going to change it. Nature has both. A lioness licks its cub with such affection. Yet three years later when the cub tries to eat at the same time as its mother, it will have its head bitten off. Things in existence are always based on this duality and the only singular light behind them all is Allah. Nothing in this existence that you perceive as good exists without the seed of potential bad. The only pure and absolute is Allah; everything else reflects that. Once you understand this cosmology, then you truly begin to act wisely, and you will choose modesty as opposed to wanting to attract everything for yourself. You will rather say 'Enough. I do not want anymore.' This is the foundation of modesty; it brings about a host of virtues.

Anger is repulsion. If you subdue it, if you are reflective about it, you find it is an immense power that can bring about courage instead of foolhardiness. It can bring about true courage and with it, the virtues of generosity, brotherhood and everything that comes from that virtue. If these two are in proper balance, then wisdom will come naturally, and justice will be the result of this equilibrium. If, for example, your intention is to help everybody to reach their highest potential, which is the purpose of existence, then you will immediately know how to tackle the issue, and whether it is the right time or not. Justice is the balance because nothing exists unless it is balanced between the opposites.

THREE KEY BALANCES

There are three key aspects that encompass everything that we experience, know, or come to know. And they are the inner and the outer, earthly and heavenly, meaning and form. They are not distinctly separate categories but these dualities help us to perceive the dynamic patterns that define our experiences and give us bearings.

Inner and Outer

The human being is an outer form, which contains the body and all the senses. We have a complex system of senses and a complex system of the mind. Beyond that, you have multitudes of layers of the mind: you have a vegetative mind and an animal mind. Your self or *nafs*, has many layers, such as the *nafs al-ammāra, nafs al-lawwāma, nafs al-mulhama*. In addition to these layers you also have the rational self.

At the higher end of the spectrum you also have a heart that contains your supreme self, the light of your 'self', which is your soul. You have a whole spectrum of the 'I' or 'self' and yet every one of us still refers to the self as I! When you were 4 years old, you announced that word. When you are forty you announce it. When you are sick, you announce it. When you are well you announce it. When you are humble you announce it. When you are arrogant you announce it. What a multi-faceted I! So who is this speaker? Essentially, it is the light that is within you, which is the soul or your *rūh* (spirit/soul) having gone through the layers of your mind or intellect or rationality.

The wise person will not react nor respond to anything unless he or she has immediately gone through a filtering process, referring to the highest. If you are connected to your *rūh* then you are truly reflective of your creator, of Allah. Your *rūh* is His resident agent within you. You are already colonised by that light, and so you have no option other than to respond to the purpose of the colonised 'you' or 'self', which is to know Allah's qualities, to be thrilled by Allah's beauty, His majesty, power, gentleness, *lutf* (subtlety), and *'ilm* (knowledge), until you feel yourself completely imbued by all of those Divine colours.

The Qur'an also tells us that it is about taking on the *sibghat Allah* or colours of Allah. You do not become God. You have turned away from your animal self towards the higher and have taken on a certain godly quality, which other people refer to as 'light'. The truth is that there is only light, which is modified, reformed, changed, exchanged, refracted and deflected. There is only light in different forms, as we now know. Matter and energy are the same thing; they are fully exchangeable, and time and space are one hundred percent flexible. There is no such thing as absolute time and space. There is, however, absolute truth (*haqq*), but anything other than that is relative.

The closer you are to the absolute, the closer you are to the truth. Every moment has a reality. The present situation between us in this hall is real, but it is a short-lived reality. After a short while we will take a break and disappear. After a few years, we will leave this world. So, this reality has changed but my love for truth—if it is consistent, persistent, and a constant reference—is a reflection of *Haqq*, Truth, because we are all the same in that we want what is permanent. This is why I have defined wisdom as sustained goodness and ease. We want goodness that is *sustainable*. The Prophet (S) says, 'Go for a goodness that lasts, even though it may be small, rather than a big thing that does not last.'

We are all utterly caught by a *rūh* that never dies, while the opposite is true for the body with which I have identified. The only certain thing about the body is that it gets closer to its departure every day. The urgency to arrive at the point of departure is reflected in the Divine Names of *Al-Bāqi* and *As-Samad*.

Earthly and Heavenly

Wisdom is appropriateness, doing the right thing. Now this is all worldly or earthly wisdom. Many people have worldly wisdom. Our Muslim leaders, our Kings all have worldly wisdom but what about the unworldly, heavenly wisdom? What about the other side of us, the immutable light in our heart? We always need to bring in the spiritual side to embellish worldly wisdom.

Worldly wisdom has to do with the highest rational ability. Machiavellian ideas are wisdom as well, but what about the other side we yearn for? Each of these two domains have their rules: worldly wisdom requires rationality, patience, modesty, justice, and courage—all of these are known as virtues. Heavenly wisdom has different rules. It requires you not to be aware of yourself, thus we have our worship. We have this wonderful bouquet or banquet of different acts of worship: in our salat we take *wudū'* to disassociate ourselves from the outer world, then you enter into dialogue with your creator, expressing love for his qualities. *Al-hamdu li'llah*, praise belongs to Allah, all the qualities we praise are His.

Then you are entering the true 'disappearing act' by bowing, going in your *sajda* (prostration) and then disappearing. When the Prophet (SAW) describes, '*As-salātu mi'rāj ul-mu'min*' (*Salat* is the ascension of the Believer), the implication being that you 'disappear'. In the act, you have no self-awareness. You have gone into the other zone which is present in you, the zone of the unseen and lights. You disappear from what you are used to as worldly appearances. You are thus perfecting the state of *barzakhīya* (interspace), which is *in* this world but not *of* this world. You do not deny this world but, more than anything else, you are acknowledging the unseen—*alladhīna yu'minūna bi'l-ghayb* (Those who believe in the Unseen) otherwise you are out of balance.

Worldly wisdom has to be balanced by heavenly wisdom, the inner and the outer. This is the first key balancing act. You have an outer presence, you have a certain colour, you have unique features. No two fingerprints are alike. Every human being is unique in that sense. However, with regards to the inner, we are all the same. We are all, at best, fumbling, mumbling, and confused. We don't know why, and as a result we end up doing things like filling our cupboards with goods and clothes we don't need and start giving these away and then we think we are generous. But why do we do this? Because of the *nafs*, the so-called ego. It lies and wants to hide the truth. The soul never lies; it is always truthful. The *nafs* will always want to appear to be generous because the soul is forever generous. Allah's generosity has no beginning and no end—it is boundless and unconditional. All our vices are the dark side reflecting the virtues which are in the *rūh*.

If you think of any idea, any possibility, or any action you take, you will find that it is either reflecting the virtue that is in the soul or the dark side. The soul reflects generosity. If you have been truly generous and open, then you are facing the soul. If you have been mean then you have been facing the other side, that black hole, and you want to hide it. You claim, 'It wasn't me,' but who was it then? It is you who has confused it all. Now you need to be *fused*: to look at the higher in you and deal with the lower in you, which requires courage.

Meaning and Form

Another key pairing that supports the foundation of all that is in the cosmos is meaning and form. Whatever appears to you has a meaning and an outer shape that betrays itself. This is true even in the field of medicine. Take the doctrine of signatures, for example. There is a signature 'tune' to the different herbs, foods, nuts and others, that look like the body parts they are good for. The walnut, for example, looks like a brain, and its fatty acids and minerals benefit the brain. So the outer and the inner relate. There cannot be an outer without an inner. There cannot be a form without a meaning.

Every physical, discernible, material form is balanced by a meaning that is non-physical, subtle, and unseen. Whether it is the subatomic world or whether it is the astrophysical world, the unseen is unknown, but it is there! There are galaxies whose light has not even reached us yet. They disappeared billions of light years ago. There is the seen, discernible body, and there is another universe that is the heavenly, that reflects the ultimate and the absolute in me and is unseen. It is the battery, the energiser within me.

Whatever exists is based on these foundations. You have the inner and the outer, earthly and heavenly, form and meaning. Our job in life is to be in balance with regards to these three complementary opposites. If you have come here with the right intention, then the attention and the results of it will be as good as your intention.

TIME AND SPACE

We have many teachings in our heritage that reflect what I am sharing with you, but we do not translate them into day-to-day action and thus we are not transformed by them. There are many religions that give helpful advice but if it does not transform the individual, it is merely information overload. Everyone thinks that what they have is the answer. This is also true because within them lies the answer and the answers always come before the question. This is Allah's way because in absolute reality there is no time flow. It is only in the illusion of our mind that time flows.

In physics there is no reason for things to not go in opposite or unexpected directions. It is just that, collectively, we are taught by our mothers that time moves like an arrow taking flight. The truth is that time and space are inventions that we are taught from infancy. The first thing a baby does when it realises that it exists in this space is when they touch their arm or their toes or they suck their fingers. This identification with time and space is the first thing we experience. This is Allah's trick. We were in the garden of non-time, non-space, eternal bliss. We did not know bliss or that eternal joy. We had to come into this melting pot to be caught, to be encapsulated, with the good and the bad and the opposites, so that we can declare our intention of wanting the best.

We want wisdom, arrival, knowledge, light, and transformation. We want the absolute; we want to be in a situation where there is no 'want' in it. We desire to be free from desire, for then we are truly performing our worship. Then we are worshipping He Who has no need, Who has no desire, Who has created us out of love and has given us desire as an excuse for us to suffer so that we accept the original offer that has always been there. Once you have discovered what has always been there now you can live. It is not a big deal that you are enlightened; it is the beginning.

EVOLVING SOCIO-CULTURAL CONTEXTS

This whole idea of being reborn, re-discovered, or awakened is a very normal and expected event. You first thought your life was according to your biological make-up, then you realise that your life is not subject to anything else other than the Life-giver Who is eternal. Then you become responsible and accountable by referring to that zone which is beyond those boundaries—heavenly wisdom.

That is why our communities and societies thrived in the past because they were in enclosed environments, even in the Arab deserts. No matter how vast the desert, you could be caught. That is why there was hardly any immorality amongst the desert Bedouins, for they would be caught. If anyone had committed an act that was considered dishonourable, for example, molesting someone else's daughter or wife, they would be caught and killed.

In a small town, however, one can hide so much more. What was applicable in the desert when we were nomadic hunter-gatherers, is very different from now, where everyone is urbanised, industrialised, technologized, and civilised. The values may be the same, but their application is vastly different. That is why our own people were on the path of *akhlāq* and *sulūk*, correct conduct by fear, a hundred years ago. They were afraid because they had so many people around them—the uncle and the aunt, extended family reprimanding them and disapproving of them. Fear was a key issue to catch the attention of a growing child.

The other aspect was obedience. Whenever they obeyed, they were rewarded and acknowledged. We all want to be acknowledged because the *rūh* (soul/spirit) is acknowledged by its Creator and therefore the *nafs* always wants to be acknowledged. We all like to be acknowledged, to be given gifts, and to be winners. It is a small, perverted reflection that the *rūh* has won by it being acknowledged. It knows its Creator and it knows that it is a drop from the same divine ocean.

Times have changed and that type of fear and obedience is no longer present. Deference and modesty are no longer norms. That is why we say that it is not possible to be transformed through the prophetic unveilings alone. So: should we give up? Do we throw the baby out with the bath water? There are always appropriate answers for every situation. The age we are living in now is based more on individuation. Everyone is for themselves. As soon as parents can spare a bit of money, they have a special room for the child with special toys or even a special laptop. We are in the age of consumerism where we are obsessed and possessed by obsession and possession. Times have changed. Individuals have been given this false pedestal of self-importance. You are a king. The focus then shifts to how to become more successful even though in the end you will still head for the hands of the undertakers. Their definition of success is something else.

For us success is about access—accessing your soul. That is success which has no failure associated with it. Every other success has within it a possible failure. In this age people are encouraged to love themselves. Every person loves their own selves, yet they do not know who the self is!

These are minor reflections of the truth that is within you—a soul that is forever loved by the Maker of it all. That is why we respect life. The fellow may have been an idiot, but we still respect the life in him. When we see the body passing by in a funeral bier, we are reminded to respect life because we have respect for the representative of the Life-Giver, which is your *rūh*. All the *arwāh* (souls) are the same. It is here that there is human equity. There is no outer equality—no two people are the same, no day is the same—but there is that essential foundation for human equity. In the eye of our Creator we are all the same. We are all children of Adam and Eve.

I grew up in an environment where the less concern I had about myself, the more I was acknowledged by my peers. Now it is the reverse. Today, everybody who stands out is acknowledged. The word for that in Arabic is *imtiyāz*. *Mumtāz*, from the same root, means excellent, from the verb meaning to excel, to stand out, but the only time it is used in the Qur'an is:

$$وَٱمۡتَٰزُواْ ٱلۡیَوۡمَ أَیُّهَا ٱلۡمُجۡرِمُونَ ۝$$

But stand aside today, Oh you who were lost in sin! (36:59)

In fact, in our original language, which has been very much distorted in the last few hundred years, one of the words that meant correct conduct is *khumul*. This meant being unknown or obscure, not showing off or being haughty, or bragging or boasting, because that would be regarded as shameful. As a kid I found it difficult to constantly raise my hand in school when I knew the answer. I felt it was shameful, until I was flung into Europe and saw these politicians constantly vying among themselves saying, 'I will represent you better; just give me your vote,' and so on. Even seventy or eighty years ago it was shameful in Europe to push yourself forward. People would accuse such a person of being self-obsessed.

Outer values have changed. We can use this. We can jump in the same ocean as the Chishtis did in the sub-continent. When Mu'in al-Din Chishti and others who had essentially imbibed the true inner spirit and transformation of Islam came to India found that Hindus had become so decadent that the only thing that was left that could open their hearts was music and song. They jumped into that pool and came up with the most heart-rending divine songs. They transformed a crude kind of belly shaking rock 'n roll into a divine communion which became the legacy of Sufi songs of the sub-continent.

YOU ARE THE PROJECT

We can do the same thing. People love themselves and they love excellence. Now take that excellence to its ultimate degree. It will reach the point of no self-concern and self-image without denying the outer project. Accept and acknowledge the outer project, but more than that, *you* are the project, and the project is to arrive at what is already there.

If you have done both then you are truly in the *barzakh* (interspace); you are doing the utmost on the outer and the inner has taken you over and you are in the ocean of bliss, irrespective of the outer. That is why you will suffer if you do not have that constant access to the zone of joy in you as you have outer involvements, whether it be in the commercial, industrial, political or the religious field.

If you do not constantly replenish by going to your inner, and basking in the Divine light, you will find that the outer is only drudgery. It may be a good drudgery. You call it *fi sabīli'llah*, (for Allah's sake) but Allah does not need you, even the poor do not need you. You now need them to soften your heart so that as we give we realise that the giver is One and the takers are countless. And so wisdom becomes enlightenment.

ON WITNESSING

We need to always be awake to the truth that we are here as conduits at best as Allah describes it in the Qur'an as:

$$إِنَّآ أَرْسَلْنَاكَ شَاهِدًا$$

Truly we sent you to witness. (48:8)

The Prophet (S) always said, 'Show me things as they are.' If it is a worldly matter, there are other people who are better experts than you. You are only wise if you call upon their expertise. If it is about an inner matter and you have learnt the art of disappearing in your *sajda* and only basking in the eternal light, then you know by your own intuition (*ilhām*) and then you also have compassion.

Allah's *Rahma* (Mercy) and compassion is based on knowledge and *Qudra* (ability) to change everything as He wishes, but He allows us to muck about a bit until we realise that we are watched, we are seen, and everything we do is recorded:

$$أَيْنَ ٱلْمَفَرُّ.$$

Where do you run to now? (75:10)

Then you know:

$$فَفِرُّوٓاْ إِلَى ٱللَّهِ$$

So, flee to Allah. (51:50)

So you have combined the inner and the outer, the form and the meaning, the earthly and the heavenly. They all meet in this ultimate creation, the ultimate gift of Allah, which is the human being (*al-insān*). But we are forgetful. Thank God we forget all the other dreadful things. However, if you remember that ultimately there is an essence in you that has created all these different layers of memory, then you are alive beyond time and you respond and act in time. That is the human interspace (*barzakhīya*), and that is who we are. Wisdom is to acknowledge that fact.

PERFECT CONDUCT

At the best of times, we are doing things that are approximately good. Absolute perfection only comes after this world has been left behind. Whatever you do now may not be right tomorrow. That is why when many people look at the lives of the *Awliyā'* (Saints) or the Prophets, they can criticize them because they say, 'Oh, they could have done such and such.'

In truth, if you are a man of light and enlightenment, you could not have acted differently to what you did at that time. You couldn't have done better because you were present, you were not in the past, reeling and suffering from your biography, nor were you in the future concerned about the uncertainties. You were *present*. So, if you were present, He who is forever present (Allah), will lead you and guide you. So, at best you are writing by His command what is already written, and then you are free from all of these illusions and confusions. Then you are truly a slave to the One and free from any other.

TRUE LEADERSHIP

The wise man and woman are ready to leave with no rancour or anger, with complete neutrality. If you are ready for that then you are authorised to be an *amīr* (leader), because you have become an *amīr* over your own cosmology. But if you have not been able to rule over yourself then you will only misrule others and this is the situation with most outer-worldly rulers. They have not yet discovered the inner treasure. If only they had a teacher who reflected that for them there would be less abuse.

We owe it to ourselves to love the higher in ourselves, to desire excellence, to want to be acknowledged and do good. Then we are unified. Once we are unified, we will find that all other diversities and dualities are perfectly in balance. They all emanated from the One, are sustained by the One, and return to the One.

CHAPTER FIVE

Global Spirituality Today

Given in 2006

- Bliss Is the Only Destination
- Happiness is a By-Product
- Give up that which You Want to Keep
- Read the Context
- Find Real Life
- Qur'an and *Tawhid*
- Information, Transmission and Transformation
- Selected Teachings from the Qur'an
- The Wisdom of a Single Reference Point
- The Turning Heart
- Purify the Heart
- One Perfection, One Supreme Consciousness
- Life's Paradoxes
- From Why to How
- Balancing Self and Soul
- Love of the 'Free'
- Transcending the Self
- Referencing is the Key
- From Uncertainty to Certainty

BLISS IS THE ONLY DESTINATION

We all aspire to the same thing. We are all looking for a way of life that gives us constancy in balance, wellness, goodness, and joyfulness. It is not a pre-destination; it is the only destination. Once that unification occurs, then your head and heart are in unison. The outer and the inner in you are unified and you don't suffer from duality. You won't suffer from perpetually being torn between 'shall I or shall I not?' So that you realise, in truth, you have no choice.

You know that you want to choose the best, and the best comes by realising that you need to call upon Him who has created the best. Even in our turmoil and in our difficulties, there are always doors and windows to ease. Here we need *tarbiya* (upbringing). Human needs do not change. The human desire to know that there is perfection does not change. Allah is Ever-Perfect. He is the Creator of it all. He is Ever-Present, so perfection must be present now.

Your access to the One is through changing your lens of vision and changing your mind to only see perfection behind what appears to be imperfect. You must always be aware of divine justice so that you do what you can to implement human justice, otherwise you end up shattered in this world of being. This *qadā'* (decree) is essential for our progress towards what was already there. It has to do with filtering the shadows and illusions of you existing as separate from Allah's *nūr* (light) which is in your heart and is your *rūh* (spirit/soul). It has to do with unifying your *nafs* (self) with the *rūh*. The *rūh* knows all the divine attributes.

HAPPINESS IS A BY-PRODUCT

As a created being you are in need. Acknowledge that we, all of us, are in need. What do we need? You say, 'I want to be happy.' Happiness is a by-product. You can never go and acquire it by wealth or power. It is the by-product of 'giving up', which is Islam (surrender). It is a by-product of 'being secure', which is *īmān* (faith). It is a by-product of knowing that you have no option other than knowing that Allah sees you, Allah knows you, so you are in *ihsān* (grace). Where do you run to? Don't deny the two, always acknowledge the One. Move from the two to the One.

Look at how we conduct our daily business: some people often wish there were 50 hours in a day because they are caught in some *shaytanic* (Satanic) energy. Put yourself in timelessness and you find you have all the time in the world. Go beyond the time and space limit, which can only happen in your heart, and you find you don't know how that supra-efficiency comes in, by Allah. You and I have to struggle in the worldly sense, but ultimately, your heart will tell you once you bring it to life. At the moment there is too much head. The head will just start, and the heart will have the beginning and the end. Allah is saying that if there is anything else in your heart then He cannot be there—'Allah did not place two hearts inside any man's body' (33:4).

GIVE UP THAT WHICH YOU WANT TO KEEP

The prophet Ibrahim (AS) tried to show us the way. He started with not wanting something temporal as his Creator—'I want a God that is always there.' Then Allah gives this awakening to him. Eventually he becomes trapped in the micro-level: he loves his son. How can he not? But then Allah inspires him, 'No, you have to be able to sever that attachment!' *Allahu Akbar!* That is why we, as Muslims, go and repeat the same ritual in Makka, until we are willing to give it up. And by that the heavens and earth manifest, and that which is not known appears, and suddenly the ram of *rahma* (mercy) is there. So that there is only *tawhīd*! The outer combines with the inner.

We are all followers of Ibrahim, Adam, Muhammed and Musa. But Allah says, 'As far as I'm concerned, they are the same.' (2:136) But there are some who have made a bigger impact than others on this earth. How can it not be otherwise? What matters is your relationship with Allah. Imam Husayn (AS) said, "Put right that which matters, nothing else matters."

READ THE CONTEXT

In the time we are living, where much is confused, individuals need to realise that they have to resurrect their heart and reconnect with the light in our heart, which is the *rūh*. How can we do that? We need to make the Qur'an accessible. We need to make the *sunna* (prophetic example) liveable, easy, now.

Every age has its outer. We live in buildings, wear clothes and travel by means that were not available 200 years ago. The truly alive contain themselves by constantly looking at the *Qibla* of the original values that Allah has given us. Live as though the Prophet (S) is with you. Don't fantasise about something that is archaic. Therefore, the new type of *madrasa* (school) will benefit from it immediately. Teach them that *wudū'* (ablution) is that which seals you from the outer world and that you must disappear in your *sajda* (prostration). The more you disappear into your nothingness, the more you can deal efficiently with what is in front of you. So, take the inner meaning of worship and live it! And live your Qur'an rather than just reciting it without knowing what the meanings are. It is about transformation.

FIND REAL LIFE

You need a structure. You yourself are a structured being with bones and muscles, but this is only as a meaning. The human being is the best of creation on two legs, otherwise they will be all be like those described as:

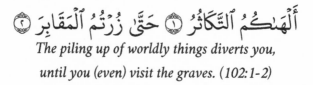

The piling up of worldly things diverts you,
until you (even) visit the graves. (102:1-2)

One of the meanings of *takāthur* (abundance) is 'like graves on two legs' or 'a grave that is walking'. Most people are dead before they die. So you need to come back to life, knowing that your *rūh* will continue after leaving the body. You are accountable at every instant. You are in this world moving back to another subtler, greater world. The question, however, is whether you are ready for it? Have you done your duties here? Have you served as best as you can? Are you ready to leave this world peacefully and with joy?

Allah says, 'Take one step towards me and I take 10 towards you.' So do not think you are clever. None of us have any choice but to maintain what Allah has promised, what Allah has decreed. We know little! If you know that you don't know then that is a great step. If you know that Allah whose light, whose *nūr*, is in your heart and knows all, then that is the completion of the next step. Then you have moved on to two legs. If you have managed to grasp this, I congratulate you and thank you, for your own sake. You are doing it all for your own sake.

QUR'AN AND *TAWHĪD*

We are fortunate with the heritage we have but with that fortune comes also the responsibility to act appropriately and to be accountable in every way. Allah has given Adam and the children of Adam the full exposure to the divine light, to that full panorama of Supreme Consciousness. With the rise of the Adamic consciousness, Allah given us the multitude of dimensions of truth and realities, which is the Qur'an.

I want to share with you the basics, the essentials, the principles of the Qur'anic knowledge and how it is entirely founded on *tawhīd* (unitive essence). There is only One Light from which multitudes of lights have cascaded, emanated, depended upon and returned to. So, with the weight, with the delight, with the glory of the Qur'an comes this effulgence, this blinding light of the Source—One Essence which manifests into an infinite variety of *arwāh* (souls/spirits), human beings, animals, the heavenly bodies and galaxies and even the ant, each of which has a soul. It is a spark, at a certain level of consciousness, relating to this cosmic consciousness of Allah. So, the entire Qur'an is founded on *tawhīd* (unitive essence) and the purpose of all of these is transformation.

INFORMATION, TRANSMISSION AND TRANSFORMATION

You have information, you have transmission, and you have transformation. We human beings, individually and collectively, seek that transformation or what is called awakening, enlightenment or whatever name you want to give it. It is to know that you are not who you think you are. It is to know that you are a *nafs*, a self which has an ego and a memory and a personality and various roles. Equally there is a source of light within you that is totally divine, which is the same in every one of us. All the *arwāh* are the same but each *nafs* is different and changing all the time. My self now is different to what it was 10 minutes ago, and it will be different when I'm ill and then again when I feel good. All these changes we recognise and experience because within us lies something that never ever changes, which is the *rūh*.

SELECTED TEACHINGS FROM THE QUR'AN

The Qur'an describes all of that to us and tells us the purpose of this life. The meaning of this life is to discover the One. It is founded on *tawhīd* and with that comes transformation. I want to share with you some of the *ayats* that are relevant to what I've been reading for you:

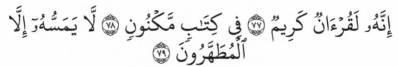

Indeed, it is a noble Qur'an, in a Book well-protected;
None touch it except the purified. (56:77-79)

Allah describes the Qur'an as the most generous thing: a gift, a book, a tablet. You cannot fathom it unless you come to it with purity. Meaning, coming to it without an assumption that you know this or that, or that you are a scholar or that you are this or that. Even in *sharī'a*, you are not supposed to touch it unless you have *wudū'*. In terms of *haqīqa*, you don't get much unless you have come with an open, empty heart.

$$\text{وَإِلَـٰهُكُمْ إِلَـٰهٌ وَٰحِدٌ ۖ لَّآ إِلَـٰهَ إِلَّا هُوَ ٱلرَّحْمَـٰنُ ٱلرَّحِيمُ} \quad ﴿١٦٣﴾$$

And your god is one God. There is no deity [worthy of worship] except Him,
the Entirely Merciful, the Especially Merciful. (2:163)

Your Creator, your Lord, your deities all end up in One because everything has emanated from the One. And then the whole story of Qur'an, *tawhīd* and transformation is encapsulated in several *āyāt*, one of which is describing the Prophetic reality:

$$\text{يَـٰٓأَيُّهَا ٱلنَّبِىُّ إِنَّآ أَرْسَلْنَـٰكَ شَـٰهِدًا وَمُبَشِّرًا وَنَذِيرًا} \quad ﴿٤٥﴾ \quad \text{وَدَاعِيًا إِلَى}$$
$$\text{ٱللَّهِ بِإِذْنِهِۦ وَسِرَاجًا مُّنِيرًا} \quad ﴿٤٦﴾$$

Indeed, We have sent you as a witness and a bringer of good tidings and a
warner. And as one who summons to God by His leave, and as a light-giving
beacon. (33:45-46)

Allah describes the Prophetic being, that profile or that reality or that model, to which we all aspire. Allah says we sent you as a witness. If you don't witness the situation then you can't move forward. If you don't realise that you are ill, or hungry, or upset, then you can't move forward. One of the most frequently quoted Prophetic supplications is: 'O Allah show me things as they are.'

Most of us quarrel with other people because we have no empathy. We do not try to put ourselves in their position. That is why everybody seems to feel justified, everybody is killing everybody, accusing everybody, denouncing everybody. There is a small amount or an extent of truth in that justification, but it won't last. Truth is that which is forever. Anything else is a short-lived reality. And that is why we want sustainable development, sustainable relationships, sustainable knowledge so that, according to changing circumstances, we still have a reference.

The good news is that you are not who you think you are. The good news is that you have come here to witness perfection upon perfection upon perfection. All of Allah's attributes, all of Allah's divine qualities, *Al-Bāsit* (the expander), *Al-Awwal* (the first), we all want them, we all desire them. The *nafs*, the human self, loves to have these which is why we love power, because the *rūh*, knows the source of Power (*Al-Qawī*). We want to acquire these divine attributes: *As-Salāam*, Forever Well and Peace, *As-Samad*, Forever Self-Subsistent, so we can pretend that we don't need anything.

We pretend we are doing that even during the month of Ramadan, until about an hour before *Iftār* (fast breaking) when you can't talk to anybody. So this is the good news (*mubashshiran*). The good news is that you are a light, you are a *rūh* (Soul/Spirit), which carries on. This is part of the process in this world. And give warning: if we don't wake up now in this world and begin to connect with the higher consciousness within us, it will be too late. If you don't work at it when you are well, you'll not be able to do much when you are ill. These are part of the meanings of several divine or prophetic teachings that 'If my slave remembers Me when he is well, I'll remember him when he is not'.

There are always these balances. You are a human being so do not deny the body but at the same time acknowledge the *rūh* (soul/spirit) and the eternal part in you that carries on. So this is the warning. Transformation is a light-giving beacon *(sirājan munīrā)*. If you are illumined, if you are enlightened, then you do what you can, and nothing else matters. You don't have anxiety anymore, you are not obsessed, you are not possessed, you do what you can, and Allah is under it all, Allah is the doer. You can only be truly *'Abd Allah* (slave of Allah), at the end of this transformation. You are accountable every instant and every minute, you are aware. You know Allah sees you, you know you are watched. You are at ease, inwardly and outwardly, you can do what you can to achieve that ease.

The outer world will always present us with challenges, it will never end. If you want a perfect world, you will always be disappointed because Allah did not create it other than for the process of perfecting the inner and outer qualities, your character, your mind, your thoughts, your limbs, so that you know nothing is in your hands. *Then* you are at rest. So, the question of *tawhīd* (unitive essence) is very crucial to our *Dīn*. Allah gives us the entire thing in the most powerful way:

$$\text{إِنَّ ٱللَّهَ لَا يَغْفِرُ أَن يُشْرَكَ بِهِۦ وَيَغْفِرُ مَا دُونَ ذَٰلِكَ}$$

Indeed, Allah does not forgive association with Him, but He forgives what is less than that. (4:48)

Allah says in the Qur'an that Allah forgives all our sins, all our mistakes. Then He says that this is not a sin. This is *kabīra*, beyond all that, it is a major crack and if you don't see the One, if you don't ask: *Oh, Allah what shall I do?* —This is fundamental. The whole thing is cracked if you cannot refer everything to Allah.

There is no doer other than Allah. There is none present other than Allah. There is none that enlightens other than Allah. There is none that guides other than Allah. There is none compassionate other than Allah. You are referring back to that which is there and here, to what was, is and always will be. Then you have truly cornered yourself and there is nowhere to run to (*fa ayna'l-mafar*). Then you have truly re-turned towards Allah (*tūbu illa'llah*). Return to the higher consciousness that is already in you, return to the *nūr* (light) of Allah that is your *rūh*, return to the higher than that which is the *Khāliq al-anwār* (The Creator of Lights), then your world is put in the right perspective.

It *is* difficult, and we *are* losing, we *are* ill. But put it in the right perspective. This Earth is 5 billion years old, humankind is maybe 50,000 years old. In the greater scheme of things, 50,000 years is nothing. The final, complete message of Islam through the prophetic effulgence is 1,400 years old and still we are not learning it. That is why Allah refers in the Qur'an to the time before the Prophet Muhammad as *jāhilīyat al-ūlā* (the first ignorance) which implies that there is a *jāhilīya thāni wa thālith wa rābā'a* (second, third and fourth ignorance) and that it continues and is not finished. We have to be cautious. We must, at all times, be humbled and ask Allah to guide us and to ask others who are better than us to lead us. We want a good healthy life in this world and we want easy access and flight in the next and we want it at the same time, because one leads to the other. I, at the moment, am a product of my past, and my tomorrow will be as good as I am now, in this moment. And the same thing applies to the society. If people turn then everything changes.

$$وَلَوۡ أَنَّ أَهۡلَ ٱلۡقُرَىٰٓ ءَامَنُواْ وَٱتَّقَوۡاْ لَفَتَحۡنَا عَلَيۡهِم بَرَكَٰتٍ مِّنَ ٱلسَّمَآءِ وَٱلۡأَرۡضِ$$

And if the people of the cities had believed and been in fearful awareness, we would have opened upon them blessings from the heavens and earth. (7:96)

But the condition is *āmanū*, or having certainty that Allah is giving you what you need, what you deserve: but be cautious and always ask whether this is the right thing. Ask "O Allah, please guide me."

Allah has given each one of us *shayātīn* (afflicting demons) in order for us to turn away from them. This is part of *Shaytaniya* (that which afflicts us with separation) and part of *Rahmaniya* (Compassion)—I've had enough, I've suffered enough at the hands of *shaytān* (affliction), I need *Rahmān* (compassion). Allah has programmed us already. We already know what to do. The Highway Code and map are clear. We just need to drive accordingly.

The purpose is so that those who are gaining this knowledge know it is the truth, meaning that it does not change. Only realities change. These are all the traces of *tawhīd*. Only Allah knows that there is goodness in your heart. Allah knows that which you have lost will be replaced with something better. Don't complain, watch what Allah is telling you. If you want to be *'Abd Allah* (servant of Allah), then listen to the Lord of Creation. What you know now you did not know a year before. Look at Allah's *'ilm* (Knowledge), ever-continuing, that stream of *'ilm* is coming to all of us all the time but we are so fickle, we forget. Whenever we are in trouble we say 'Allah, Allah', and whenever we are relieved we forget. We give credit to everyone other than Allah.

Accept creation but recognise that the Light behind all, within all, before all, after all, is Allah. Thank creation but make sure that your constant gratitude is for Allah. You are a *muwahhid* (one who unifies), you have connected the communal thing, the *farq* (differentiated) with the *jam'* (gathered). Now you are gathered, recognising the differentiated, simultaneously.

You know who you are, you know your level, you know what you are keeping in your heart, you know your fears, you know your anxieties, you know all of it. Get out of it! Do your *wudu'* (ritual ablution) and enter into the sublime *sajda* (prostration) and you will see everything is wonderful. When Allah says in a Divine Tradition, 'I was a hidden treasure and I loved to be known', this is what it means.

If you and I believe that our Creator is perfect, that the Creator is in charge of everything and within everything, then why do we not realise that every moment is perfect? Our lenses need to be changed. We go to the optician but what about the lens of the heart? The optician is easy, the lens of the heart is more difficult. Only you and I can work on it.

Now, the prescription is that if you don't rise to *Janna* (state of paradise) and see the perfection now, then you are asleep and all you will see is agitation, disturbance, confusion and chaos. Anything that comes to existence, from the moment it is created, is moving more and more towards chaos. It is called entropy. It starts all perfect. Before the Big Bang, there was only absolute perfection. However, everything that moves within a closed system is decaying. But then something else arises, which is an aspect of the ever-present Perfection.

The more we refer to the higher in us, the more we refer to the *rūh* in us and the less we refer to the causal side in us, which is the mind and the intellect, the more we are in balance. Again, we are reminded to give what we can, perform our prayers, perform our duties, and whatever we are doing will be reserved for us as credit. We will see it, we will experience it.

THE WISDOM OF A SINGLE REFERENCE POINT

Allah gives us an example: One man has one boss who is consistent and is a single reference. Then Allah refers to another person who has constantly quarrelling bosses. He doesn't know who to listen to: the bank manager, his wife or the car dealer. Allah asks whether these two men are the same? He who has one reference point or he who is continuously confused? And then He says *Alhamdu li'llah*, give praise to the Maker of it all, most people don't realise that they are suffering from emotional blackmail and many other things in our hearts. Forget the mind, which is clogged up anyway. Then Allah hammers it all home: whoever is confused and does not know the source is lost!

Allah reminds us also not to think of this as a small matter. Most of those who have faith and trust in Allah, are in *shirk* (associating others with Allah). They asked the Prophet (S), 'What is this subtle *shirk*?' They call it *shirk al-khafi* (Subtle association). His reply was that it is like trying to catch a black ant during the darkest part of the night, crawling on a black rock. It is not a small matter, but this is our *Din*. Our *Din* is based on the Qur'an which is based on *Tawhid* (Divine unity), and the ways and *sunna* of the Prophet (S).We have to live that *tawhid*, otherwise we are only Muslims in name and deed but in our inner state we are confused.

THE TURNING HEART

The root of the word *qalb* (heart) is also repeated in the Qur'an. So the entire business of *qalb* is *inqilab*, to turn or revolve, which was the way of the Prophet Muhammad (S). His was the biggest revolution ever. He came to people who had bad habits and a culture that could not continue and had to collapse. There were personal habits and societal habits—love for wealth, love for power, abuse of women, of children, of new-born baby girls, etc. —and he turned that around.

Trust in Allah, seek Allah's *Rahma* (mercy), be accountable to Allah, do your duties and you will see the *āyāt* (signs) completely true to that trust. If you are truthful you only see truthfulness. You will experience in the outer world your inner state. That was the *inqilāb* of *Rasūlu'llah* (messenger of Allah). *Inqilāb,* however, can go the other way, which has also happened. There are those Muslims who became rulers who were inwardly in love with Caesars and Pharaohs but outwardly built mosques and palaces and pretended to be *'Abd Allah* (servant of Allah). So this is the biggest *nifāq* (hypocrisy).

Allah describes it for us so beautifully: He describes how we take bits of the Qur'an that we like and leave the rest. This is the cleverness of some irresponsible Muslim speakers and teachers. They take the bit that suits them without giving the whole context. This is the most dangerous thing, because you are using the Qur'an, you are using the *sunna* (prophetic tradition) but for other devious reasons. These are the dangers. These are also *nifāqu'l-khafī* (subtle hypocrisies) and so on. Allah sums it up for us: 'Return to Him who has brought you forth.' Specifically:

$$\text{فَتُوبُوٓاْ إِلَىٰ بَارِئِكُمْ فَٱقْتُلُوٓاْ أَنفُسَكُمْ}$$

Return to your Maker and kill your selves (egos). (2:54)

This is what it means! It also means to watch out for that outer *nafs* (ego self) of yours, that boasting, self-obsessed ego. There was a specific purpose for these *āyāt* that were revealed, and also a more general one which is the more subtle one on the level of inner meaning. The implication is for us to be truly in *tawhīd*. We must only see One. Therefore, if you see any aspect of yourself, you are not close to the door of *tawhīd*. All of our rituals are practices in order to leave the self behind. Do not deny the self, simply leave it aside and you will find the other side. When you put the two together you will once again end up with Humpty Dumpty! Then you are *in* this world but not *of* this world. You don't deny this world, you are not stupid, but more than that, you are illumined and enlightened.

What matters most is how you leave this world. Will you leave it with a joyfully empty heart, or with fear and anxiety and concerned with who is going to do what?

In conclusion, I share with you this business of return and *ghufrān* (forgiveness). Those of you who truly have trust and security in that, Allah will give us, Allah will save us, Allah will show us, Allah will guide us, respond, answer back, go forth, join in with how Allah and His Prophet are calling you to live.

$$يَـٰٓأَيُّهَا ٱلَّذِينَ ءَامَنُواْ ٱسْتَجِيبُواْ لِلَّهِ وَلِلرَّسُولِ إِذَا دَعَاكُمْ لِمَا يُحْيِيكُمْ$$

Oh you who believe, respond to Allah and His messenger when called to that which gives you life. (8:24)

The key here is *Yuhyīkum* (gives you life), the implication being that at the moment we are only semi-alive, only biologically alive. Allah says, 'Come to life!' Meaning you must come to realise that you are a *rūh* (soul/spirit), encapsulated in this prison for a while. Don't denounce anything but more than anything recognise your *dhāt*, your essence. Once you begin to recognise what your essence is, the rest becomes easier and easier because now we have put it into context. Once you put it into context then it loses that heavy demand upon you. The teaching of Imam 'Ali in this respect is that the bigger the issue you are facing, the more you should make it insignificant. We are all going to die, not a big deal, so don't make it such a huge problem, you don't know what happened there. Make light of it, be light-hearted, then your heart becomes fully alive.

PURIFY THE HEART

If the heart is full of pus and anxiety, full of hatred, then there is no light, nor space for light. The heart is the place where the soul and the *nafs* (ego) meet. It is the marriage chamber. So make sure it is clean and nice and full of flowers, otherwise there will be no marriage, no wedding. Some Sufis call the day they die the *Urs,* which is union. The outer human marriage union is a small *mithāl* (metaphor) which often goes wrong anyway. The greater *mithāl* for you is the inner reunion, between your *rūh* and your *nafs.*

We have the heritage, we have everything that is needed, we have the map, we have the highway code, we have the living beings who followed it and lived it. Now you and I have to begin to taste it and enjoy it, and give gratitude to Allah and love and thanks to the Prophet of Allah, and those who were before us who also absorbed the same thing and came to life.

ONE PERFECTION, ONE SUPREME CONSCIOUSNESS

All human beings in this world are challenged and caught by the most important questions in life; why are we here? What is the purpose of existence? Why can't I be happy all the time? Why do I feel insecure sometimes? Why do I get angry? Why do I feel hatred occasionally? Why do I feel good when I love? Why is it that I want to maintain balance but I can't always maintain that perfect harmony? We are all the same.

From the beginning to its end the design is that there is One perfection, One perfect pattern, One Supreme Consciousness, One Light of lights from which multitudes of different modified conditioned lights emanate and to which they return. This is how these waves of energies cascade, reform and return to the same source.

In science, the biggest challenge today is to find the unifying theory behind it all. How do our normal classical physics connect in a seamless way with quantum mechanics and what about other things which still puzzle us all the time? What about this amazing miracle of light itself? We talk about photons, wave bands, multitudes of colours, all the other spectrums, other similar band widths. We are still trying to uncover bits and pieces of an entirely unified field. The seeker is part and parcel of this unified field. We are trained as human beings to think rationally, to think causally—what is the beginning, what is the end, what brings this and ends up with that— and we get accustomed to the passage of time. There is a direction in time.

In science, in physics, there is no incongruity if you think the reverse or that time is going the other way. Indeed, without that theory you cannot resolve so many modern issues. In particle physics things must go the other way.

Here we are as human beings in this whole world. If you think back two to three thousand years, there was nothing other than tribalism and care and concern about existence. And then there were cycles of civilizations coming and going, growing up to a point, to a pinnacle of ease and comfort and beauty and arts and all kinds of luxuries and then recycled. Some shorter, some longer. The average age of empires is, we can discern now from our history, around 250 years. This is the cycle of life. Every insect has its cycle, every bird has its cycle, every human being has their cycle.

LIFE'S PARADOXES

There is a beginning and an end to everything and yet none of us want the good things to end. How do you resolve this impossible paradox? If you feel good and happy and content and well, then you don't want that to end. If you have an intimate relationship with your relatives, your children, family and that love that unifies you with others, you don't want it to end. So how is it then that we still don't want it to end even though we know every minute we live is bringing us closer to the physical end? Intrinsically, we are essentially schizophrenic. Part of me does not want to end and part of me wants to adjust and be prepared for the end. The two things are not easily reconcilable. Part of me wants expansion and control and wealth beyond measure and yet, in a moment of contentment, there is nothing in my hand.

We all love those moments of giving up where we can do nothing. I have personally heard from friends and other people close to me that the best ever times in their lives were moments of almost near-death experiences or when they were in an operating theatre and there was nothing they could do. Those are moments of real surrender and relief. Lovers at moments of true intimacy or early discovery, before they get repelled from each other again, would like to die in each other's arms. Why? Because they want to preserve that unity as a memory, as complete. But why not have that all the time? Essentially, we are all the same, we want to find a way out. And the way out is the way in!

FROM WHY TO HOW

The world altogether now has reached a point where it is the end of a line. It is an end of that fantasy that if you have enough insurance, enough salary and enough for retirement, you'll be happy. You know it is not true. In my whole lifetime I have seen more happiness, more contentment, amongst poorer people.

The world we are living in is like that. We are all bereft. Don't be taken in by outer paraphernalia. I assure you, if you have the right inner-state and meet anybody who is well-dressed or well-off, just say quietly to them, 'You know, I know that you are not really happy deep down.' I tell you they will immediately attach themselves to you. This is true especially if they are concerned with the outer, if they have a Mercedes and something Gucci, that sort of thing. South African Indians are definitely a part of that or aspire to be part of that. But go to them and say, 'You are not very happy, really,' and they will hang on to you. Similarly, if you want to run away with somebody else's wife, go and tell her that she is really not appreciated by her husband. 'He doesn't really appreciate you! He doesn't really know what a gem you are. What a special being you are.' You will create havoc in the land!

Come to realise that we are all bereft. Be honest with yourself. You cannot be sure that you are truly sustainably content. Why? We are now going back to the original question. Why are we here? It is like asking the child when he asks why shouldn't I have this honey? A clever parent will postpone that question. 'Let's see how we are going to eat it without dripping.' Turn the question of *why* to *how*. You will read and experience magic. Why we are here? Let us turn it to how we can live joyfully. How can we live such that you can at all times, irrespective of outer events, access a zone in you that gives you that contentment and joy? If you manage to transpose the *why* to *how*, I guarantee you access to the soul which carries the spark of the Divine light. This is true irrespective of who you are and what religion you have, and what race you come from and your socio-economic standing or political manoeuvring or anything else. Turn the question of why to how I can live so I am well.

And you have to start with the outer. You have to start wanting to be well physically and mentally, on every level, and then socially and then at heart. Then you find that you are programmed wanting wellness, wanting 'foreverness', wanting the eternal bliss which is here and now, but it is access to it that relates to the inner. As Rumi says: 'Passionate love was easy, but then problems arose.'

We all want to have access to something that never changes. We don't want this side or that side. We want to have the constancy of access to something that gives us contentment which is not outside of us. The outside world is a *mithāl*: it is a sample, a parable, an example of what exists in a pattern from within the soul. So we human beings are essentially made up of, or composed of, an aspect of limited consciousness, conditioned consciousness, and contaminated consciousness, which is the so-called 'me' and 'my mind', and 'my memory', and this amazing entity I have which is called the brain, and then another side of me which is the source of that energy, which is my soul. The other side of me is cosmic, universal, and is the same with everyone. That is why we always question each other on justice because we are all the same essentially but always different outwardly. If we can immediately resonate with these two dimensions, then you are unified. People will regard you as consistent.

One aspect of one of our greatest saints in Pakistan, Baba Farid, whom I visited many times, emerged when his closest companion was asked about him after his departure (death). He said, 'All that I can tell you is that (whatever happened) he was the same.' Even when there was a famine in the area and his son was dying. They came to him and asked what they could do? It wasn't that he simply sat back and did nothing; he did what he could but he was undisturbed. We have to have a certain measure of stress but depression and distress and all of that is impossible to deal with. Nearly half of us now require some sort of medications which only increase because you develop dependencies. Do what you can and leave the rest.

BALANCING SELF AND SOUL

We are all made of these two dimensions of self and soul and we find that most of us cannot maintain that balance and need to practice. Then you need to do whatever it takes. Whatever spiritual path you have, religion you have, get to that point of constancy. It does not matter, but get it. If you have got it, you have won. That means that the higher in you has won over the lower, without denying the lower. The lower is always there, I always know that there is a greedy fellow in me and if I allow that to dominate I will be unhappy. So I want to have the so-called generous fellow in me predominate a bit more because that makes me happy. Why? Because the soul has access to the most Generous entity ever, which is the Creator Himself. My soul knows all the Attributes of God: the Ever-Generous, the Ever-Present, He Who has no beginning and no end, the Most Powerful, He Who Knows all, He Who hears all, He Who is Able to do all. Who doesn't want these qualities?

Then when the self, the so-called I, the biological I, the egotistic I, realises that I can only adore these qualities but I can have a little bit of them, it will take 'sibghatu'llah', its colour from Allah. Then you will take on a little 'halo', a little more intelligence from the source of intelligence, which is the Creator, which is God. All of these great Divine Attributes are in the soul of every individual being on this earth. Those qualities are then brought to the forefront and put on the altar of your worship and if you truly follow and internalise them, you will be transformed into something else. That is the process of years of suffering and accepting the divine offering. That's something else. But once you get the map that we—all of us—are essentially the same you will realise that this is what matters.

We want happiness, we want wealth, we want security. For the last 20, 30 years all of us have been hoodwinked into seeking outer security but we find that we are still insecure. You are searching for the right thing in the wrong place in the wrong way. This reminds me of the story of Mullah Nasradeen's lost ring. One night he was looking for it under the street lamp. People saw him and started to help him look for it, because there are many who want to do good especially if they are seen by others. Soon he had many people looking for the ring. Then one wise person asked Mullah where he had lost the ring. He said, 'I lost it over there!' So the businessman asked, 'But why are you searching here?" Mullah said, 'Because it is more convenient, there is light here under the street lamp.' This is what we end up with. It's convenient and easy for us to be hoodwinked by outer security.

LOVE OF THE 'FREE'

We all love to get something for nothing. Why? Has God designed us in such a foolish way? Why do we love to get something free? You know the shops and the bazaars in cities like Damascus and elsewhere, they know how to hoodwink people. They immediately offer you a cup of tea, it's ready for you, come, just come, so you get obligated. You don't need it but maybe the wife will have that shawl. Another tea, yet another tea, some fruits, and by that time you have begun to spend money. You started with free, you have ended up being free of your money!

Why do we love to be given something for free? The soul has been given the freedom of access to the infinite treasures of Allah. The soul has access to boundlessness in every aspect, whether it is knowledge, whether it is glory, whether it is majesty, whether it is beauty, but the self is limited. It's for that reason if you and I do not accept and concede the limitations, we will not be given openings to the limitless.

This is also why the true spiritual path becomes difficult because it is about submission, acceptance of boundaries. It is not just a simple esoteric thing. The more you limit the outer, the more you find the inner will possibly open up. These are the laws of nature. The more you can say no to temptation, the more will be the horizon of the yes, of glory and magnificence. The less involved you are, the less concerned about your personal life, the more you find that 'pre'-light behind your life is now inspiring you, illumining you.

I have had various teachers in my life and I often try to summarize all that I learned from them. The one-line summary from the 7 years I spent with Krishnamurti is: 'Do not concern yourself with yourself. Have least self-concern!' Everything I learned from that man, following him into the United States, at Ojai Valley, in India, in the UK at Brockwood Park, it was just this: Stop being concerned about your self-image or yourself. Give it up, stop it!

TRANSCENDING THE SELF

'Transcending the self'—these are all words. You know you exist, you have an image, you have a role, you have some duties, don't deny them, but they are instant by instant, they are not important. They all come and go.

If you identify yourself solidly with that self-image, then you are fossilized. Then you have already become an idol. You have become this 'personality'. Worst of all are these religious personalities because they have now assumed an extra-terrestrial dimension. Don't you know I was ordained so and so many years ago?! You haven't seen my books? You don't know who I am? That is why if you really want to hoodwink anybody then you must tell them 'I know you!'

Watch out for the *nafs*. Don't ever think that you do not have *nafs* (ego) because then you do not exist. Please, you must vanish. *Of course* we have an ego. Thank God for the ego! Thank God for the suffering from the ego. Do not ever deny that, do not ever say the *nafs* is purified. There is purity in you beyond purity. It is a divine presence but do not deny the personal absence; you and I are absent, otherwise we won't do all the foolish things we do. We won't eat, we won't get married, we won't fast, we won't walk, we won't have any of these, we won't *do* any of these things.

Can you imagine if you knew at birth you are a light and then your poor mother stuffs this breast into your face? If you are lucky it is not just a bottle. You would wonder who the hell is this person and what is she doing? Can you imagine? So thank God for veil after veil after veil so that you end up realising that these veils were all providential. It's fantasy and half madness if somebody says one experience was a big providential thing. That means everything else was not providential. That means God was absent all these years, all of these months. Then for an instant, once in every 40 years a pip of light came and now it is providential. It was providential that we met, of course, and it was providential we parted, of course. It is providential that you came and you died. Stop all this fantasy, this religiosity. These are veils upon veils upon veils.

Trust in that there is only One, and the only access to the One is by recognition of the two and realising that the two have emanated from the One, are sustained by the One, return to the One and therefore you are also One.

REFERENCING IS THE KEY

That is all there is to it! And everybody has to do it to themselves. You can't impose it on others. In my own lifetime, I have met people whom I really liked and was drawn to. I can give you many, many examples and I knew I had to wait. They had to go through major, major experiences of suffering because they had put their heart and trust in some fantasy, whether it was a big worthy project or a family trust or their children's endowment. You have to look after your family, you have taken some responsibility. Thank God for that, otherwise it would be something even more foolish.

To serve others is to reduce the possibility of over self-indulgence, so you have certain limits, a modicum of comfort. Anything more than that and you'll end up with no reference point and therefore, no idea how you got there. The key is reference, reference, reference.

My consciousness is a limited consciousness and is founded on my experiences. It is founded mostly on my culture, partly on my background, the language, the people, my religion, where I was born. So I am conditioned, but another part of me has been illumined unconditionally. That unconditioned consciousness is beyond limitation. It's for that reason I want freedom beyond freedom, and it is the wise person who discovers that freedom is to recognise that you are not free. Why? Because you want to do the right thing, at the right time, in the right way. There is no freedom in it. There are no degrees of freedom in it. There are no degrees in perfection.

Perfection means there are no ripples. Perfection is when there is no past and no future. Perfection is the eternal present. Perfection is there. You and I have it in our heart but as a template. The rest has to move on to realise it by reference to the perfect, eternal consciousness. This is why those of us who have a religion are fortunate because we believe in life after death. We have certain accountability. We have a certain measure of ethics and morality. I can't get away from it. I may cheat everybody now but what about later when I face the Maker? There is a certain advantage in these sorts of beliefs and religions but you need to be illumined by it rather than become stuck to the structure. A rocket has to have a structure but it is useless junk if it does not fly. If it does not go beyond a certain speed, it's of no use.

I have a structure: I have bones but it is light that has been condensed and conditioned. All of it is light. There is only light! There are only atoms in which the moving parts are the electrons and the other entities. There is only light. There is One divine light with multitudes of infinite levels and layers upon layers crisscrossing in different dimensions. It is not linear, it is not three dimensional; its dimensions are beyond count.

Just think of this beyond the dimensionality of our brain. We are told we have over a trillion neurons in our brains! Now, apparently the ways they can connect, the permutations, number more than all the atoms in existence. I don't know how much it is -10^{73}, I think some fantastic number where you run out of zeros. So the possibility, the potentiality, is limitless but you and I have to acknowledge our limitations. There is a certain time, a certain place, and God in His perfection has made us go through these cycles. You know your breathing cycles, your heart-beat cycles, your sleep cycle, your day, your week, your month, your yearly cycles. There is cycle after cycle after cycle after cycle. You can't deny any of these. There are waves after waves. Some small, some large and they are all there. You can't deny them. You can't deny the cosmic configurations.

FROM UNCERTAINTY TO CERTAINTY

There are certain days where you think things are easy and certain days when things are difficult and it is not only because of humanity. There are other factors as well. We are all limited. We must accept our limitations. The more you give in to that limitation, into your inner silence, the more the possibilities for the limitless soul within us. This is who we are and if you do not see the map, read the map, then you cannot drive according to this map. That is why you find people who are driven by religious zeal do not know what is driving them; it is just zeal because if they stop their zealousness they would become more confused, more lost and more upset.

If anybody wants to believe in something, therefore, as Krishnamurti used to say, 'If you start with certainty you are most likely to end up with uncertainty. Start with uncertainty, you are likely to end up with certainty.'

Always start with doubt. Whatever you are going to do, you will be certain. It is often said—I've seen it as a Chinese proverb, an Arabic proverb, an Indian proverb, an Eskimo proverb—: 'If you are certain then you are most likely to be a fool, but if you are uncertain then you are likely to be a wise person.' There are different variations of this proverb. Be uncertain, be uncertain. Give yourself a break. Access to the higher is between thoughts when things stop. That's why we have this wonderful practice in our *salāt* (prayer) to disappear. Go into your prostration and disappear. If you can disappear on a regular basis then the chances of that inner light appearing in you is more likely. You need the constant outer discipline until it becomes your habit. Until you realise that your joy lies in accessing inner limitlessness by this outer limitation. Outer conditioned consciousness accessing inner limitless consciousness.

Sometimes in gatherings you get a high. Especially during nights of *dhikr* or vigils. That is just your personal consciousness, that beam of energy that has now broken through like lightning, from the infinite divine soul, God consciousness. So you experience joy, a bit of an electric charge, until eventually it becomes constant. It is for that reason the traditional Sufi masters would not allow youngsters before puberty to be in a circle of *dhikr* because they cannot take this high voltage. They had courtesies, rules, and regulations but in this so-called liberal world we are living in, what rules can you impose? What *adab* can you portray and what do you reference? So I pray to Allah for all of us to recognize the way He has:

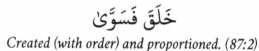

Created (with order) and proportioned. (87:2)

He created from the One, to the One, by the One, appearing as twos. I pray to Allah to enable us to have unification of these twos and unison between all otherness. I pray to Allah to show us that human beings have essentially come to know Who has created, by realising the perfection of His creation!

CHAPTER SIX

Gnostics and Politics

Given in 2007
as the opening talk

- Origin of the Term Gnostic
- What is Gnosis?
- Condition and Unconditioned Consciousness
- Gnostics and the Self, Politics and Others
- The Rising Tide
- On *Zuhd*
- Original Love: A Unifying Field
- Sufi Teachings
- Duality Underpinned by Unity
- Dual Consciousness
- Witnessing Perfection
- Confusing the Two Dimensions
- The Way of the Middle People
- Quantifying Enlightenment
- The How of Enlightenment
- Divine Politics

ORIGIN OF THE TERM GNOSTIC

The Gnostic is the one who goes in search of knowledge. In historical tradition, there were people who followed certain parts of Jesus' teach-ings and they became the heretic Gnostics of earlier days. In the last 50 years, yet these heretic Gnostics have become popularly revived after the Nag Hammadi discoveries in Egypt. We owe it all to a peasant called Mohammed Ali, who discovered these parchment scrolls in ancient jars hidden in a cave. About a third of them were destroyed through the centuries by lighting, fire and the rest became the most valuable museum pieces for hundreds of scholars to try and decipher and thus bring us the most pristine teachings and utterances of Isa (AS) translated into Coptic. The language we are the inheritors of once again. I tell you this as a dramatic prelude or perhaps a metaphor for this opening address.

WHAT IS GNOSIS?

I will try to share with you what gnosis is, or rather, I want to focus on the *why* and the *how* of gnosis. I can sum it up for you: you can never 'get' gnosis; you must allow it to manifest in having 'got' you.

It is not that you have attained gnosis, but rather that it has got you. Interestingly the last question of *why* is the most important. Why gnosis, why enlightenment, what is all this business about? Why all these religions, why all these apparent differences and thousands upon thousands trying to find where they connect, where they relate and where they are unified? We will come to that, *inshallah*, and you will find that that too is paradoxical, in that the why comes after you have already got the answer. It is, why should I eat in order to live, why should I live in order to be fascinated, why do I need to be fascinated in order to see miracles, why do I need to see miracles in order to be ready for the ultimate magic of leaving your body? That is the whole story! Do I need to carry on?

Back to the message of gnosis and politics. Politics, again, in its classical meaning is 'how best to relate to people and others in a manner which is conducive to sustained goodness'. In classical times there were a lot of good references to politics or how you related to yourself. In Arabic, the word politics (*siyāsa*) originally meant bringing up children. Meaning how you co-exist, how you bring up children so that they ultimately discover the light within themselves, so they graduate into full humanity, which is spirituality plus physicality. This is the original meaning of politics. This was why Aristotle wrote 'Politics' for his student Alexander the Great.

CONDITION AND UNCONDITIONED CONSCIOUSNESS

You have to see how we human beings have gone up and down and sideways about the purpose of life, the balance of life, the harmony of life. From the time of Socrates until now we have been, in a way, on a downward spiral, but I am very optimistic that the suffering will not have been in vain. The hundreds of years of oppression, the inquisitions, and everything else that we as human beings have been through, is going to yield fruits that we did not expect. It is where we are going see the connection, the fusion between science and spirituality.

I am immensely optimistic but not in the way that you imagine. I am not talking about a re-resurrection of structured religions, where they will be battling it out in some form of Hollywood type fantasy arenas. None of that will happen. Essentially you will see that we are reduced to the original elements that the human being is made of: the two complimentary elements. One is physical, material, limited, defined, conditioned, which is Conditioned Consciousness. The other is Pure Consciousness. Every single one of us has a specific conditioned consciousness which changes and evolves or devolves along with the desire, the quest, and the desperation to have access to pure consciousness, divine consciousness, God consciousness, supreme consciousness. That is all it is.

The children of Adam, no matter what background, what colour, what texture, what culture, what religion, share exactly the same thing. Each one of us has ever-changing awarenesses and these awarenesses vary in their depth and extent. We may have an awareness that we are sitting in a hall, an awareness that we are listening, an awareness that we have come with a quest, a hope, or a desire, that we will now access a zone in us that is forever reliable, forever constant, because we know that we are not constant. One minute I am awake, one minute I am asleep, one minute I am well, one minute I am not. One minute I am responding, one minute I am playing another role, one minute I am uncertain, one minute I am insecure… Sometimes I am these infinite varieties of shades and shadows behind which and within which there is an eternal light. This is really the whole story.

GNOSTICS AND THE SELF, POLITICS AND OTHERS

We have tried to camouflage the real purpose of life. I think we have run out of those titles: 'the purpose of life', 'the quest of being', 'seeking higher…'. So we camouflage it with 'gnosis and politics'. The two are never separate but rather ever complementary. Politics includes a relationship to myself, my body, my organs, my mind, my emotions, my intellect, my higher reasoning, my heart and my soul. This is politics. They are never, ever separate, like psychology and sociology.

If you are interested in saving yourself, to know who you are through psychology, you will end up being concerned about others, because in truth there is no otherness. It is sameness disguised as being different; that is why if you are not able to treat others as you would treat yourself you are not close to self-knowledge. That is also why we are repeatedly reminded that whoever wants to know their Lord must know themselves, meaning to know their soul. The soul is the agent to the Divine within. It has been Allah's representative in the heart of Bani (the tribe of) Adam for four and a half billion years. I think we can collectively and globally relate and help each other to the unveiling of that which is self-effulgent, which is self-disclosing. This is why I think, genuinely, we are heading towards a wonderful time of spiritual awakening.

THE RISING TIDE

The rising tide of spiritual awakening does not mean that the political systems, or city boundaries or country borders, or nationalism, or religions, or all of these things will be swept aside. No: there is a huge lead time, maybe another one, two, or three hundred years before we realise that people will be allowed to cross frontiers without all the misery to which people are being subjected because they are poor and cannot buy their way out of this or that. My optimism is spiritual optimism. In the meantime, the excesses of materialism that we are all suffering from, or complaining about, will continue.

I have absolutely no doubt that the golden era of the Gnostics or the Sufis or the teachers saying 'Turn away from the world' is coming to an end. That is why you find most of the old *Khaneqahs* (Sufi Halls) are really the same as freemason lodges, and will soon be up for sale, or lie empty. The time has come. You cannot tell people, 'Turn away from the world, don't be materialistic.' Junk is going to fill every bedroom, every living room, every garage until they have a garage sale and inflict it on Oxfam and other unfortunate receivers. This is unavoidable. Now, does it mean that God's mercy has stopped?

ON *ZUHD*

مَا وَدَّعَكَ رَبُّكَ وَمَا قَلَىٰ ٣

Your Lord has neither forsaken you nor is he displeased. (93:3)

Your Lord is Ever-Present. Wherever you turn is the light of Allah, the *Nūr* of Allah, the light of eternity. What it means is that we take on the materialistic side and come out of it from the other end. It was alright a hundred years ago in a village in India or somewhere in North Africa, for the Shaykh to be sitting on a mud floor and say turn away from everything. Not anymore! Imam 'Ali summed it up 1400 years ago, '*Zuhd* (asceticism) does not mean that you should not own anything, nor turn away from anything. It is that nothing should own you!' So by all means take it, take the material, but do not let it take you. Have it if it is there, but do not be sad if it is not. Who is imprisoned by whom?

It is a question of the heart: look at the father of all of the major religions in the Abrahamic tradition, look at Prophet Ibrahim. Here was this great, healthy young man brought up in this wonderful clan. They moved to Haran which is now Southwest of Turkey and there he found his uncles and traders and Idols. He found that the whole thing was rubbish, so he created a coup and he was set to leave and go South to Palestine and from there to Egypt. At that time Palestine was in an immense state of poverty. He went to Egypt and there he was honoured by the Pharaoh who took a fancy to prophet Ibrahim's wife.

The entire story of the Abrahamic tradition is based on this wonderful being, this hunter-gatherer nomad whose main livelihood was grazing and main occupation was caring for his clan. The only thing that he was attracted to was his son and that distracted him from the constant openings and thrill of the Ever-Presence of the Creator. So he had to carry on the tradition of the day and be willing to sacrifice his son. As he was willing to do that the ram of mercy appeared, to prove to him that it was about his intention. Turn away from that which you love and then you will find Original Love is the actual medium.

ORIGINAL LOVE: A UNIFYING FIELD

Just as space is the medium for things to move through, love is the medium of all of the Attributes we love. How does the connection between clemency, generosity and forgiveness meet with other attributes of beauty, majesty and so on? Where do they meet, where is the unifying field? It is called love. This is the meaning of the divine dictum (*hadīth qudsi*), 'I was a hidden treasure, and I loved to be known.' What is it that Allah loved to be known? Qualities which we human beings are endowed with that give us the possibility of understanding and being transformed by them, such as the patience.

SUFI TEACHINGS

Two major Sufi teachings are first to stop fearing for provision and secondly to stop the fearing the loss of reputation. This is Imam Abu'l Hasan Al-Shadhili's teaching. He said, 'If you promise me these two things, I promise you enlightenment. One, no fear of provision, second, no fear of human beings or what they think of you.'

Another most important Sufi teaching is, 'Time is like a sword, if you don't cut it, it will cut you.' In other words, go into patience, which is one of the great divine Attributes, *As-Sabūr* (the Ever-Patient). What is 'going into patience?' It means going into timelessness. You wanted something, now postpone it for two million years or even billions. I mean, what is a few billion years between you and your Creator who is beyond time and beyond space?

It is a child who wants everything *now*. Because they have just emerged from being a soul they have not yet learnt the camouflage of identification with the body, mind, limbs and memory, so they want it immediately. A two-year-old is a tyrant. He wants instant gratification because the soul is ever gratified and the two-year-old is still identifying with the soul. He hasn't learnt the tricks of growing old and being wise. They are still totally within their primal state. Why can't it be instantly done? I want constant and instant and perpetual satisfaction! You say no, you have to wait until the season comes, etc. This will only be the case of course until the commercial people can figure out that they can give you anything that you want, out of season, so that you fall sick from all kinds of disturbances, out of time, out of space.

DUALITY UNDERPINNED BY UNITY

The key issue for us is to be able to understand what we mean by gnosis. What is that quest and how can we reconcile paradoxes? You like to be known by others but if you are too well known then you have to spend a fortune to go to a deserted island where nobody knows you so as to fool around for a few days. You want to be known, but equally you don't want to be unknown. You want to be depended on and you like also to depend on others. Paradox, after paradox, after paradox. They will only be resolved if you truly put in front of you, within you, above you, below you, the original template that you are both sublime and ridiculous.

You are a both a Soul that is timeless, indescribable, a flash of light depicting the sacred Creator, and a Self, a human being with a biography, a beginning and end and a biological genealogy with DNA imprints. Don't deny either. How can you? Deal with yourself! Can you subdue your anger and turn that amazing power into a useful tool, rather than just blurt it out? How can you turn around your love for attraction? Bring everything to you, gain everything, own the whole world, the cosmos or realise the owner of it, the representative of the owner of it all resides in your heart? This is politics, the politics of the being human.

A few lines of Umar Khayyam reflect the underlying unity of the duality of our nature:

For in and out, above, about, below,

'tis nothing but a magic shadow-show,

played in a theatre whose candle is the sun,

'round which we phantom figures come and go.

This is duality behind which, within which, and after which, there is only One. All of Gnosis is based on *tawhīd* (divine unity), only One. There can only be One and the twos are in order for us to be puzzled, to give up and to yield, and to submit to the Ever-Present One. The Tao Te Ching tells us that hard and easy only complete each other, long and short are relative to each other, high and low are dependent on one another, and that first and last only succeed one another. It is a process, it never ends.

DUAL CONSCIOUSNESS

The story from a modern point of view, from a conscious-oriented point of view is that there are two levels of consciousness: one is primal, basic and the other is supreme consciousness—otherwise you will never be able to understand the cruelty of a lion devouring without any remorse. Nature is immensely cruel, so where is God's mercy then? We say that God is All-Merciful. Go to the jungle for a few days and then see. What does it mean? Does it mean that God is not there? No, it means that basic consciousness covered the first movement in creation about maybe 400 or 500 million years ago of the cell when the cosmic rays began that energetic movement within the cell to multiply and grow. It is at that basic consciousness level where every entity is only conscious of its self, meaning, it only wants to propagate itself. It is only concerned about self-survival. The idea of survival of the fittest is true. Absolutely. At that level, fitness is brute force. But what about this other consciousness, the one that hit us maybe a quarter of a million years ago?

That awareness of awareness of awareness, the human consciousness, double consciousness: I am aware I am a specific entity, but I am also aware of a zone that is beyond me, which we call Supreme Consciousness, God consciousness, Pure Consciousness, or any other name you like to give it. These two consciousnesses coincide in the human being. And the quest if you like of gnosis and politics are in order to get these two consciousnesses in unison.

This is why you find religious scriptures constantly refer to the higher, referring back to Allah.

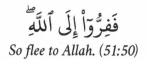

So flee to Allah. (51:50)

What does it mean? Is Allah somewhere else? What sort of Creator, All-Powerful, All-Permeating, is 'somewhere else'? No: it means refer to the higher within you. Deal with the lower, recognise pain and that conditioned consciousness, that local consciousness, but also refer to the zone already in you that is beyond up or down, or change or movement, or pain or pleasure. With the two together, then you have the right perspective. Say yes, I have pain but there is not too much I can do about it, so it is not so important.

So you have married the two together, as the great Shaykh Muhammad ibn Al Habibi says in his Diwan:

جَمَعَ الضِّدَّينِ في مَشْهَدِهِ

It [the heart] gathered the two opposites in its vision

WITNESSING PERFECTION

The two extremes are now connected in that witnessing and this is witnessing perfection—the perfection of your pain and witnessing the perfection of that which is going to relieve you of pain at the same time, simultaneously. That is why I am optimistic that once we get out of this excessively structured religiosity into the zone of self-redemption—saving yourself from yourself—there is going to be a global awakening of consciousness amongst human beings and then morphic resonance will take place once again.

More and more people will come to know each other without having to interrogate or subject them to some sort of an inquisition: Who are you? How do you pray? Everyone has been created somewhere, somehow, with some religion, some belief or disbelief, it does not matter. What matters is whether you, together with your inner-awakening or enlightenment and your awareness of the outer world with all its dualities and politics, are you doing the right thing. Is it the right time? Is it the right place? Are you putting things, such as politics, where it belongs?

I would also like to share with you the wonderful culture and background we have inherited at this time and age all accessible through media technology. Look at what William Blake says, when we talk about how all is in one and one is in all:

To see the world in a grain of sand and heaven in a wild flower.
Hold infinity in the palm of your hand and eternity in an hour.

St. John of the Cross says:

> *I abandoned and forgot myself, laying my face on my Beloved;*
> *all things ceased;*
> *I went out from myself, leaving my cares forgotten among the lilies.*

So do not deny the lilies; transcend them. Without that transcendence, we are stuck in this duality and this materialism. Do not deny materialism, because then the energy which has caused them will deny you. That is why my hope and expectation come from the 100 odd sciences, especially where quantum physics is completely resonating with classical physics.

Equally, do not deny the uncertainty of life (Heisenberg's Uncertainty Principle). We have no idea about the foundation of matter: it does not exist, nor does it matter. It is energy, pure energy which is in the atom. Everything is built on these wonderful little things called atoms and they get together and become molecules. What about the physics of it? At the end of the day you realise that whatever is matter and material is actually the energy which has gone into that form for a little while. It has been captured and imprisoned, as we have in our bodies, and after a while it will be released. Energy is on its way to becoming matter and matter is on its way to becoming energy. It is *bayna bayn* (in between and between, or neither/nor).

Imam 'Ali in his teachings instructs us that it is both and neither: you are *in* this world, not *of* this world. Buddhism teaches to abide not by this dualism, but to carefully avoid pursuing it. In other words, do not say only this is good and only this is bad. The Qur'an tells you there is something you may hate yet you think it is bad for you but it is the best for you. What do you know? You only know this moment, what about next year? Time changes. Do not abide by dualism; acknowledge it, do it and go past it and carefully avoid pursuing it.

As soon as you have 'right' and 'wrong', confusion ensues and the soul is lost. This is the teaching of Buddha. It is beyond all mental reasoning, beyond your intellect. It does not mean that you should not have an intellect or reason. Have it, but go past it. Have the car, remember that the car is there to deliver you somewhere. Don't stand there all day admiring it or take it to bed with you. It is a vehicle. The same applies to a teacher, or your *Dīn* (path). Step on it and fly with it, but don't be caught by it. Cause and effect are necessary for us to deal with in the kitchen, but anything more than that is detrimental.

Rumi says,

> *Reason is the chain of travellers and lovers, my son,*
> *break the chain and the way is plain and clear ahead for you, my son.*
> *Reason is a chain, body an illusion and the self a veil and when you have risen*
> *out of reason, body and self,*
> *you have gone forth past shadows and illusions, my son.*

Do not deny anything, but more than that do not deny the light that is beckoning to you, that is illumining everything, that is causing you all, if you like, this so-called temporary confusion. This fundamental duality is something that we have to reckon with and this is what is called politics of the self.

CONFUSING THE TWO DIMENSIONS

You have to accept there are two of you. There is a meanness in me that wants everything for myself and there is an occasionally generous person in me who likes to give, and usually when you give you like to be photographed with the other person thanking you! The world is this composite situation of both physical realities and emotions and the inner, submerged uncertainties of the quantum world that we are made of.

When time stops, all there is is the Now, of which Meister Eckhart says,

...the now when God made the world is as near to this moment,
the last day is as near to this now as was yesterday.[2]

If you know the meaning of cutting time, go beyond patience into timelessness.

This is why we love meditation and prayer. What does it do to you? It recharges you. How? By stopping the draining of your batteries. By giving up your 'this is good, this is bad' labelling. You stop it all. You become recharged by the ever-present light within you. So all you and I need to do is to stop. The problem is that in this world of ours, of secular education and all of the other wonderful things that we enjoy, we are taught to always have a goal, a plan, a strategy in place. Occasionally, if you are foolish enough, you even bring in consultants whom you pay heavily to kick you this way and that. Nowadays you can get all kinds of executive coaches.

We are taught all the time how to get something, how to capture what we require and we transpose this type of thinking into the other zone, into the spiritual zone, and that is where the problem lies. Most religious people are confused because of that. We are dealing with this world which is all about acquisition and we take that into the spiritual side. But the spiritual side is not about acquisition. It is about relinquishing, it is about death, it is about not having anything. It does not have to be literal; assume yourself dead, practise death. Learn the art of stepping aside from yourself fully—no self, no image, no idea, no thought, no identification. Lose your identity in the divine entity within you, then you have combined the two, worldly and non-worldly.

Here is what Jesus talks about the kingdom of God when he says the 'Kingdom of God is within you'. Imam 'Ali says that your sickness is from you though you do not realize it, and your remedy is within you but you do not perceive it, and you claim you are a small entity but within you is hidden the whole cosmos.

---

2. From The Complete Mystical Works of Meister Eckhart, 2009, p.341.

When we read such things it becomes pure poetry, very nice and uplifting. That's not good enough; it is not about 'uplifting' but rather about stopping being down-lifted. Stop that! That is why many gatherings, including that of *dhikr*, do not do much good other than give you a false upliftment for a while. What about later?

We need to realise that the roots are not there. The root has to come from you realising that you are both sublime *and* ridiculous. You are both: you are mean *and* generous, you are *in* this world but not *of* this world. If you do not realise that then there is no use. You may then try to hang on to somebody else whom you think is an enlightened teacher, or a Guru, or a Shaykh. eventually it ends up in disaster because nobody can give you anything. It is you who can stop having all that you think you have.

This is why I said that the greatest confusion is these two dimensions. One is a worldly dimension that is acquisitional: 'Go and get it!' In the meantime, you have stepped on a few heads and made a few enemies. So, you get a few bodyguards, you get the bank to protect you and the government runs after you. The other side is completely different: it is about negation, nothingness, the eternal void which is beyond the cosmic space. If you do not develop that taste, then you remain half-cooked, and you start learning it after you leave the body.

THE WAY OF THE MIDDLE PEOPLE

The mercy of Allah does not end. It continues. There is another life after you leave the body. That is, life in the grave. There is an evolution there also, both a material evolution, as we have come from mineral to human, and a spiritual evolution until the whole cycle comes to an end and then that is called the day of reckoning or *yawm al-qiyāma* (The Day or Resurrection or Moment of Account), or the end of ends.

We are now in the middle. One of the meanings of 'middle people', or *ummatan wasata*, similarly in the Buddhist teachings as the Islamic, is that you are in the middle between the material and non-material. You are sandwiched between the unseen where you *were* before and now you are in the seen until you develop your insight moving towards the next stage where you can no longer act, but you have insight, after death.

We are now at a stage that we have to willingly quest for that enlightenment and yet at the same time take appropriate action, have appropriate relationships, follow appropriate courtesies, and adopt appropriate human qualities. Most religions dwell upon these issues, virtues like generosity, kindness, help, service. They are absolutely essential. They were the foundation of cohesion of societies or communities but we are heading towards a zone, or a time, where you don't have family around, the extended family. You now have plastic cards that you can wave at a machine and get by. No longer do you have those situations where you are constantly acknowledged as you give up your self's desires moving towards the zone of self-purification, accessing pure inner-consciousness. Nowadays it is another zone.

It does not mean that we do not uphold all of those virtues; we certainly do, but they are not sufficient. You must have that preference of others over you, you must have love for others rather than the so-called ego. These are necessary conditions but not enough. What matters then is your ability to truly let go of everything. Be Ibrahimi, truly walking in the footsteps of the prophet Abraham. Make a list of the things you really want most and be willing to give them up. Look at what Bayazid Al-Bistami says about the *what*. He says:

> *I searched for God for thirty years, thinking that it was I who*
> *desired him*
> *but I now know that it was He, God, who had been calling me all*
> *along.*

It is your soul that is calling you; nothing is going to be enough. However much wealth you have is not going to be enough. Power is not going to be enough, no matter what. Why then is there this discontent? It is because you have not been dancing with your partner, with your soul.

That is why the Sufis consider the day of departure from this world, as *urs*, the day of your wedding. Meaning what? Meaning the 'wedding' of the *nafs* and the *rūh*. Why don't you complete that union now? You're without a wife, you're without a husband; it is a metaphor, it is a 'sample' of that inner wedding.

We are repeatedly told by all spiritual beings, all prophets, all masters, all scriptures, that this world is a little sample of the next world. So why don't you fully live that sample? Are you married to your *rūh*? Are you truly in ecstasy with your inner or are you confused? Is there a bit of anger, a bit of rancour, a bit of guilt? Why guilt? Guilt is the distance or the difference between what you could *have* done and what you *have* done. So, whilst you are doing something, be aware, so you won't have guilt. Whatever you are doing, be aware of why are you doing it, as if it is the last thing you do in your life, so you won't have regrets. Then there is that term 'if only'. Whenever somebody tells you 'if only', or if they say 'unfortunately', then please run away from them.

Everything is fortunate, there is no 'unfortunate'. There is Divine Presence forever, but you and I don't see the perfection of that now because we have an agenda. So I am carried away by my agenda instead of Divine will. Once I make my will subservient to Divine will then there is total unison between the self and the soul, and the entity and the original Divine identity. There is only harmony and peace. Peace is already there. It is we who create noise, movement and action and disturbance. Look at chaos, you will find order within it. There is no separation, in the truest sense. The now is ever-present, it is eternal. Distance does not exist. This is God's laboratory. Time and space are God's test tube: He created this entity which is beyond time and space and yet is within time and space.

QUANTIFYING ENLIGHTENMENT

Now I come to the question: who is enlightened? For hundreds, if not thousands of years, many battles, quarrels, killings and communal warfare were had over who is and isn't enlightened. Our man is more enlightened, my shaykh is better than yours, my prophet is better than yours, our scripture is better than yours. Everybody is killing everybody else without realising the whole business is about killing your attachment, your mental expectation, your idea. Change your attitude and show gratitude about who you are and what you are even in ignorance. You will find that your attitude is easy to change and you will see wonder upon wonder. You will then learn more from your enemies than your friends.

Rumi has said that repeatedly. He would always make *du'ā'* (supplication) for his enemies. His companions responded, 'But we are your friends, we love you, we have been with you,' and he said, 'But you have done nothing for me. It is my enemies who have really taught me. If it weren't for my enemies and the outer world kicking me in my teeth, I would not have been able to leave the love of the world. It is they who knocked me and pushed me and kicked me so that I realised I can't rely on this world, this is unreliable. I want something that is reliable.' As for the question of who is enlightened or the degrees of enlightenment there are infinite varieties.

Gnosis begins with the baby's gnosis: knowledge that this is a nipple, this is the mother, and later on they begin to know this nipple is not everything they want. Later on in life it is the treadmill that you want or something else, other remedies. It changes; there is no end to Gnosis. You cannot say that he is enlightened. If you say that then it means that you have fixed it, it is another zone, you can say no, this teacher is more in *tajrīd* (isolation), he is more willing to give up everything, he is not concerned about the number of *murīds* (students), or wealth or power or internet hits. Then you say, alright, he is possibly a bit more liberated than the other Shaykh who is always concerned about how many do we have, how many have come. Maybe these are worldly measures that echo the non-worldly state. Do not mix them up.

To measure and qualify gnosis is impossible except by this allusion to it. How far are they from this world? It does not mean that you are denouncing and spitting on the world. The world is Divine but appears as "Bovine" so don't denounce anything; denounce only your attachment, your expectations, your fears.

THE HOW OF ENLIGHTENMENT

Now we come to the question of how you get enlightened. *How* is the key issue that I have already partly covered. It is by turning away from all the shadows. To be enlightened you must turn away from all shadows, this is a non-worldly question and it is through self-knowledge, soul awareness, and sacred presence. This is the *how*: self-knowledge, know yourself.

Then he inspired it to understand what is wicked for it
and to have cautious awareness of what right for it. (91:8)

You know that you are also degenerate and decadent and yet you also love to be wholesome and healthy and pure. Once you realise that, you become more and more soul aware. You refer to your inner soul. You refer to God within you and then you realise that everywhere is sacred presence, a sign of God, the cosmic soul.

Now you are beginning to accept duality and live unity at the same time. Now you are going to transform yourself, less self, less egotism, more self-abandonment, then you start to have glimpses of the ever-present, eternal Light. In the gospel of Thomas, one of the gospels of the Gnostics, Jesus said: 'Blessed are the solitary and the chosen and the ones who are chosen, so that you attain the kingdom, for you are from it and to it you will return'.

Solitary meaning not having expectations from others, being meek and weak at the time you are exercising your inner-connectedness. Being spiritually meek means when you are acting in the world be fully present. In the kitchen, be the cook. When you are a father, be the father; and when you are the mother, the friend, or the businessman, be that role, but in the awareness that you are not only that role.

Rumi describes his inner journey as follows: "Since within you lurks a hidden enemy, only by repelling the monster, by harshness can you be saved.' The man who beats a rug with a stick is not aiming the blows at the rug. The purpose is to rid the rug of dust. Layers of dust are within you constituting the veils, such as egotism and others that cannot be eliminated with only a single blow. That is why you and I receive one blow after another; you think you've solved it and then something else happens. The Jews, who were really the elite in Iraq, had a famous and wise saying, 'You try to close it at one end, it opens somewhere else. You think you've got it, but you haven't. Admit that it has got you and then be a guardian. Be a steward (*khalīfa*) of Allah with whatever is in your custody, whether it is wealth, children, house or friends. Be a custodian, be a steward, be responsible'.

We all know the rarity of such human beings in this world. But as I said earlier, I have a strong notion that enlightenment and awakening and Gnosis will be normal not, as it is nowadays, unusual, so that everybody tries to compete how many hats, turbans or whatever else are on their Shaykh's head.

DIVINE POLITICS

In these last few minutes, I want to share with you divine politics. All we experience in the microcosm is within the macrocosm and that is where divine politics comes into it. As I said earlier, true Gnosis and politics are never separate. In all situations, the extent of a person's enlightenment relates to the frequency of reference to the higher within. That is divine politics. All of us will *suffer* until we learn to access the ever-present divine *offer*. We are all designed for that. We have been created for that and, as a great mystic Baba Kuhi said, 'See the One and you will be spared the two. You will be amused by and enjoy the two.' He says further:

In the market, in the cloister - only God I saw.
In the valley and on the mountain - only God I saw.

Him I have seen beside me oft in tribulation;
In favour and in fortune - only God I saw.
In prayer and fasting, in praise and contemplation,
In the religion of the Prophet - only God I saw.
Neither soul nor body, accident nor substance,
Qualities nor causes - only God I saw.

That is why I said earlier witness perfection. Perfection is beyond the good and the bad. It is perfect, it is not any more subject to a little good or a little bad; it is ever perfect.

Now we come to the last point, why we seek Gnosis. Why do we seek Gnosis? It is like trying to describe the taste of honey. Until they taste it, then 'oh, I know'. So, the answer to *why* comes after you have got it, and you only get it after you give up everything else and accept that it has got you.

This is the ultimate spiritual pilgrimage. That you have entered into a new phase of living and in this phase you are witnessing perfection upon perfection. You are bewildered. Somebody comes and tells you that something is very bad. You descend to their level, as the Prophet describes, to the people's level and say, 'Yes, you are right' but within you, you see only goodness. You don't play God anymore. Deal with the world and let the Creator of the world deal with it for you, and then wherever you turn is perfection. The most amazing fact about life and creation is the ever-constant presence of utter perfection, in spite of personal faults and misconceptions. The outcome in every case is due to normal laws, decrees and channels of manifestations—don't ever deny those—emanating from the same source, the ever-present fountain of Life, ever True, ever Harmonious, ever Perfect in its Oneness, Nearer than nearness itself, Present before time, permeating heavens and earth with Light and Supreme Consciousness. There is none other than that One.

CHAPTER SEVEN

Power of Devotion, Prayer and Worship

Given in 2009

- Awareness of the Unseen
- Otherness: Disguised Selfhood
- The Same Genetic Source
- A Short History of Spiritual People
- Space, Time and Context
- Prophetic Unveilings of Singularity
- *Al-Insān Al-Kāmil*—The Complete Person
- The Illusion of Separation
- Globalisation
- Evolution towards the Unseen
- Scientism, Rationality and the First Level of Evolution
- Unveilings of Love
- Hierarchy of Needs: Body, Mind & Heart
- Balance between Self and Soul
- Catch Yourself: What is your Intention?
- Unity of Action
- Poem: Allah

AWARENESS OF THE UNSEEN

I express my gratitude on my behalf and everybody's behalf to the essential, original Essence of creation, Allah, God, who has created these amazing visible and invisible realms, the universe. I thank Allah and I thank you who took time off for your own sake to discover further that which is beyond the limits of discoveries.

We are all on the same journey. That journey involves integrating both outer and inner horizons, the seen and unseen. Being able to perceive the seen and unseen implies that there has to be a 'middle people'. Being the middle people, or *ummatan wasata* as described in the Qur'an, means that we do not deny physicality, sensuality, realizations of matter, energy or any experience whatsoever. While we do not deny these, we can also differentiate and appreciate, as well as judge, what is beneficial and what is not, what is appropriate and what is not. This allows us to enter the horizon of the Unseen. We are in the middle, between heaven and earth, a *barzakh* (interspace between the seen and unseen). It is all in the middle. Life is a work in progress and we are all on the move. There is no such a thing as total or fixed conclusion.

The Qur'an says:

$$وَأَنَّ إِلَىٰ رَبِّكَ ٱلْمُنتَهَىٰ ﴿٤٢﴾$$

And to your Lord is (the beginning and) the end. (53:42)

There is none other than that. All other so-called realities are helpful illusions: that I exist, I am separate, I'm doing or saying something good. There is no doer except the One; no attribute that you and I like, except that it belongs to the One. There is no beginning and no end in truth—it's all our fantasy.

Nowadays the real progress in spirituality is coming from astrophysics, from nuclear scientists, and from quantum theorists, and increasingly less from theologians. Thirty to forty years ago no physicist in his right mind would have dared to mention 'God' in their discourses. Over the last 10 years it has become fashionable. We are realising more and more from the field of science that there is ultimately that singularity, which we call *tawhīd* or Oneness, that engulfs all apparent dualities. We also have the notion of the Big Bang, and the Big Collapse, that are replicated repeatedly by every one of us.

The Big Bang was when you were perceived or conceived; born the same way as life began on Earth, 3.8-4.5 billion years ago. The same thing also applies to each one of us; we will experience personally this local collapse at the point of death. Yet at the same time we all love immortality.

Egotistic persons start building monuments; which they can even disguise as schools or mosques or churches, it doesn't matter. They like to see their name in light—'This is in the name of my great father!'. Yet another idol! But never mind, it is better than other worse idols. We all seek immortality, every one of us, in different ways. It is just so that we can declare that we are passionately in love with that entity which *is* eternal, *Al-Hayy* (The Ever-living), Allah, God, whatever you may wish to call it.

OTHERNESS: DISGUISED SELFHOOD

As middle people we have to be rational, using our mind and reason. We have to learn compassion and to co-exist with others and we have to do this in order to learn that there is no otherness. Is this not a real paradox? If that is not a puzzle good enough to occupy a lifetime, I do not know what is. We have to survive; human beings can only survive with others, with community, with society. The progress of our evolvement is such that we have this notion of serving others, for others' sake, or for God's sake. Often religious people use that to browbeat others when they say, 'I am doing this *fī sabīli'llah* (for the sake of God).' So now everybody must crawl because you are doing it 'for God's sake'.

I say 'they' but who is 'they'? Who is the self? Where is the self? Whatever you do is in reality instigated by the love of the self; whether for the most selfish person or the most selfless person. It holds true even for the loving mother who dies during birth. All of it is for the self. The self is a spectrum; one end of it is this identity, which we call "you and I". When you were 4 years old you said 'I', when you are 40 you say 'I'. So the sound does not change but the entire cosmology and the context changes radically. That's another magic.

This is the situation we find ourselves in. We have this lower self, identified with the body, with the genetic background, with the culture, religion, and all the other things that give you and I, he and she, an identity, self-respect, status, which is important for us human beings. Do not ever deny the ego. Ego is what will lead you to ego-lessness or it will trap you and suffocate you. Both are the same. Like water which is 70 to 80% of the Earth's surface, you and I are composed of water and yet floods cause more deaths than any other natural disaster. It is the same with fire. Fire is in us, it is wonderful, and most important for heat. Without the sun there would be no life and yet fire consumes whatever is in its way.

THE SAME GENETIC SOURCE

We are simple beings, the Adamic being, the children of Adam. All of us genetically come from the same source. This is also true linguistically; all our languages have a common root. It is an amazing recent discovery. It is only in the last 10 to 15 years that we began to realise that it is true that we are 'one people'. Colours vary because within 10 to 15 generations the colour of your skin will change according to UV light that you are exposed to. At that time, these human beings were running around innocently. 'Innocent' meaning ignorant, but ignorant without even being aware of what knowledge is.

A SHORT HISTORY OF SPIRITUAL PEOPLE

The Great Flood, the Flood of Noah (AS), or Gilgamesh and many other names given to it in cultures worldwide, including in South America, caused great devastation and generated a legacy of mythology surrounding it.

As the Qur'an tells us, people had begun to transgress because everybody wanted power. You see, the unseen is powerful, we all want to know the unseen and as a result, in the last 5,000 years we created classes of people who claimed to have access to the source of power, such as priesthoods. The priests are those who think that they alone can connect you with God. They claim to have a better lubrication in the process of communication with God, as if God is somewhere, or nowhere, or wherever.

Then of course you have the shamans who spread further than all. These beings would enter into another state of consciousness by which they would resonate with their ancestors, or with other beings, or unseen beings, and come up with statements that were most fascinating, shocking, accurate or complete nonsense. So shamanism was one of the earliest attempts of humanity at large to connect the seen and the unseen. Then you have the seers who read the future for you and all kinds of other levels and layers in between.

Around that time, 5,000 to 6,000 years ago, the notion of prophethood began to occur. Amongst a large population of people were beings who were both sensitive to the unseen and charged with guidance: seeing what is visible, tangible, discernible, and also having insight into what is beyond the limitations of space and time. A sudden flash of insight going back and forth in time. It's only now that the physicists tell us that there is no real reason in nature or natural laws that the direction of time should be exactly as we experience it—in that you are born, you grow, and you die. There is no natural reason for time to move along the direction that it does.

SPACE, TIME AND CONTEXT

Space and time are inseparable. Remove one, you lose both. And they are the womb in which you and I are being cooked, developed, in order to recognise the seen, to get to the edge of the unseen. And within that there is a hierarchy, to see, to appreciate, to be wise, all of which means appropriateness in the right time in the right place. Religious people have serious problems when it comes to the verbal prophetic traditions. To correctly interpret them you need to get the exact context: when was it said, to whom, how it was said, and then to understand whether it is subject to time or meant for all times. That is why we end up in considerable theological confusion, debates and animosities.

I used to think that religious wars have caused more death, more mayhem, more slaughter and more violence that anything else. So I asked a few of our young people to do a basic and crude search to check the numbers of those slaughtered 4,000 to 5,000 years ago in the name of God, mine or yours, to the present time. We discovered that in fact secular wars have killed more people. God was spared, especially during the last century. Far, far more people were slaughtered for the sake of acquisition and human greed.

PROPHETIC UNVEILINGS OF SINGULARITY

To come again to our little historical snapshot of what happened in the last few million years: we have these great prophets coming one after another, with strong cultural inclinations. They spoke what was relevant to their people, connecting with the seen, but always referring to the unseen. All prophetic messages were talking about the needs of the day, about the requirements for living in a fairly harmonious society, being safe and helpful to each other, bringing about a certain bonding. Of course religion is the greatest connecter, but it can equally bring about the greatest animosities, if people leave that 'clan'. Suddenly 'if he is not one of us, then he is against us' isn't even enough, now he has to be slaughtered!

Essentially, this advancement, this growth, this plethora of messengers, apostles, prophets were saying the same thing in essence: that there is oneness, or singularity as the physicists call it, an all-permeating unity but it can only be known through accepting, studying, and realising dualities and pluralities. God does not play hide and seek; He's not hiding behind us, but this is the way things are.

This is also the story of the descent and ascent of Adam. Life will not continue unless there is total selfishness. The genes are 100% selfish to propagate themselves. They are replicating and singing the divine name of *Al-Bāqī* (the Eternal) or *Al-Hayy* (The Ever-Living). That's all they know. Then *Al-Wāsi'* (The Vast), in a hierarchical sense, until you get to the primates, the beginning of the higher attributes start. It is for that reason also, if you look back in history, 3,000 years ago the bull was worshiped. He's virile, reproducing, big testicles, physically huge, powerful; so the king was represented as a flying bull. That's interesting—earth and heavens. Very strong and powerful here but it can also fly. The flying bull was one of the key deities. Other deities included the cow and other animals such as the crocodile, the cat, and especially the dog. The dog has amazing qualities such as reliability, loyalty and other senses like its hearing, far sharper than ours, also smell, etc. These were created as attributes.

We get this notion of 'the One', 4,000 years ago when the great patriarch, the Prophet Ibrahim (AS), emerged to declare that there is only One. Prior to that, the notion of One was there, but not declared, or clearly defined. This One is behind all the twos: you don't see Him, you can't touch Him, you can't define Him, and that is the only power that gives you the ability to think, see, walk, sleep, eat, and to return to Him after you die.

It was the Prophet Ibrahim (AS) who brought the notion of humanity and divinity together. Do not forget your humanity. You are a human being, but don't ever lose sight of the ever-present Divinity. From the Judaic patriarch comes Isa (AS) where, again, human beings suddenly see humanity and divinity completely united.

AL-INSĀN AL-KĀMIL—THE COMPLETE PERSON

The same notion carries on with the Prophet Muhammad (S) where we talk about *Al-insān al-kāmil*, often wrongly translated as the 'perfect person'. There cannot be perfection in a person, it's an oxymoron, a conflict of two terms. You can have a person who knows, who refers to the zone of perfection in their hearts or to the prophetic model, but you and I are decaying. Just go back to 100 year old physics, the Second Law of thermodynamics—the Law of Entropy. Everything is disintegrating and the efficiency of the system becomes less and less until it returns to its origin because the pool of energy and matter is constant, which is also the First Law of Thermodynamics—Energy cannot be created or destroyed. So we find this amazing movement in humanity in every way you look at it. It is the sandwich between physicality, the world which we want to know more about, and the unseen. So we have no option, other than to surrender to it, other than declaring *Islam*.

I like to see well, I would like to improve my sight, my ears, my senses, and my common-sense. But more than all of that, I'm totally gripped by that passion for the unseen. It is passion that is driving us. We are all the same, but suddenly we may take a detour or a distraction, a diversion and become passionately in love with whatever, a woman, a man, a job, a project, or a mosque, or a religion. Forgetting that the passion is for Him Who created the force and the power, the passion to unify all. It is through that passion that we are all able to talk about some sort of friendship, connection, kindness, gentleness, compassion; all of these are different versions of the same glue, called love culminating in *'ishq* or passion. The whole thing is driven by the soul's passion because the soul is never separate from its Maker.

THE ILLUSION OF SEPARATION

You and I have this fantasy and illusion that we are separate. We say that he is closer to God, another far away from God. What sort of a God is measured by a ruler, by centimetres or inches? There is none other than God! Everything else is shadows reflecting that light because the sample of that light is within them, called the soul or the spirit, the beginning and the end of the whole story. So that is why we are endowed with all of these faculties and these limitations which we now call our world, our great world, with its ups and downs and all of the elements and the rise of science.

Physical science became prominent during Victorian times because people woke up from the oppression of the dark ages in Europe to under-standing how things work; you put this and this together and experiment and then there's an explosion, or you put some substance together with another and they will fuse. Suddenly by 1900 you had this idea that *everything* is science and so God was fully retired without a pension; now everybody is scientific and technologically enlightened. A great awakening!

GLOBALISATION

Now we are caught up in a bigger wave called globalisation. What is the intention of this globalisation? Is it to uplift humanity? Spirituality? Give people the basics of food, shelter, clothes? What was it? No, it was the great movement of so-called Reformation. Go on, do it, make money, as long as you put the name of God on the highest skyscraper. For the sake of God! We glorify God, but slaughter God's creation. That's what we have done. When you have exhausted all possibilities due to your intelligence and mind, you may realize that all that is left is reliance on God. That state is most powerful and potent and opens up new channels of consciousness which you may not have been aware of.

Many of us had many times in our lives where you don't know where to turn. Every one of us is honoured by situations like this. How about you maintain that honour? Admit that you just don't know where else to turn! The Qur'an and all the Abrahamic traditions are full of this, as well as Eastern religions.

EVOLUTION TOWARDS THE UNSEEN

The Unseen desired to be seen, therefore creation and consciousness. Which can only produce awareness if there is an identity and a ego-self. Awareness of the unseen is to know that there is only Allah, to know that there is only the eternal light, that has no beginning and no end. All other lights have boundaries; useful for the little animals we are, to grow to realise the magnificent magic and miracle of the Light which is in us. This is also why the magicians were very prominent for most of our history. The magician or the sorcerer who, along with the shamans, were in it for power.

That's why the new generation is fortunate; most of these hypocrisies will evaporate. We all love money, we all love power, we all love status because we are passionately in love with the unseen Source of power, wealth, status, in the heart, called your *rūh* (soul). Recognise the duality, the two facets of the self and the soul; the consciousness and the higher consciousness; the first evolution and the other evolution; knowing that there is only that eternal light that calls and holds and permeates the universe. If you don't recognise it, then you are only semi human. You don't deny the pain, you don't deny the anguish, but it does not overwhelm you. You deal with it rationally, wholesomely and you move on.

SCIENTISM, RATIONALITY AND THE FIRST LEVEL OF EVOLUTION

We come very quickly now to the 19th Century, to scientism and the rise of technology and how clever we are. All that we have done is trying to see within what is see-able. We have very quickly reached the point of the electronic microscope, and soon after that we have moved on to particle accelerators and so on. The more we find something, the more we find that there are another hundred things to be found, which opens gateways for the future PhD students. It's wonderful. The one that grows geometrically is the PhD type of project because it is an addition to knowledge, that type of knowledge we call the 'seen'.

Equally with 'seen' knowledge is another form of knowledge, that of the 'unseen'. But we have to be careful, we can't impose that. Suddenly you come into the room and say that you have seen the angels come through that door. One of my main prayers in my life has been that Allah may spare me such people. It is unfair and incorrect to bring in the unseen and your so-called power into the seen. It shows you are unfulfilled, miserably clutching at straws. It may well be true you have perceived something, but you have created it. Your dreams are your creations, your visions are your own creations, otherwise how do they occur unless you have empowered them? Do not impose them upon others! Run away from whoever tells you, 'I have seen this thing around'.

When the Prophet Ibrahim's son died, the sun disappeared because of a total eclipse. Was it because the heavens were crying for Ibrahim? Was there some huge change in the planetary system? He said, 'Don't be stupid, the heavens have nothing to do with Ibrahim. My son caught an illness.' Be correct, don't mix up things, otherwise we end up with obscurantism and all kinds of fantasies where we mix up religion with reality. There is One Real and that One Real percolates into hundreds of lesser realities with a small 'r'. Therefore, even the lie that we perpetuate has a reality. It is only reality. There is only truth. Everything else draws its energy from the same truth. It is then diluted, diluted, and diluted until it comes to you and me and we see darkness, but darkness can only be perceived because there is light. They are never separate; where is it that Allah is not?

We are essentially, divinely inspired creatures, whether we like it or not. In a way, the West did the right thing by taking away the search for knowledge from the theologians 600 to 700 years ago. They established the universities and now they have the theology department within the university so as not to taint it with all these superstitions.

Your job and my job is to be rational, correct, kind, gentle, and to rise from the first level of evolution of simple survival and power into the second level of spiritual evolution and awakening to the thrill that is always there. The problem is that we do not grasp it because we have only grasped the drudgery of work, or responsibility, or fear of losing status and other such things. We have to truly, constantly, act at the level of the seen, maintain that, and look at the horizon that has no end. Put the two together and we have put Humpty Dumpty together. We are both: humanity and divinity unite in us.

UNVEILINGS OF LOVE

Surah Ar-Rahman says these two oceans meet in you; one does not overcome the other. No matter who it is, whether a prophet or some other human, they are subject to mistakes on fundamental levels but those mistakes are insignificant. The mistake of whoever is awakened to the unseen is better than the best action of those who are not. These are hierarchies, different levels of awakening to the real authority, to the real author, Allah *Azza wajall*. There is nothing in life other than trying to unify the seen and the unseen through the power of love, which enables every duality to disappear and all notions of freedom to be lost. That is what love is.

If there is true love and *'ishq (Passion)*, you no longer have duality. You don't know who you are. But equally there is this notion that we are free, independent. It is Allah Who is *As-Samī'* (The All-Hearing); you and I are not. We have to pray, supplicate, and ask.

Essentially there are 3 levels of connectedness and love. One is the divine level, the second is the human level, of mutual respect, availability, condition, and the third is causality. One level is constant, boundless and divine; the second is conditional and necessary for life on earth. The third is the causality of connectedness due to chemical, physical and other forces.

Thank God that haphazardness is not accepted; we'd have nothing other than chaos which was probably the case when the sorcerers, shamans and seers were rampant during the time of the Flood. Everybody asked them and they could manage to do things. So there would have been a lot of chaos and instability. It's very important for our outer to have some stability, some reliability, and for the inner to realise we can't have it. Therefore we are soft at heart. The reverse of what we are now: outwardly stable, rock-solid investment, but inwardly totally uncertain, disillusioned and unhappy.

No matter what you and I experience in this life it is a mixture, a combination, of dualities and pluralities, which complement and oppose each other. The mixture is of the good and the bad, birth and death, right and wrong, just and unjust, beautiful and ugly. It is also all of the countless visible, tangibles as well as the meanings of concepts that complement and emerge from the source and return to the same source.

I would also like to remind you that the best way you can discern and understand the definition of love, which is the force of unity or singularity that permeates dualities, is through a multitude of degrees, of strength, density, intensity, quality and quantity, but ultimately it is that which unites every type of opposite. If you want to glue two pieces of wood together, that is an aspect of connecting two different pieces into one. The glue here, the medium, is love. For human beings it is something that is not easy to define. It is something from the heart, beyond our mind's confines. That is why the mind has its ways, logic and reason, and the heart has its way. The human being is a mixture, a combination of both. If you deny one, you'll be denied the other.

HIERARCHY OF NEEDS: BODY, MIND & HEART

All of us grow from babyhood to adulthood to old age to death. We take on these ladders and staircases of reasoning, understanding, wisdom, and then we reach the point where its root was there from the beginning, which has different qualities, different domains of reason. But it is not the same as mental, causal, or discernible reasons. This is who we are. We were extensively discussing aspects of *du'a'*, supplication and human needs. It is the biggest gift of God. We all have needs, some of them are real; for example, you need to be able to breathe. Try to put something heavy on your chest for 5 minutes and see what happens. Try to deprive yourself of food for a few days, or drink, and see what happens. You will be beside yourself.

We all have needs that are discernible, physical, material. But we also need to know how to get a clearer mind and better mental images, better recall of memories, so we can wipe out all the stupid things, otherwise we will be mixed-up and confused. With most people in this life, you will notice, half of them are in the past and the other half are worried about the future, therefore there is no presence. And this is why they all say I need time, I need space. What an ungenerous God Who created people who are always caught in a frenzy of space and time! Make it your habit that all you have is space and time. You'll be amazed. The rest is fantasy of your mind.

It is a question of mental hygiene and the right attitude towards your wellbeing. Your wellbeing is at all of these levels of body, mind and heart. You cannot deny any particular one. And they are hierarchical. If the physical is distorted, in pain, then the subtler, which is mental, cannot be brought into equanimity and balance, let alone the heart. And the three go together, until such time as you transcend them. We do not continually want to think that 'I'm well in my body, I'm well in my mind and my heart is pure, I don't have much enmity or hatred in it'. This is boring; you need to have done this homework. If you've done your house-work, the cleaning up, then you will see how the seen and the unseen are in perfect harmony.

So even if you are not dancing or your heart is not overflowing with joy, you will begin to capture flashes of the perfect harmony and joy that is in nature, seen and subtler, such as the way the ant moves. Just before I came here, I was looking at the most amazing long-legged spider climbing up this fairly smooth wall with 40 to 50 eggs dangling from it, struggling. What was it doing? It is *Al-Bāqī* (the Everlasting) worshiping survival. Incredible! Tiny little things you could not recreate. Wherever you look you can be fascinated forever. You don't need outer silly entertainment; you need a bit of access to inner attainment and you will be in ecstasy at all times. And then you'll take on your outer responsibility with light heartedness. If you can do it, do it. If you can't do it, don't complain all the time, establishing your victimhood. It becomes a habit of your mind—everybody is carrying their own miserable biography with them.

BALANCE BETWEEN SELF AND SOUL

Now, there is a very serious paradox with the seeker—people like us, who call ourselves 'seekers'. It is the question of, 'Who am I?' And then, how do I reconcile my lower humanity and all of the chemical, physical things that are going on within me, whether in my body or in my brain and all the amazing interaction of enzymes and hormones? How can I reconcile my so-called humanity with what I aspire for as a seeker, which they term

Divinity, that which is Sublime, that which is beyond space and time, that which is Absolute, that which is Ever Real, that which is True, beyond any measure?

The dilemma, the paradox of the seeker, essentially, is how to reconcile the love of independence, the Independent (*As-Samad*), the Strong (*Al-Qawī*), the Powerful (*Al-'Azīm*), those divine attributes, with the lower aspects and behaviour of the ego, which want to assert themselves.

As a shadow, your lower self, your ego has no reality. It is there simply because the real light in your heart, which is your soul or your spirit, that shines upon that shadow, wants to be the soul. This is the paradox. You are both. You are a soul that is divine, with no beginning and no end, that gives rise to an aspect in us that at best can be called 'bovine', which is this lower self.

So, there are two elements in me. One is a shadow that is ever changing, ever restless, ever pretending, ever wanting to assert itself; that is the idol. That is the ultimate idol. You see some people coming, wheeling their statue in front of you, boasting, 'Don't you know who I am?' And the other is complete transcendence. Of course, that shadow element, that trouble, was the ultimate source of vices, but yet it leads us to the door of virtues. If you can spot your meanness at the moment it is occurring, you will be neutralised and you will then act correctly in a generous way. I guarantee you, you do not need to do anything other than that.

CATCH YOURSELF: WHAT IS YOUR INTENTION?

Corrective teaching can come from the unlikeliest of sources. Once many years ago, my luggage was being carried by a porter in Bombay airport. In those days, Bombay airport was like some *mash'ar* (pilgrimage centre), unlike now. One passenger might bring with them 1,000 people to the airport to say goodbye. Another passenger arriving could attract 2,000, anticipating gifts from the traveller. So this porter carried my bag after I had arrived from London, transiting to a local flight to Kerala. It was hot and he carried the bag very fast. I had 10 to 15 minutes but the flight was always late. When we arrived at the departure gate I wanted to tip him. The problem was that I only had a large bank note which was 5 to 6 times his daily wage. So now I became this wonderful, successful, business man, giving this poor Indian porter a big tip. He spotted the ego and declined saying, 'No thank you!'

These sorts of people were my teachers! Don't think that it was just these great Shaykhs; these were my teachers. I said please, take it. He said, 'No, I have a salary, I don't want to take anything from you.' I ran after him, leaving my baggage, to beg him to take it.

It is your intention that matters and it shows with adults or children. Don't fool around. Be real: what is your intention? Are you trying to show off? Are you trying to appear that you are *Ar-Razzāq*, the Provider? Shame upon us! We are all veiled upon veiled, upon veiled into this confusion. Where did you get the energy from to be the giver or the teacher?

UNITY OF ACTION

I was sharing with someone today Ibn 'Arabi's main teaching that you must see the essence of all actions as One, which is One source of energy. In Arabic it is *Tawhīd al-Af'āl* (Unity of Action). Meaning that I can lift my hand because there is energy in me and the source of that energy is a software that converts food into this heat and so on. All of it has emanated from the One Source that is Ever-Present.

Allah is the source of actions *and* my understanding of the attributes. Why is it that I love beauty? It is because Allah is the source of beauty. Why do I love majesty? Because Allah is the ultimate source and He is majestic, that entity is majesty itself.

The essential issue in all of this I'm trying to share with you is that you need to put things into context and read the map appropriately. The map shows that we are both. The more you watch the lower do so without judgement because if piety in and of itself doesn't lead to *Rabbānīya* (divinity), it becomes a burden.

One of the big dangers of supplication is precisely this. 'Oh, Allah I'm always a wrong doer!' Then stop! 'Oh Allah, I'm always faulty!' This is how the lower ego adds to its illusory image and veils with an additional halo of spirituality. Yes, I know I'm always faulty, I'm always unjust, I'm always mean, but look at your fault *diligently*. What is the real intention of what you are doing, of what you are saying, or how you are acting? What is at the end of it? If there is an element of the 'you', the ego in it, there is an element of poison in it. If it is just for its own sake, you will not say *fi sabil illah* (for the sake of God) and all that other nonsense.

If within you there is humanity, compassion, self-examination, self-criticism, and self-correction, illumined by the ever-effulgent Light of the ever present, One and Only Creator and Sustainer of it all, then you are really at the edge of humanity and divinity. You do not resolve the paradox. It dissolves. Of course everybody is mean, but are you acting and looking through the lens of meanness? If you do, take the lens away and put on the lens of generosity. See Allah's generosity upon you. Then open it up and then you'll begin to taste what is called *baraka*. It is not superstition.

Another danger of this funky, distorted, distracted *du'a'* is that you believe that whatever you ask Allah will give it to you. As if Allah is your delivery clerk.

If you are a seeker I warn you. You will fall much worse than he who is messing around at the casino but eats *halal* meat. The thing is that you must always be aware of pulling rank and power upon others in order to make up for your own inadequacies. If your self and soul are truly in unison, you don't need anyone, nobody needs you, and you are then truly *'Abd Allah* (In service of Allah). And if you can do something, without it adding more to your ego, or expectation, or anger, or disappointment, it's fine. If it's going to add to your disappointment then again, you are less and less free from your lower self and the ultimate freedom is freedom from the self. Also, love will end that freedom, because you know, *la ilaha illa'llah*. There is none other than Allah. You don't even talk about it anymore.

These are some of the subtler ways that we seekers on the spiritual paths use religion. As an appropriate methodology for boundaries, rituals, and practices, all of which are helpful to contain the outer in order for the inner to declare where its origin is. Which is unity, which is the One-ness. It is already unified, but you and I have to deliberately, with will, connect these seemingly diverse elements into the One-ness from which they emerged, by whom they are sustained, to which they return and which we call by different names, the most common amongst those on the Sufi path or Islam being *Allah*.

POEM: ALLAH

In everything
part of nothing
not affected by anything
in need of nothing
unlike anything
Aware of everything
Knower of all things
Creator of everything
Sustainer of all things
Before everything
After everything
Apparent in everything
Absent in nothing
Above and below everything
Within and without all things
And non-things.
The ultimate desire
of all creation
is to disperse
along the path
of Passion and Love

For Union and Gatheredness
For the Perfection of His manifestations
the root of tranquillity and peace
the only door
to freedom and release
the Originator
of Darkness and Confusion
the only Guide
to bliss and spiritual fusion
the only Reality
Always True
Unique in Power
Enabling all into existence
to realise Eternal Presence
Independent of all pasts, futures and the present.
the First and Final Destination
the Controller of all affairs
undistracted by any affair over another
the Creator
of Life and Death
the divine Soul His messenger
in life and death
the Bestower
of the human heart
as a temporary abode for the Soul
the ocean of Tranquillity
at the root of all agitation and mobility.
From Boundless Nothingness

burst out transient everythingness
before time
and after all timelessness
our human soul reflects this Truth fully
with the self identifying with the body and matter
and heart recalling the passion
that shatters all illusions
so the purified seeker can recollect
the Original Perfection
and Timelessness
of Eternal Life and Mercifulness.
For every creation there is a beginning and an end
for every law there is an exception to bend
His Light is without beginning or end
the human Soul reflects His Closeness to no end
bound by His Love
for those who transcend
the veil of the self
and the illusion of otherness
from the One Eternal Light
whose shadows are only indications
of the veils of separation
twoness and other shadows
covering Eternal oneness
Allah.

Thank you for taking the time for yourself to realise that there is timelessness in your heart and not to deny that which is caught in the prison of the body for a while. The ultimate maker of all is Allah Azza wa-jall. So this is the good news, and if we do not realise that, then the bad news is misery upon misery, drama upon drama, one difficulty will bring another ten, and so on. You are not the same as yesterday. I thank you again and I thank Allah for His mercy upon us all.

CHAPTER EIGHT

The Qur'an's Universal Message: A Mercy For All the World

Given in 2010

- Unity of Body, Mind and Heart
- A Brief Socio-Anthropological History of Spirituality
- Passion & Suffering
- Qur'an: A Book of Reminders
- Truth and Apparent Reality
- Save Yourself from Yourself
- Primordial Qur'an
- Human Maturity and Inner Evolution
- The Five Inner Senses
- Maps of the Inner and Outer
- The Essential Message of Qur'an
- True Worship: Transcend Self Consciousness

UNITY OF BODY, MIND AND HEART

The only business that is worthwhile in this life, and to which all other businesses come second, is how we as the children of Adam, as human beings, can live the life that fits this ultimate complex creation. How can we live here, inwardly and outwardly joyfully, with no regrets, no remorse, no fears, no anxieties, just correctly? 'Correctly' is a very easy word to use, but it will take many volumes to define. We need to do this so that you and I, he and she, whoever are present, know how to conduct ourselves, so that you have both your outer and your inner senses: you have your mind, your head, your intellect *and* your heart. All of them need to be in unison. So we do not go back and forth in time, in fear of the past, in anxiety about the future, missing the present.

A BRIEF SOCIO-ANTHROPOLOGICAL HISTORY OF SPIRITUALITY

The Qur'an is a revelation which describes to us, in multi-faceted ways, these numerous dimensionalities and spectrums of consciousness. It comes almost at the end of tens of thousands of years of evolvement of *Homo Sapiens*. A very brief history of this is that from the beginning human beings were driven towards another zone that transcends existential struggle and survival. Recent discoveries in the last 10 to 15 years by anthropologists, archaeologists and others show that humans have always quested for spirituality, for the beyond, for Allah or for God, or for that power that is both manifested and veiled by matter, flesh, as well as the non-manifest, the seen and the unseen.

Their discoveries have been going back further and further in time. Twenty years ago they used to talk of about 8,000 to 9,000 years ago—and the city of Jericho was very important as being the first main example of this. Then they began to discover that actually Jericho, like many other great old cities, has 7,8,9,10 layers of other cities that have been burnt down, accidentally or by invading people. Now I think the general consensus is that earlier settlements precede those settlements, probably 12,000 to 14,000 years ago. We all often talk about agricultural settlements, when people finished all the seeds and all the animals around them, and of course they knew about seeds germinating, so they begin to cultivate through the plough and before that through the hoe. The main users of the hoe were women and thus matriarchy was prevailed at the time, reflected in the effigies of female gods.

Soon after that, man had to drive the plough so society became much more patriarchal, and men managed to continue that high handedness and continue to keep women subjugated. Today women are generally behind the sink and treated like sex objects. So this is the human trend. The Qur'an tells us that all of these lower natures are in man, but if man, if human beings, do not refer to the design of it all, —the Permeator, the Supporter, the Creator, the Beginner, the Ender, Allah—then most of this comes to nothing. It is just cycle after cycle, after cycle. The Qur'an also enjoins us to travel the land, to go and see how civilisations were built. Look at the Pharaoh! It is not until very recently we managed to get an idea how these enormous stones, in their millions, were carried up to create the amazingly stable structures of the pyramids.

PASSION & SUFFERING

The Qur'an is a book of signs, both on the horizon in human history, in our hearts, and in ourselves, through a complete package of revelation. It connects the ultimate truth that in truth there is only truth—*lā ilāha illā'llah*. In truth there is One and only One.

The idea of two-ness, so to speak, according to the Christians, is also not quite authentic in that sense and is similar to original sin. Adam sinned, so he had to be imprisoned in this world and suffer for a while until redemption. The Latin word for suffering is passion. The implication is that if you have passion for the truth, you will suffer from yourself, from personal relations, human relations and all of the other things until you do not care for them anymore. You have passion for the light, you are no longer buyable or sellable like a commodity in the name of progress.

These days you are bought and sold from one company to another because you are a performer, which also means that you are ambitious, which means you can tread on other people's heads, while carving this miserable career for yourself. You might well end up like Henry Ford who, in the last year of his life, had such a phobia of dying alone. He created shifts to ensure that people were with him all the time, paid nurses and others, and built this immense place not very far from his factory in Detroit. In the end, he died at night alone. Strangely, there was such a flood that nobody could come near the place. So who do you think you and I are? Every week you have an example of a despot or a king or a ruler or a great corporate magnate just being totally and utterly relegated to the cemeteries or dustbin of history.

QUR'AN: A BOOK OF REMINDERS

The Qur'an reminds us that you, I, he and she, are as good as our realisation of absolute goodness. So it is the book of books. It is a book that gives us signs within ourselves and human history, in our present day, contemporary dealings on the horizon and beyond. And you and I have to take it according to our ability to digest that spiritual message. It's no use pretending to have more knowledge simply because I have a big hat or a big turban or certificates or whatever.

To get back to the message of the Qur'an: It comes at the end of a line which has been fairly well defined, from the Prophet Ibrahim (AS) about 4,000 years ago. It does not mean there were no prophets or apostles or messengers before or in the wider geographical area. It just happens that in this area around the Mediterranean basin, Mesopotamia, about 200km to the East and 400km to the West it was fairly easy to eke out a living. There were lots of places you could hide from the vicious animals, caves or corners or rocks or hills, and it was fairly easy to live on a few berries, fruits and all the old, biblical trees, figs, or all the other things that we know and relish and of course also wheat.

Prior to that, you could hardly control agricultural growth. Then came cross pollination; by rubbing the wheat, it can fall down and settle into the earth and so on. So we have these 4,000 odd fairly clear years of similar, repetitive, messages that there is One Creator and all of us are the children of Adam and, metaphorically, Adam was designed and created in the Garden, in Paradise. But look what we have done since that time? There have been more killings in the name of God and Paradise because it is assumed that before Paradise you have to have such passion, readiness to die, that it has to be apocalyptic. People have to be killed, left, right and centre before the awakening and when the truth and the final day arrives, and you are in Paradise. This has been the prevailing idea. Look back at the history of wars. And incidentally, they only started when big kings emerged. Earlier on there were only nomadic people.

The Prophet Ibrahim (AS) moved with a smallish tribe, mostly with some animals, doing some hunting but mostly herding and they moved to Haran, which is now not so far from the border between Turkey and Syria, at that time about 30 days from Ur, southern Iraq. Ibrahim (AS) had the notion that he must leave his people because they had become too involved with the actual physicality of the objects that they were using as symbols of deity or God. His uncle ended up being one of the main manufacturers of these idols as well as with trader in them. So Ibrahim (AS) went down to what is now Palestine and further down to Egypt and then, from there he came back and lived in that area, and died in what is called *Madīnatu'l-Khalīl*, which was named after him.

From there emerged many other local tribal chiefs who combined the outer and the inner. Inwardly they were ready to relegate what was not theirs, realising whatever we have is a loan to us and that everything belongs to Allah. We have it so beautifully in the Qur'an, the *Ayat ul-Kursi* (the throne verse) and many others.

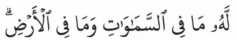

To Him belongs whatever is in the heaven and the earth. (2:255)

So what are you quarrelling about? None of it is yours, including your body, including your mind, including your heart, including your intellect. It is loaned to you. If you realise that, then you will begin to do what Ibrahim (AS) and his followers in their thousands constantly echoed. It is the same message in different languages and different cultures but mostly related to each other.

You are a human being; you have needs, you have things to fulfil. Adam in the garden did not know what differentiation (*furqān*) was. You had to come to this zone of consciousness within space and time where you have to eat to survive, you have to have shelter, you have to have some relationships, otherwise you cannot grow as a human being. We are the only animal that cannot survive or grow in any way without social contacts. So this message was regularly repeated with all the great prophets. We have Musa (AS), and the apostles after him, until again as the cycles of initiation, growth, flowering, degeneration took place.

As you all know, this is a new cycle in human life, in every life. The 14th century Arab Historian, Ibn Khaldun exemplified it very well in his introduction of '*Al-Muqaddima*'. Initially there was also the interaction between the open spaces and the nomadic people and the settled people. When you are nomadic, you can get by with very little, and go for days without any food. Interestingly, one of Lawrence of Arabia's main strengths and reason for being respected by the Arabs is that he would not take any provision with him whenever they travelled for one whole day. If you are travelling from any place to another over desert terrain, you find usually the distances are anything from 30 to 60km between these oases or caravanserais. And if you are travelling that distance you won't take any water or any food. No self-respecting Arab ever did that. Lawrence wanted to be accepted, so he did the same.

This was the case that anytime, within those early cultures, there was hardship, there was self-reliance and doing with very little. Soon after that, people got a bit more settled in towns and cities, as you know, they became more pampered. This is a natural cycle. We are not reminded all the time to have less, and constantly practicing doing with less. We have now reached a point where the consumption and waste is such that people are now talking about ecological crises.

What about your own personal ecology? Are you aware how much water you have drunk? How much tap water are you using? How much power you are wasting? How many extra clothes you have? For what? For whom? How? The Qur'an is the constant reminder that you are human but within you lies a *rūḥ* that is sublime. (38:72)

So the Qur'an is, if you like, an original, timeless declaration of truth and Islam is the way of application. Therefore, you can't talk about the Qur'an without talking about Islam. The Qur'an is the declaration that there is none other than original truth and it is absolute. From that come all the other relative issues—up and down, good and bad, and human justice as a tiny little flash trying to represent divine justice. The only way to this is the package of Islam which is based on accepting the truth that I am insufficient: at all times I have needs and my needs have got a hierarchy. Ultimately what I really want is to be needless.

TRUTH AND APPARENT REALITY

Everything in this life is false. It's all shadows. All of us are shadow-chasers. The only difference is the extent of that shadow. The Truth cannot appear in its absolute form. The Qur'an says, 'If this Light descends on a mountain it will vanish.' (59:21) If the Light of the Absolute, which is timeless, descends on the so-called me, subject to space and time, I cannot exist. As Ibn 'Arabi says, 'Don't constantly denigrate the lower self. Without it, without a bit of it, you will not survive.' So, accept the lower self as a key to the higher self. In other words, also accept that all of us are subject to vices and mistakes and errors, but use that insight to humble the lower self and honour the higher self by its light so you can recognize what is nearer the truth. Then you are between humanity and divinity.

Because of this idea of realising the divine potential within us, soon after the early effulgence of these lights, we had this idea of man-God, and Jesus, for example, became a cult issue. Christianity was really a cult in that he is both man and God. I agree with that also, in my own little way. I have accepted the trinity; that there is true father, son and holy spirit. One of them is called the absolute consciousness, pure consciousness, sacred consciousness, the ultimate consciousness, the second one is myself, as a human being, personal consciousness, and the connecting link between us is unknown and it is the holy spirit, whatever it is. This is a way the idea of trinity can be understood.

SAVE YOURSELF FROM YOURSELF

But all of these attempts for thousands of years, by different cultures, were based on the same fundamental issue, which is the Qur'anic issue. The name Qur'an means to read, gather that which is there. We must relate things to their original inception. Human beings wanted the unseen, unfamiliar, unknown God.

Early on, during the first 50 years after revelation, people were illumined by the Qur'an, they lived the Qur'an, they knew it was about the eternal life, not about a few years here and there. In the early years it was not about you having a bigger camel, or a bigger horse, or so many wives. It was about saving one's self from one's self. Therefore, whenever they were under a real threat or attack, they rose to it fearlessly. There are the ayahs in the Qur'an that say they were thousands or more. Different numbers are given also of angels. It is to illustrate that we are all metaphoric, that amazing power can come about if you put a person utterly in a corner, where there is nothing else for them to do.

Amazing force comes about because we have already reconciled with death. If you are not afraid of death, then you have your wits are about you. You don't calculate how many they are or how many I have. Numbers did not matter during the battle of Badr but during the battle of Uhud they began to calculate. It's not certain how many came from Makka, maybe up to 10,000, mostly on horseback. And the poor people, the Muslims, managed to gather about 1,000, a third of whom turned back and the other two thirds were uncertain, from the two tribes of Ansar. This is a human dilemma; if you are not constantly willing to totally, utterly, give in to Him Who possesses and owns all, then it will soon end up in dynastic rulership, as happened 50 to 60 years after Hijrah.

PRIMORDIAL QUR'AN

What are you, not *who* are you? What is it that I'm made of? Here again, Islam excels in explaining that you are sublime *and* ridiculous, you are a human being. The truth is that we've got wonderful traditions in our culture and our *din*, our human cosmology. You are a self that is *shaytanic* because it is a shadow, it is flickering, restless, an ego, and lower than that.

We must get back to the true Islamic cosmology. Who are we? We are a shadow of an ever-changing so-called you, while the real you never ever changes. And the real you is your *rūh*. This concept is the same in all religions, not just the Abrahamic line, except that different words are used for *rūh*. If you go back to the Aramaic, you go back to *rūh*. When we really look at that Abrahamic line of which the Qur'an is the culmination and final, complete version, we will realise that it is not a new thing. Islam was not invented by the Prophet Muhammad (S), nor Christianity invented by Jesus. The same goes for Judaism. These people simply echoed the truth that is from time immemorial. It is primordial.

HUMAN MATURITY AND INNER EVOLUTION

In the Muslim world we find that most cities and towns are built around a shrine. The shrine is usually for a martyr, especially in Iraq, where we did a good job of burying our luminaries. We have thousands of these messengers and prophets whom we prefer dead because we make more money out of them than when they were alive. If they are alive then they need to be fed, have children, and make demands, unless of course they are true ascetics. One of the greatest leaders of Kurdistan, when Saddam used to bomb, would remain put when everyone ran away. Mulla Mustafa Barzani, whom I knew well, would never move from where he was praying until the dust settled and they would find him. He would then simply say, 'I trust if my time has come I may go.'

Once, when he was sitting near a wall that was collapsing, Imam 'Ali suddenly moved out of the way. Someone who was with him said, 'You've escaped your decree.' Imam 'Ali responded, 'Allah has shown me that my time has not come. I saw the wall about to fall, so I moved along with my destiny. I did not go against anything.' So you and I have to also accept what is appropriate for us at the right time.

Now is the right time, really. It is beginning to happen more and more: the rise of Islam through the rediscovery of the Qur'an, the rediscovery of the unity, of the origins of all these terms indicating the interconnectedness of all elements. The human being has to unify both outer and inner senses. We spend so much time trying to improve our outer senses—our eyesight, our hearing, our taste, our touch. How much time do we spend on our inner senses, to improve on our *khayāl*, the imaginative faculty, which we have neglected?

People ask, 'Is it allowed in Islam to paint?' And of course, if simply regurgitating what was appropriate 1,400 years ago, we say, 'No! It was not done at the time of the Prophet.' But neither did he drive in a car. Why are our mullahs (theologians) and others riding in cars? The essential issue does not change.

Essentially you are a human being, here in order to perfect the knowledge that what you are seeking is beyond here, within here, and without, yet given time and authority to arrive. Both! This is what it is. You are both human being and another entity beyond it. This is human dignity, but we fall under the Western hypnosis of the idea that unless something is measurable, unless it is repeatable, then it does not exist.

What is real? Are you real? Why are you not the same tomorrow? Why aren't we the same as two years ago? Tell me what you did on 6 July 2009? You may have suffered, that day may have been a heavy day for you. What is real? It was real for you, then! Because you identified with your outer, 'I'm this, I have accumulated this, I've lost this, so half of me is gone.' Half of you gone? Please go away, restore it and come back, because I cannot talk with half a person. It is bad enough to talk with a so-called 'whole' person. Because the inner and the outer had not been unified, because we have not realised that if the creative faculty in me, my *khayāl*, has not been awakened, I will never be whole.

It is for this reason, in this time and age, that it is very important to encourage the young people to be creative in the arts. A thousand years ago it was irrelevant, it was not possible. Look at the statistics of people who had to work in agriculture, at least where figures and statistics are available in the West. Look at how many people worked in agriculture in America 110 years ago. That number has been transposed; there were 11% to 12% involved in agriculture and now that number is people involved in the car business, in spare parts and garages. and just about 1% are in agriculture. In the East, most people had to make this leap.

THE FIVE INNER SENSES

Times have changed and it is for that reason it is easier for young people now to move into the unifying field of One-ness and lap up the Qur'an, as long as they are given the map of who we are, the map of self-knowledge and if they are given certain indications of transformative worship. I, for one, confess that I would not do my *salāt* unless it recharged me, especially in my *sajda* (prostration). There I go into perfect oblivion. You get recharged. The rest of the time is 'discharge'.

The map of self-knowledge enables us to recognize how we perceive things. We are all aware of the five outer senses, but not so much of the five inner senses. The first is that sense which combines all the other inner senses and helps us integrate everything into a whole, known as the *hiss al-mushtarik* (combining sense).

Young people need that creativity and to be given the opportunity to read the fairy tales, to imagine things and talk to the fairies, so that the second inner sense of the *khayāl* (Imaginative Faculty) develops, in order that the *wāhima* (Evaluative Faculty), the third inner sense, also evolves. This is giving a value to something and then being willing to change it.

One of our greatest Sufi Shaykhs says it is *wahm* (evaluative conjecture/illusion) that stops you from seeing the original light—'But the illusion of other-than-Him hides Him'.[3] This is because we give values to specific things. Perhaps I consider this fellow to be a 'bad' person—a bad person, meaning his actions have been so continuously offensive to everyone that we have now labelled him. We will then always be surprised when suddenly we are proved wrong. The worst sometimes turn out to be amongst the best.

We have historical examples. Look at the wonderful backing that our great Prophet received from Omar as well as Khalid bin *Walīd*. Khalid bin *Walīd* was the general of the Quraysh at Uhud, the battle that devastated the early Muslims and nearly killed the Prophet. Khalid showed amazing military brilliance against the Muslims and then he flipped, he embraced the *Dīn*. It is actions, you see. That is why *wahm* must have the ability to change. I always thought it important to teach the principle of changing your mind. Actually it's not important to teach, it is more important to be taught! Wonderful! Therefore, the teacher is also taught. The Giver is One, the takers are many. From the One comes twos and these twos are complementary.

The fourth important sense is the *hāfidha*, the Faculty of Memory. People often suffer from their memory and occasionally are given electric shocks to move them out of that. It is my memory that tells me that when there is a hall, there is a gathering, people have come, you are supposed to have the right courtesy, *adab*. They've come for their own nourishment. Give them that which you think is best, give them your best. Don't be concerned about reputation or name; be free from that and constrained by outer *adab*. Then comes the *mutafakkira* (Contemplative Faculty) the fifth inner sense.

---

3. From the Ode 'Withdrawal from All that is Other-than-Allah', by Shaykh Muhammad ibn al-Habib.

This entire heritage is available to us.[4] For the young generation to really regain access to the Qur'an and to the *mizān* (measure/balance) and the *maqām* (station) of *iḥsān* (excellence), they need to discover their own authority in the heart. They may give lip-service to their parents and grandparents but in truth they are fed up with a system, a way of life, that has done its work. It worked for their parents, but not anymore. They do not know what the traffic jams between here and Johannesburg are like now! They had a very easy time, they could relate to each other, it was a small community that trusted one another. There was faith, there was generosity, it was one band, but no longer.

MAPS OF THE INNER AND OUTER

You will have a different version of young people if they are given the map of outer and inner self knowledge. If they are given the benefits of transformational *'ibāda* (worship), they will learn that you go into your *sajda* (prostration) to be free of thoughts, to disappear from your self; otherwise, repeat it. Or else do *nafl* (supererogatory) prayers or renew your *wudū'* (ritual ablution), because all of these are the preparations. When you go to bed, you remove your clothes, you take off this and that and prepare yourself, switch off the light, relax, and then you go into that sleep state. What is the will that *you* have to go to sleep? Tell me how is it that *you* are claiming sleep? Try tonight that you are going to describe how you have managed to unlock this new consciousness, this wonderful consciousness, of going to sleep. You don't know how you do it! You can't say 'I'm demanding sleep' or 'I'm demanding God consciousness'.

What you can do is recalibrate. You can turn away from *shaytān* consciousness, from lower consciousness, from your stupidities, from your anxieties or your fear. That is why the Prophet's ultimate teaching con-

---

4. For a fuller explanation of the five inner senses see Shaykh Fadhlalla Haeri's book 'The Journey of the Self – *A Sufi Guide to Personality.'*

nects the Qur'an and *furqān* (criterion)—'Die before you die!'. It is not about the bodily death which just is some physical manifestation that will be very inconvenient for the people who take you and bury you, and stand there looking very sad.

Many of the Muslims I see here divide their time into 3 portions: one portion in attending funerals; another in attending weddings which are failing as rapidly as they are performed; and the third one in hospitals. What a wonderful life and then we call ourselves a great culture. It is not Islam that is at fault. It is that I, as a Muslim, have not imbibed it. Historically whenever Muslims and Islam coincided there was great effulgence.

You must rise to the true purpose for which you and I have been created without denying your childhood, or the ego. By the time you are in your 30's, 40's, or 50's, you must become uncomfortable enough to laugh at your ego and treat it with humour and be shocked by how dreadful it is, how much it has caused you endless trouble.

There has been an endless lack of sight or seeing things as they are, because it has not moved to insight. We have not been truly alive! Then we say we are a great Muslim civilization, and yet more Muslims have killed other Muslims than any other religion. Why? Because reference to the light was not there? Islam is effulgent all over the world now because of the global scene. Globalization was entirely instigated by human collective greed. But look at its side effects. Many side effects are painful, but one positive side effect is that human beings all over the world are beginning to discover their own true spiritual origin, and that it is Divine. If you do not refer to the Divine in you, the human passion and human compassion and tolerance and humility and joyfulness will not take place. You cannot have this without the other. This is our *Dīn*!

Living Qur'an is living Islam. The Qur'an was the original declaration of Oneness. There is only One Creator and human beings have been designed and created in order to perfect their worship. Islam is the package of how to practise that. It has in it a great deal of cultural beauty. The way you bury your dead, the way you behave, these are not in the Qur'an. They were essential complements to the Qur'an, for that reason if you want to truly absorb the Qur'an, live the Qur'an, you must combine the book and the *sīra* (Life) of Muhammad (SAW). How best did he do it? And the Prophet (SAW) was also so enlightened in a historical sense as well, that he occasionally changed his ways.

THE ESSENTIAL MESSAGE OF QUR'AN

What we have between the Qur'an and Islam is a complete cosmology. If you truly love God, save yourself from yourself, groom the lower, pay attention to the tendencies of the animals in you, all of which are in you, because you are the culmination of all creation. Then we are sublime in the sense of light, *rūh* (soul/spirit), which is the same in every one. That is where the culmination of the Abrahamic tradition comes about, which is that all of us are the children of Adam, all of us are the same.

The Prophet says, 'And those who are most loved by Allah, are those that do the most for others.' Serve others! Why serve? So that you cleanse your heart from your own selfishness, so it becomes transparent, so you begin to have that authority shining from you, upon you, from within you, by Allah's mercy which encompasses all the seen and the unseen. That is why it is a universal message. It is not a universal right but a universal responsibility. All of us have that responsibility, each one to themselves. Nobody can help anybody else, not a prophet—no one—unless you decide, by your own will, you are going to submit to the truth, that we are all *fuqarā'* (ascetics), we are all *miskīn* (impoverished).

Mu'min (believer) *miskīn* (impoverished) in the case of the Beatitudes is now translated as the 'weak in spirit.' Why would God like the weak in spirit? We need to look at the original meaning in Aramaic, *miskīn*, exactly that word. The same word is also in Hebrew, the same word in the Semitic tongues, and therefore Arabic. *Miskīn* is from *sukūn*, meaning calm, collected, content. *Muskan* is a house. It means one who is in every way reliant upon their *īmān* (faith) They know Allah is with them, Allah wills them what they need at the time they need it according to His perfect knowledge, not their own whims. There is a huge difference between my own whims and His knowledge.

All over the world people are beginning to understand this distinction and not just in the Muslim world. Why? Because of the internet, the availability of the knowledge, and original languages. If you look back 30 to 40 years ago you could hardly find a single book in Aramaic. Books were in Syriac and most languages were only spoken. They used oral tradition, they didn't write it, and it's only happening now. If you go back you find most of the Abrahamic lines have the same message, in essence. But the cultures began to change it, so we end up in a culture where if the diet is different, you are considered different, "not one of us".

TRUE WORSHIP: TRANSCEND SELF CONSCIOUSNESS

I am so optimistic about the rise of the light of the Qur'an for young people provided they are given a chance and encouragement and the time to absorb it. They must also be given the chance to perfect the transformative aspect of worship and faith. Faith is not something to talk about smugly. If you are *mu'min,* you won't talk about it because you don't know who you are talking about! You've already jumped into that ocean and you are covered by it. Like Bistami, when they came looking for him, everybody was asking where is Bistami. He also started looking, eventually somebody pointed at him and said it's him. Bistami replied, 'I don't know who he is!' Because of that *tawhīd* (unity). Lose yourself in the higher self and you find everyone else is exactly the same. You have moved from differentiation, identification, separation, and dispersion and otherness, into the ever-present One-ness. Then you have done whatever you can.

This is called *al-insān al-kāmil* (the complete person); it is not a fantasy or illusion, or something that lies somewhere else beyond the mountains, or you put a chain on your neck with either a cross or a verse from the Qur'an. If you have absorbed it, you no longer do anything other than what you can do at the right time, in the right way, free from your lower self.

CHAPTER NINE

The Original Meaning of Sacred Messages I

Given in 2011
after the dhikr

- The Overflow of Grace
- Humour the *Nafs*
- Play the Role but Go Beyond It
- Oneness: Sameness in Otherness
- Purify the Heart
- Turn Away from the Self
- Recognizing the Overflow of Grace
- Poem: Creation is Sacred Expression
- The World Now and its Past
- Nature of Creation and Human Condition
- Self-Realisation

THE OVERFLOW OF GRACE

$$\text{لَئِن شَكَرْتُمْ لَأَزِيدَنَّكُمْ}$$

If you are grateful, I will add more unto you. (14:7)

We all know that the more we are in gratitude, the more we are attuned to the source of grace and blessedness, the more it will flow. It is a matter of resonating with that which is at the beginning, which is present, which is at the end, which has no boundaries. The more we resonate with that truth, the more we realize that it is all about that truth, and it becomes not just our habit, but the only possibility for life. It is, however, a matter of *dhawq*, or taste.

HUMOUR THE *NAFS*

The *nafs* (ego self) is the shadow of the soul, or the shadow of spirit, which is the shadow of Allah on earth, this apparently independent entity has to be humoured. Seen as a child—in a spiritual sense—you have to encourage it, you have to exercise a bit of *jamāl*, beauty, and show it a bit of gentleness. But when you grow and become more steadfast, you realize that no matter what, the self moves, changes, and that it is only a cover for that which is ever-present. And how can you ever know that unless that pattern is within you? The entire creational pattern, Allah's *fitra*, Allah's *sunna*, is within us. So, the *nafs* has to be occasionally humoured, occasionally pampered, until such time you can stifle it every now and then and suddenly you exercise *jalāl* or majestic firmness. This is *tarbiya*, disciplining.

Initially the love of ease and comfort dominates, until you begin to transcend experiential, essential ease and comfort to the perfect ease of the condition of paradise which is ever-present, here and now. But if all my energy and attention is somewhere else, how can it plug into that ever-present energy? If I am always concerned about *jamāl* (beauty), how can I ever catch that amazing counter-balancing factor called *jalāl* (majesty). So that is why we need to first taste, then enter into the *maqām* (station), and then leave it, go past it, otherwise we become a stiff personality—the 'pious' person, the 'scholarly' person, the fatherly personality, the gentle person, the giver and so on... These are all parts in a play.

PLAY THE ROLE BUT GO BEYOND IT

وَمَا ٱلْحَيَوٰةُ ٱلدُّنْيَآ إِلَّا لَعِبٌ وَلَهْوٌ وَلَلدَّارُ ٱلْأَخِرَةُ خَيْرٌ لِّلَّذِينَ يَتَّقُونَ أَفَلَا تَعْقِلُونَ ﴿٣٢﴾

And the worldly life is nothing but amusement and diversion; but the home of the Hereafter is best for those who are God-conscious, will you not understand?
(6:32)

One of the meanings is that while we do play the roles, we should not get fossilized in them. In essence you are another entity. You contain all matter: you have all the initial basic elements of air, water, fire and earth, but you are also *Nūr* (divine light). And remember always the numerous models that we are given in the Qur'an, as to who this being is. The angels' objection to the rise of Adamic consciousness was that this was a new being who had a will, and was not totally and utterly in alignment with essence at all times. This being was not contained within the patterns that they knew.

This human creature has a separate will. It is the ability to tune yourself to the ever-present perfect Will. This is the meaning of *Astaghfir'ullah* (I seek forgiveness of Allah), in other words taking cover under that perfection. That is why we are allowed all the ups and downs, the mistakes and the continuous errors.

قُلْ يَٰعِبَادِىَ ٱلَّذِينَ أَسْرَفُواْ عَلَىٰٓ أَنفُسِهِمْ لَا تَقْنَطُواْ مِن رَّحْمَةِ ٱللَّهِ إِنَّ ٱللَّهَ يَغْفِرُ ٱلذُّنُوبَ جَمِيعًا إِنَّهُۥ هُوَ ٱلْغَفُورُ ٱلرَّحِيمُ ﴿٥٣﴾

Oh my servants who have transgressed against themselves [by sinning], do not despair of the mercy of Allah. Indeed, Allah forgives all sins. Indeed, it is He who is the Forgiving, the Merciful. (39:53)

Al-Ghafūr, the Forgiving, comes from *ghafara*, meaning to cover. All mistakes can be covered and forgiven, but then you have this amazing declaration,

$$\text{إِنَّ ٱللَّهَ لَا يَغْفِرُ أَن يُشْرَكَ بِهِۦ وَيَغْفِرُ مَا دُونَ ذَٰلِكَ لِمَن يَشَآءُ وَمَن يُشْرِكْ بِٱللَّهِ فَقَدِ ٱفْتَرَىٰٓ إِثْمًا عَظِيمًا ﴿٤٨﴾}$$

Indeed, Allah does not forgive association with Him, but He forgives what is less than that for whom He wills. And he who associates others with Allah has certainly fabricated a tremendous sin. (4:48)

What an amazing exception! You cannot reconcile *shirk*. *Shirk* is the seeing of the twos and that is the entire foundation of confusion and trouble with the human being, within the collective psyche on earth and any-where else.

ONENESS: SAMENESS IN OTHERNESS

Once we have deviated from seeing the two through the sight of the One, then there is trouble. This distortion occurs within the same person: on the one hand this and on the other hand something else. It can also be found within the same family and it is endless, until you begin to see sameness in otherness and you find otherness is beautiful and the sameness is perfection.

$$\text{فَلَن تَجِدَ لِسُنَّتِ ٱللَّهِ تَبْدِيلًا وَلَن تَجِدَ لِسُنَّتِ ٱللَّهِ تَحْوِيلًا}$$

But you will never find in the way of Allah any change,

and you will never find in the way of Allah any alteration. (35:43)

Nothing ever will change. This is how it is. So all of one's lifetime is to properly focus one's sight. On what? On the fact that there is only One pattern, One reason, One design, One object, One direction, One purpose, One love.

Every other love emanates from the sacred passion for us to be totally in unison with that which is eternal. We need to be totally in unison with that reality that has no needs, totally in unison with that which is beyond measure in wealth, in knowledge, in ability to communicate, to hear, to know. It is boundless and that is why we have to remove any notion in our minds or intellects.

$$ لَّا يَمَسُّهُۥٓ إِلَّا ٱلْمُطَهَّرُونَ ۝ $$

None touch it except the purified. (56:79)

Of course, we love knowledge; we are acquisitive with knowledge but when it comes to spiritual awakening you need to drop it all and be totally bereft and it's easy to realise that we are all bereft. The breath which goes in may not come out. Just remember that any minute, anyone of us can die. Any one of us is different from a second ago.

PURIFY THE HEART

No two people are ever the same at any second and yet there is that perfect constancy, ever beaming in your heart.

$$ ٱللَّهُ نُورُ ٱلسَّمَٰوَٰتِ وَٱلْأَرْضِ مَثَلُ نُورِهِۦ كَمِشْكَوٰةٍ فِيهَا مِصْبَاحٌ ٱلْمِصْبَاحُ فِى زُجَاجَةٍ ٱلزُّجَاجَةُ كَأَنَّهَا كَوْكَبٌ دُرِّيٌّ يُوقَدُ مِن شَجَرَةٍ مُّبَٰرَكَةٍ زَيْتُونَةٍ لَّا شَرْقِيَّةٍ وَلَا غَرْبِيَّةٍ يَكَادُ زَيْتُهَا يُضِىٓءُ وَلَوْ لَمْ تَمْسَسْهُ نَارٌ $$

The example of His light is like a niche within which is a lamp,
the lamp is within glass, the glass is as if it were a pearly [white] star lit from
[the oil of] a blessed olive tree, neither of the east nor of the west,
whose oil would almost glow even if untouched by fire. (24:35)

This *zujāja* (glass) is your *qalb*, your heart and all paths attempt to purify this *zujāja*, this *qalb*.

$$ إِلَّا مَنْ أَتَى ٱللَّهَ بِقَلْبٍ سَلِيمٍ ﴿٨٩﴾ $$

But only one who comes to Allah with a sound heart. (26:89)

All of the other struggles, the *jihads*, all of them lead ultimately to having nothing ever in your heart because what is already in it is enough for you, from the beginning to the end and from no beginning, before beginning, to that which is beyond the end, which is the *Nūr* (light) of Allah.

But we are constantly occupied by doing this, that and the other as preludes to reaching a point of exhaustion. Then, at that point, I may begin to hear *Lā ilāha illā'llah*, none other than the same reality, the same entity, the same light. And I will realise I have been chasing shadows after shadows. Some of them are so remote, they just contain a spark of that truth until such time you realize that wherever you turn,

$$ فَأَيْنَمَا تُوَلُّواْ فَثَمَّ وَجْهُ ٱللَّهِ $$

Wheresoever you turn, is the face of Allah. (2:115)

This is the whole story.

TURN AWAY FROM THE SELF

The beautiful, magnificent, delightful journey of stepping outside of the self and into what is reality and truth, which is this *rūh*, is what we all seek. No matter who it is, on this earth, as all of human beings, we want the same. We just don't want ideas or beliefs; we want to know in such a way that is not subject to discussion or any discourse about it. That is the truth and good luck to you. May you, in every way, wherever you return, have a confirmation of that. It has been there before you and will be there after you. It is the only *hudhūr* (Presence).

RECOGNIZING THE OVERFLOW OF GRACE

There are four points to my talk. The first one I will try to share is that it is not so much through reason and logic but more through some intimate, inner voice that all of creation is sacred and whatever expressions come within it, is energized by that sacredness. So the entire thing is an overflow of Grace. And if we begin to feel it, see it, then we will truly always be thrilled by this passion and yet maintain a measure of sanity, sensibility, and humanity, all at the same time.

The second part is, why are we where we are now? How did it come about? In other words, what is our past? If you want to know the present, you must look seriously into where it came from. The entire thing is a flow, a stream, whether you are looking from an evolutionary point of view, a revolutionary point of view, or the point of view of humanity. There is a total connectivity and a stream that aims towards the ultimate highest level of consciousness, God.

The third part is the nature of this world and creation and all the amazing interlinks, and therefore, what is the nature and make-up of human beings? Who are we? And for the last part I touch upon this vague term of 'self-realization', awakening, enlightenment or whatever other name you may like to use. It implies having been touched, having been in a state that is not the usual, limited consciousness. In other words, the state of enjoying access to pure consciousness, to God consciousness. These are the four issues.

POEM: CREATION IS SACRED EXPRESSION

Every instant or event
reveals itself and tells its own story.
A spark of truth veiled by movement, change, other distractions,
emerging peacefully, or with a bang,
only to merge or submerge,
with or without a trace.

Countless realities,
evolving or devolving with veils or patterns that repeat, multiply
or vanish
in the mist of no-thing-ness, with or without trace.
The intelligent voice asked about the meaning and purpose of
human life,
with all its fears, struggles, desires and hopes.
Is it all futile absurdities and sense-less illusions?
What is the truth of the moment?
What is really real?
Who are we?
Where are we?
Why can't I play with the angels?
Why does my curiosity have no end?
Why can't I enjoy durable rest?
I want to know the truth.

The powerful pleading reached my heart and soul,
and my voice tried to convey what I know as true
and real within existence,
with or without trace.
The essence and root of life is self-effulgent,
in all appearances,
and is ever-present,
externally and internally.
The truth leads the senses to discern creational realities.
All of what exist is relative and are ever-changing entities.
Measurable forms and energies,
with or without trace,
everywhere, at all times.
Whatever there are in the Universe

— celestial, terrestrial, stones, plants, animals and humans
— transmit and receive expressions and signals
of their condition in time and place,
driven by souls or energies
which overflow by Grace from the Universal Essence, Allah.
The truth and the real declare themselves in countless ways
and can be known in countless levels of clarity or depth.
All are emanating from the One supreme consciousness;
sacred expressions are beams of light which declare truth
in as many ways as there are creations.
There can be no existence without a sacred connection.
All is within Allah's grasp.

This is a very detailed description of how everything—whatever is or not—is within that eternal absoluteness, experienced as changing relatives.

THE WORLD NOW AND ITS PAST

I'm going to sum up for you the history of 7 billion years concentrating on the last 500 years. Throughout our life—past and present—we constantly review and modify human values and references to ethics, morality, personal responsibility, guilt, regret and other emotions. The ancient primal drive for survival is constantly modified by ideas, notions and expressions which are the result of breakthroughs in higher consciousness. All meanings are attempts at spiritual arrival. Human consciousness of thousands of years ago began as self-awareness and the experience of needs, mainly for stability, as well as excitement. The migrating nomadic clans roamed and multiplied. Their languages were transmitted along with skills of adaptation to the environment, always longing to belong and to be forever content and happy. They were seeking safety and ease, and the comfort of their traditions and cultures.

History gives us an illusion of continuity. They are all stories. Looking in the mirror of others for acknowledgement. It is reassuring to see glimpses of unconditional, sacred love and acceptance. With agriculture came the raising of fences and the relentless drive for acquisition and increase to the point of self-annihilation and almost the end of humanity. Noah's ark floated towards an uncertain destiny and landed precariously on a promised land. Thereafter, a few prophets were inspired with higher insights of truth and brought contentment and light to some hearts.

Then came the beginning of religions: love of power and fear of the other induced kings to evoke religion as a cover for greed and plunder. In 1512 Charles I used the imperial crown to rally lesser despots against the Turks for the glory of Christianity, just as did many other rulers and despots of different persuasions, before and after him. They make a mockery of religion to justify their crusades and collective organised warfare. It ushered in centuries of practising personal and collective aggression, vicious invasion, killing, rape, and devastation of lands and forests that once gave life to a vanquished people who were described by the victors of history as being anti-progress, civilization or religion. This is the dark side of the self-disclosure of humanity—the fear for survival fanned by the fire of anger.

The human gene is etched with the traces of this past. It has been so for millions of years and we ourselves can recall the nomads' innocent laughter, living and dying, as a continuation of eternal life. During the past few thousand years, we have become accustomed to voices of authority 'descending from on high'. For the last 500 years powerful forces have been driving our lives toward greater and higher personal ambitions, individualism, specialism and the acquisition of ever-increasing outer wealth. Our minds are accustomed to measuring things and objects to the detriment of the heart crying to return to the inner sanctum of the ever-present contentment of the soul.

NATURE OF CREATION AND HUMAN CONDITION

The sublime and the ridiculous can be one, as you all know. Whatever exists signals its presence and is linked with the rest of creation in subtle or obvious ways with or without noticeable trace. Every star, every stone, transmits its frequency and colour and receives what relates to its nature at that time. The desert bush protects its leaves with thorns and spikes and yet it invites the insects and bees to its few flowers through scent and pollen. Sacred Oneness appears as balanced in the dualities of attraction and repulsion and appears with every message by which we witness the dynamics of life's theatre.

A scientist may see much of nature through chemistry and physics, but Rumi calls it Divine Love, the power that unites and holds the universe. A man of faith simply says it is God—Allah. Whatever is sensed by us represents a facet of these dualities, all of which are energized by One reality, One sacred message with different intensities. As we live and die within the womb of space and time, we experience all these complementary opposites with their distinct tunes, countless sounds emanating from a magisterial supreme silence. The most crucial paradox in this life is the self/soul dynamic where the soul or spirit is veiled by the biography of ever-changing self or ego. And the individual is like a photon, an entity, but exists only because of the wave.

Man is shaped by nature and nurture as well as the seen and the unseen, but miracles are how matter and energy are inseparable and one in essence, the same as the rest of creation. It is that One Essence whose traces are in the Universe but itself remains absolute and bewilderingly unique, the One without definition and boundaries, Allah. Natural evolution pursues a path towards higher-consciousness and closeness to the ever-present sacred essence. Human beings have the additional ability to recognise the lower self as a shadow of the true inner light. And then by that recognition, exercise will to turn away from that which is unacceptable to the soul and to continuously refer to sacred presence. Nature and nurture have completed their plan. The rest is about us completing our perfectly intended destiny.

SELF-REALISATION

To know is to understand through mental comprehension and the heart's connection. The soul knows all and the self has the potential to know what is within reason and causality. We call it logic and intellect, creativity, or great insights or breakthroughs, which are due to the light of the soul beaming through an opening in the heart. Then the mind is sparked and illumined with an 'aha!' and a sigh of relief. The soul is the transmitter of life, knowledge, ability, will and all modes of subtle or discernible connections and communicating the self's desires and all of these qualities, which become available through the unison between head and heart, or self and soul. The soul/self unison is sometimes called Self-Realization. Others call it 'Enlightenment', yet others speak of 'Knowledge of God'.

The soul is Truth's presence within you and confirms that all worldly experiences are passing shadows and illusions emanating from its ever-present perfect conclusion. Truth and reality are one ever-permanent, eternal, perfection. Life's journey is an experience to realise that outer desires will end and not lead to lasting contentment. Whatever is needed for inner joy and happiness is already here, there and everywhere, ever-present. Yet we struggle with faith, deny, lie and become habituated with self-delusions, personal veils and our individual biographies. The grace of the soul is here within time but its nature is timeless not confined to space. It is a brilliant, ever-there, self-declaring reflection of the One.

Everything beams the truth of Oneness, always and everywhere, showing gentleness or harshness, no matter where or how. Self-knowledge begins by responding to the call of the lower self or ego and then to evolve by turning away from all outer manifestations or justifying distractions towards the original passionate attraction of the soul within. This divine love and passion will burn away all remaining traces of earthly shadows. The baby is now adult enough to realise that all previous phases were rites of passage, to be transformed by the original inner Light that calls to itself by itself. The human being carries the sacred message which simply declares in every tune you can imagine '*Lā ilāha illā'llah, Muhammadan Rasūlu'llah*' (there is not deity but Allah, Muhammad is Allah's Messenger).

The Original Meaning of Sacred Messages II

Given in 2011
Closing Talk

- The Qur'an: A Grand Affair
- The Synergy of Gatheredness
- On Silence
- On *Astaghfiru'llah*
- *Mā sha' Allah*: Seeing Things as They Are
- *Subhān Allah*
- *La Ilaha IllĀ'llah*
- On Ego
- Gatheredness

THE QUR'AN: A GRAND AFFAIR

The Qur'an tells us:

$$\text{إِنَّا سَنُلْقِى عَلَيْكَ قَوْلًا ثَقِيلًا}$$

Indeed we will cast upon you a heavy word. (73:5)

It is so heavy that it is beyond measure.

It also tell us:

$$\text{لَوْ أَنزَلْنَا هَذَا ٱلْقُرْءَانَ عَلَىٰ جَبَلٍ لَّرَأَيْتَهُۥ خَٰشِعًا مُّتَصَدِّعًا}$$

If We had sent down this Qur'an upon a mountain,
you would have seen it humbled and coming apart... (59:21)

The Qur'an has such an unfathomable power that it not only pulverizes our mind to imagine, it just annihilates everything because it is the source of it all.

THE SYNERGY OF GATHEREDNESS

When hearts are open and minds are partially left aside and personal identities recede in significance, something else happens as you all know. One plus one becomes something far greater than two, or three, or its countless variations. This is when the souls resonate and that magnified resonance brings about the beautiful illusion of the closeness of Divine Presence. These moments, these days, are so precious that as you internalize them they open up that space to the higher consciousness within you. You can always recall it.

This is an immense gift in which I consider myself very much privileged to participate because this joy is part of boundless Joy. It is not worldly pleasures or a bit of openness or a bit of excitement, rather, it's something else which is the purpose behind all the stages in life that we go through. We consider these stages as having been our life's journey and everyone considers this as having been the most important thing for them. These great biographical privileges, difficulties, challenges and ups and downs are, in essence, all the same. They are all, if you like, preludes to apparent experiences or heartfelt openings to that which is never ever closed and that is the grace of Allah.

ON SILENCE

If you manage to enter that unfathomable silence, then you have gone to Nirvana and then all you can do is courageously return to the apparent world of movement and change and only see perfection upon perfection within it. You will witness perfection in spite of your personal identity, the need for survival or growth, or contentment, or any of those interesting, 'useful' objectives. But you reach a point which was before the beginning: perfection upon perfection upon perfection. In all the great scriptures and original teachings we can find what we are trying to share between ourselves.

If I am to sum up what for me has been the most fundamental issue in my own life, it is that the sameness of all these sacred messages is the original sameness described in the Qur'an in numerous ways. Look at the beautiful, simple way the first *Ayahs* (verses) in *Surat Al-Mulk* are expressed:

فَٱرْجِعِ ٱلْبَصَرَ هَلْ تَرَىٰ مِن فُطُورٍ ۝

ثُمَّ ٱرْجِعِ ٱلْبَصَرَ كَرَّتَيْنِ يَنقَلِبْ إِلَيْكَ ٱلْبَصَرُ خَاسِئًا وَهُوَ حَسِيرٌ ۝

...Look back again. Do you find any fault?

And look again, and again, until your sight comes back dazzled and exhausted

(67:3-4)

Meaning now you will realize it through insight. Your insight returns to you in the abandonment of glorification. This witnessing happens according to your stage of receptivity. As we have heard, unless there is *isti'dād*, unless there is readiness, unless there is also appropriate timeliness, it will not happen.

The first stage is realizing your own duality—hence *Astaghfiru'llah*—in your conditioned consciousness. The second is self-soul duality. The third is not seeing, not being at one with Cosmic Oneness. Now you are at the gate of silence.

ON *ASTAGHFIRU'LLAH*

All of us can be within the protection of *Astaghfiru'llah* (I seek cover with or forgiveness from Allah). We take cover because every one of us occasionally displays an aspect of meanness, forgetfulness, impatience and intolerance. We take cover in Allah's absolute patience, in Allah's absolute generosity. When I say *Astaghfiru'llah*, remember that *ghafara*, the root verb means to cover and *ghufr* is a cover for the head. I take refuge means I take cover in Allah's perfect unfathomable generosity from my limited small meanness.

What is the effect, what is the importance of a little shadow when that brilliant light shines so that my meanness completely disappears in Allah's ever-present generosity? *Astaghfiru'llah, Astaghfiru'llah!* That is why the Prophet (S) has said that no day had passed without people hearing him repeatedly taking this great entry point to the vast *Rahma* (Mercy) of Allah. *Astaghfiru'llah!*

MĀ SHĀ' ALLAH: SEEING THINGS AS THEY ARE

We all want to see things as they are, which is why we are all curious from the point of birth. We want to discover, uncover, travel so as to see things as they really are. And the prophetic prayer for that was and is: 'Oh Allah, show me things as they are'. So as you see things as they are in the immensity of the Now. Whether you like it or not, this is it.

You are a mixture of both a biography which you are going to carry and suffer from, and a light that is totally utterly resonating with the sacred universal spirit or Allah. This is how it is. It all depends how much you are exercising a will to recall, to reconnect with that light which is in you and then you can see things as they are. Those two people over there, they are quarrelling, why? They want the same thing, fighting over a scarce resource, or the one is scared of the other. There is nothing other than perfection if you see things as they are.

Then it comes to your participation: you can participate but then is there anything you can do? I can assure you, each one of my close friends has been through experiences like this. Keeping away from issues like this is not out of cowardice or out of lack of compassion. It is that there is nothing we can do but wait a day.

So: 'Oh Allah, show me things as they are' is *Mā shā' Allah* (As Allah wills). That for me is the most important, key issue of living, being in the state of recognising and accepting *Mā shā' Allah*. This is how it is. This is also the reason why many religious paths teach: 'Don't complain, don't ask people, wait and ask Allah.' This is *Mā shā' Allah*—wait.

This is especially so for spiritual seekers, who, as soon they have some opening or any other insights, want to blurt it out rather than let it grow until the dam fills up and then it may overflow by itself. Because for hundreds of years now we have been taught to outwardly compete and that more is better, we also transpose that onto the spiritual side. Amongst the ugliest things I have come across in my life is religious or spiritual one-upmanship. It is horrible, as you all well know, and you want to run away from it. There were eighteen different sizes of head-gear during the Ottoman empire for various levels of Muslims, although there is not supposed to be anyone between a person and the Creator in Islam. And look what they did! It was really a mockery. So *Mā shā' Allah* reminds us, 'This is it, here it is.'

SUBHĀN ALLAH

All human beings are inspired from the same place, to be sure. As Prophet Ibrahim (AS) says,

$$لِّيَطْمَئِنَّ قَلْبِي$$

...that my heart may be satisfied (2:260)

Allah is the cause, the beginning, the end, the power, the soul. He is the giver, He is the taker and so it is *Mā shā' Allah* (as Allah wills). The glorious transcendental aspects of some of our *'ibādāt* (worship) have us taking refuge in Allah from Allah. What are you going to do now? As the Prophet says, 'I seek refuge by You, from You.' Where do you go then?

Then there is nothing else left other than the true insight and glorification of the *Mu'min* (one who has faith) which takes you to the third stage or the third complementary level of *Subhān Allah* (Glory be to Allah). *Subhān Allah*, how wonderful it was, I didn't know anything, *Subhān Allah*. I was a bit concerned, *Subhān Allah*. I went there without knowing what was waiting for me, whether good or bad, *Subhān Allah*, *Subhān Allah*. Admission of limitations, admission of high expectations, admission of the duality of *Rabb* (Lord) and *'Abd* (slave) dancing together forever—it is *Subhān Allah*. *Subhān Allah* takes you into a song in the garden beyond, much higher than 'Show me things as they really are', or *Mā shā' Allah* (as Allah wills). *Subhān Allah* is beyond it all, encompassing it all.

LĀ ILĀHA ILLĀ'LLAH

When you have done that, then all that is left to complete the circling of the *Ka'ba*, is *Lā ilāha illā 'llah*. Whatever occurs, seen and unseen, emerges from the Divine Master of the universe. It is wisdom to respond appropriately, to interact within space and time in creation, and to refer it back to its origin, the Divine.

ON EGO

Stop for a minute. What is your real intention behind all of this? To help someone else? To serve? Then it is alright because it doesn't add more to your ego and that is good. Do good, until such time you find that the ego is actually an indicator and a door to ego-less-ness, to the perfect freedom of the *rūh*. Then it's perfect; you will then never denounce the ego any longer. For a child you have to build the ego, but for the adult you have to show them that it's give-and-take. It is, of course, the opposite here, as I said earlier. So only take because you truly see Allah is the Giver; all of it is from Him to Him onto Him by Him.

The ability to act is Allah's way of showing us that we can pretend to be little creators and doers, developers and evolvers, the gardeners and builders. We enact all the attributes we love until we realize that they were all already beaming from our own heart. The more you practice this awareness, the more you find it is real, the more you can refer to that zone of pure, perfect, effulgent light, and the more it becomes the real you, the more you become like *Bayazīd Al-Bistāmī*.

GATHEREDNESS

There is no separation except for us to realize the ever-permanent, timeless Gatheredness. Everything has been gathered in that instant, that instant is still here and now. From that instant comes this one form of universe. How many multi-verses there are, we don't know! We are in only one little slither of this apparent movement of the Big Bang and the Big Collapse and we are in the in-between.

It has been, is, and will be. Inner contentment is contagious because it is not meant for any purpose—it is not meant to raise you to a higher state or become a guru. It is Allah's *Rahma* (Mercy) upon all of *Banī* Adam (children of Adam), and no wonder the angels objected!

CHAPTER ELEVEN

Celebrating Life Through Sacred Expression

Given in 2012

- Sacred Expression in Qur'an
- The Story of Qur'an in a 'Story'
- Death
- God is not a Man in the Sky
- Uncertainty and Trust
- The Complete Person
- Take Refuge in Presence
- Change your Space
- Well-Meaning Sensate Distractions
- Wheresoever you Turn is the Face of Truth
- Real Life
- States & Stations
- The Place of No Place & No Time
- Truth Cannot Be Measured
- Seamless Connection

SACRED EXPRESSION IN QUR'AN

Growing up, I had the trust and the faith that the Qur'an has it all. The Qur'an is a blueprint that gives us the description of how situations are and what the fundamental foundations of those situations are, as well as the prescriptions needed. You hardly find any *ayahs* in the Qur'an, unless they tell you this is the situation and this is how you can resolve your misery, fear and anxiety. Often it is very condensed.

I thought therefore to share with you a fictional story, many elements of which I have encountered as true. I am not a creative writer, but I thought I would do a metaphysical spin on a human story and, in between, show you the *ayahs* of the Qur'an that truly unplug and unpack the whole issue. This is really to encourage every one of us to return to the Source.

And if there is any hope for the Muslims, wherever they are in the world, then it is that. Otherwise with this business of 'we are Muslims let us unify, we are Christians let us unify, let us have interfaith', there is a lot of good will but at the end of the day it doesn't last. It seeps out. And once they leave the meeting place, they are back again at each other's throats because that is the *sunnah* (pattern) of Allah. No two people can accept, because there is no two-ness. In truth there is One-ness. You will revert back to the very basic issue of identity—Who is he? Who is she?

When you begin to see the whole story, the whole truth, through the lens of one-ness, then two-ness—difference, otherness, duality—becomes enjoyable. In fact, it becomes amusing. Otherwise, it is miserable and you know what that means: everybody has had enough of it. Maybe not enough.

The story starts as follows:

THE STORY OF QUR'AN IN A 'STORY'

After harrowing days of bombardment of Salzburg there was a day of calmness. Half of all the buildings in the city and many thousands of homes were reduced to rubble. They actually estimated that more than 17,000 houses were destroyed.

And at that time, Salzburg didn't even have a population of 100,000, such a beautiful city of high culture. *The American and allied forces caused mayhem. The 'friendly' allies who were supposed to save the city, actually destroyed it. The early morning sun sprayed its rays of hope upon the devastated city.*

Max the musician was making his way cautiously to the centre of Residence Platz (it's a very famous square in the middle of Salzburg) *with its elaborate baroque fountain and surrounding buildings, most of which were now in ruins. He walked towards a broken bench and adjusted his sitting position for his cello in preparation for his musical improvisation celebrating cycles of life and death on earth's eternal life's source. Max was already a well-known figure in musical circles and festivals, especially in celebrations of Mozart and Haydn. A gentle breeze blew some of the dust off the piles of rubble and Max produced his red silk handkerchief and placed it firmly on his mouth. The stench of dead domestic animals and birds had become more intense with the rise of the sun. He was playing the changes of seasons of the human dramas on earth within an eternal truth.*

DEATH

وَهُوَ ٱلَّذِىٓ أَحْيَاكُمْ ثُمَّ يُمِيتُكُمْ ثُمَّ يُحْيِيكُمْ ۗ إِنَّ ٱلْإِنسَٰنَ لَكَفُورٌ ۝

He it is who gave you life and will cause you to die and then revive you to a new life. (22:66)

كُلُّ نَفْسٍ ذَآئِقَةُ ٱلْمَوْتِ ۖ ثُمَّ إِلَيْنَا تُرْجَعُونَ ۝

Every soul shall taste death and then to Us you shall return. (29:57)

I am not being grim, but following the Qur'anic pattern, in that wherever there's life, death is mentioned, especially, for example in *Surat Al-Mulk*:

ٱلَّذِى خَلَقَ ٱلْمَوْتَ وَٱلْحَيَوٰةَ

Who created death and life. (67:2)

This is to show you that, as far as Allah is concerned, it is not necessarily sequential. Allah is not in time. He does not follow a time sequence. So the *ayah* says, 'He created death and then life.' So they are ever together. And these *ayahs* tell you personally, individually, as well as collectively as with the city of Salzburg, that life and death circulate, cycling up and down. If it is not a natural disaster, then more and worse human-inflicted disasters. More than 100 million people were slaughtered in Europe in the last century, in the name of something or other—progress or 'civilization' or fear.

He looked around the empty square and thought to himself that he could represent all of creation—he continued playing. After a while, he felt a passing figure on the other end of the square. A mother and her young daughter were clambering over the rubble making their way out of the square. The young girl began to pull her mother towards Max. She was wearing a long grey frock, obviously a hand-me-down. Max greeted his unexpected audience with a gesture and carried on playing. Beautiful Isabelle was looking at Max attentively and as he felt her glance, he stopped playing and looked at her sad face tinged with fear and tiredness. It was her birthday and her mother was taking her to the outskirts of the city to her cousin's house which was not bombed. She smiled at him and said, 'I am Isabel and I am twelve years today. Do you think music will come back to our city?' Her anxious face was mixed with hope. 'I am playing "requiem for the dead",' Max spoke softly, 'and celebrating life at the same time. Do you like it?' Isabel's eyes welled up with tears and her mother gave her a little hug, trying to resume their arduous journey. Max held Isabel's hand softly and promised she would have an enjoyable birthday. Mother and daughter began walking amongst the piles of stones and debris and the smouldering stench. A little grey kitten emerged meowing to Isabel; she kneeled down and asked her mother's permission to pick it up and take it with them.

GOD IS NOT A MAN IN THE SKY

ٱلَّذِى خَلَقَ ٱلْمَوْتَ وَٱلْحَيَوٰةَ لِيَبْلُوَكُمْ أَيُّكُمْ أَحْسَنُ عَمَلًا وَهُوَ ٱلْعَزِيزُ ٱلْغَفُورُ ۝

He who created death and life to test you as to which of you is most righteous in deed. He is the Almighty, the All-Forgiving. (67:2)

Now 'righteous' or 'best' here means presence, as Max was to acknowledge.

That you celebrate that which is gone, that which is not, that which will come—the Eternal Presence. This is celebration, this is the test. Otherwise, a test for what? Is there some big, fat, giant creator, sitting somewhere laughing at us? Testing and trying—misery! What is this? All that it means is the return to your presence: ready to declare you own nothing, you control nothing, you have no idea how life came and when and how. And how it will also continue, not end. It is your body that will be returned, out of loyalty to where it was made, from where it emerged, which is the earth.

UNCERTAINTY AND TRUST

$$وَمَا تَدْرِى نَفْسٌ مَّاذَا تَكْسِبُ غَدًا ۖ وَمَا تَدْرِى نَفْسٌ بِأَيِّ أَرْضٍ تَمُوتُ$$

No soul knows what it will earn tomorrow, and no soul knows in what land it will die. (31:34)

Nobody knows, you can never tell! The air that goes in may not come out. This is again another *mithāl*; these are the true similitudes and true wonder-ments of the Qur'an, for you and me to remember, to be aware. What is the most precious thing you have? Your so-called life. What does it mean, 'your life'? In order for that to resonate with Eternal Life. If you don't resonate with that, you have missed your capital, you have lost it. It is not about longevity and many more years. Many more years of the same misery?

THE COMPLETE PERSON

Except that, as you get older, you are less capable of dealing with it. You are less healthy, less strong. When you begin to resonate with Eternal Life, genuinely, truly, within your own heart, unconditionally, not wanting to impose on others, or impress others, you just know it, then you have arrived.

That is the meaning of *insān al-kāmil* (the complete person). We have so many of these examples, eulogizing the prophets, the imams, the 'perfect' beings, but how does it apply to you? If you yourself have not ended up at the point from which everything began, you have not completed that journey. *Insān al-kāmil* does not mean a 'perfect' person; it means completing the journey and fulfilling the purpose of your life, which is to know that life is eternal, that Allah is Ever-Present, eternally, beyond limitations of place or time.

TAKE REFUGE IN PRESENCE

Within three years Isabel was a promising student at the music academy and played in a concert celebrating Max's 80th birthday. On that occasion Max gave her a red silk handkerchief and told her whenever she felt sad and depressed to put this on her face and fly into perfect harmony and bliss.

$$\text{وَلِلَّهِ مَا فِى ٱلسَّمَٰوَٰتِ وَمَا فِى ٱلْأَرْضِ ۚ وَإِلَى ٱللَّهِ تُرْجَعُ ٱلْأُمُورُ ۝}$$

To God belongs all that is in the Heaven and Earth and all matters shall revert to God. (3:109)

Then what ownership do you have? What is that upon which you can truly, utterly rely? What is your security? Other than, that is, the inner joy of knowledge that life is eternal and you have been given a spark of it.

CHANGE YOUR SPACE

Some years later, Isabel was on holiday in Salzburg and was showing her kids the city and its beautiful surrounding mountains. Upon visiting the old market square, they went into a new museum and amongst the main exhibits there lay the beautiful cello that had belonged to Max. She could not stop her tears from flowing. She sat down, hugged her children and told them the story.

أَلَمْ تَكُنْ أَرْضُ ٱللَّهِ وَٰسِعَةً فَتُهَاجِرُواْ فِيهَا ۚ فَأُوْلَـٰئِكَ مَأْوَىٰهُمْ جَهَنَّمُ ۖ وَسَآءَتْ مَصِيرًا

Was not the land of God wide enough for you to emigrate? (4:97)

ٱلَّذِى جَعَلَ لَكُمُ ٱلْأَرْضَ مَهْدًا وَسَلَكَ لَكُمْ فِيهَا سُبُلًا

He who made the earth for you a cradle and marked in it paths for you. (20:53)

Ten years after Isabel's parents emigrated to Canada and had enjoyed their new life, news came of the death of their favourite uncle Ignacio. He was a Jesuit monk, the last in the monastery when it had been sold to a hotel group. Ignacio had decided to join Albert Schweitzer at his leprosy colony in the Belgian Congo. After a few months he died, broken-hearted and disappointed.

WELL-MEANING SENSATE DISTRACTIONS

Isabelle had married Zeki, a successful tax consultant whose father was a Turk and mother a German. Soon they had two children and Zeki was enjoying his material success and the family holidays to the Caribbean and the occasional skiing trip.

زُيِّنَ لِلَّذِينَ كَفَرُواْ ٱلْحَيَوٰةُ ٱلدُّنْيَا وَيَسْخَرُونَ مِنَ ٱلَّذِينَ ءَامَنُواْ وَٱلَّذِينَ ٱتَّقَواْ

For those who disbelieve the present life has been made to appear attractive, they mock those who believe and those who fear God. (2:212)

ٱلَّذِينَ يَسْتَحِبُّونَ ٱلْحَيَوٰةَ ٱلدُّنْيَا عَلَى ٱلْأَخِرَةِ

They embrace fondly this life in preference to the hereafter. (14:3)

This is Zeki. He is engrossed in the outer life. You understand Zeki! There are many of them here and there and everywhere. They all say, 'Never mind, I have children to feed, I have got to get the money, I need a tax consultant.' You need Zeki!

When the children were in their teens, Isabel was feeling the emptiness in her life and often remembered Ignacio's last words to her before leaving for Africa, 'Be patient for it will take you 40 years before you begin to have lasting fulfilment beyond pleasures and pain'. She thought to herself that she still had a few more years to attain this prophecy. She was a frustrated housewife with a husband who was pursuing his worldly obsessions and pleasures and yet, a good man.

A Turkish Sufi group was visiting Toronto and Isabel was thrilled by the singing of the communal dhikr and Shaykh Mustafa's booming voice. Zeki was not interested.

Once Krishnamurti was asked about this. I was there. The wife was becoming spiritual because she was unhappy and suffering. The wife asked, 'What can we do if he is not interested and I'm interested?' He said, 'Both of you are heading for a collision.' And went silent.

Zeki was a rational, sensible, worldly materialist. A year later, she changed her religion again and joined a Rifa'i Sufi group in Toronto. On her birthday, Zeki had arranged a special party for her but she became ill and locked herself up in her room. She even thought of suicide a couple of times. The local Rifa'i Shaykh, Shaykh Salim was her new spiritual connection and she was fully absorbed into the new teachings. She loved the Qur'an and began to pronounce the Arabic with some fluency.

WHERESOEVER YOU TURN IS THE FACE OF TRUTH

وَلِلَّهِ يَسْجُدُ مَن فِي ٱلسَّمَٰوَٰتِ وَٱلْأَرْضِ طَوْعًا وَكَرْهًا

And to God prostrates all who are in Heavens and Earth, willingly and unwillingly. (13:15)

Zeki and Isabel all are in prostration, he to *Al-Ghani*, He who has wealth and power, *Al-Qawi*. She for other aspects, *Al-'Alim* (The All-Knowing), and *Al-Ghafur* (The Clement, Forgiving).

إِنَّ ٱلَّذِينَ ءَامَنُواْ وَٱلَّذِينَ هَاجَرُواْ وَجَٰهَدُواْ فِي سَبِيلِ ٱللَّهِ أُوْلَٰٓئِكَ يَرْجُونَ رَحْمَتَ ٱللَّهِ وَٱللَّهُ غَفُورٌ رَّحِيمٌ ﴿٢١٨﴾

Those who believed and those who emigrated and exerted themselves in the way of God. These can indeed expect the mercy of God. God is All-Forgiving, compassionate to each. (2:218)

Zeki was quite understanding, but the emotional and spiritual distance between them grew wider. Isabel went for Hajj and was trampled over, near the position of the stoning of Satan. She possibly passed out, but vaguely recalled angels lifting her up out of the torrent of human congestion. She recovered soon and decided it had been direct divine intervention. Shaykh Salim referred to this instance in a few of his talks and his repertoire of spiritual miracles grew in number and intensity. Isabel unpacked her Hajj suitcase, which was full of scarves, prayer beads, prayer mats, eastern perfumes and other bric-a-brac. She put aside a few of the items for herself and distributed the rest. A few months later, she decided not to keep any of these souvenirs as she began, more and more, to feel the presence of the light of the Ka'ba beaming out from within her heart. A while later, she remembered the wisdom that when you have a diamond mine, you have no interest in pebbles. She longed for the ultimate arrival.

يَـٰٓأَيُّهَا ٱلَّذِينَ ءَامَنُواْ ٱتَّقُواْ ٱللَّهَ وَٱبْتَغُوٓاْ إِلَيْهِ ٱلْوَسِيلَةَ

O you who have faith! Be wary of Allah and seek means of recourse to Him
(5:35)

إِنَّ أَرْضِى وَٰسِعَةٌ فَإِيَّـٰىَ فَٱعْبُدُونِ

My earth is wide and it is Me that you must worship. (29:56)

وَلَوْ شَآءَ رَبُّكَ لَءَامَنَ مَن فِى ٱلْأَرْضِ كُلُّهُمْ جَمِيعًا

Had your Lord willed, all people on the earth would have believed. (10:99)

مَنْ عَمِلَ صَـٰلِحًا مِّن ذَكَرٍ أَوْ أُنثَىٰ وَهُوَ مُؤْمِنٌ فَلَنُحْيِيَنَّهُۥ حَيَوٰةً طَيِّبَةً

Whoever does good, male or female, while having faith, we shall make them live a good life. (16:97)

Now, 'good life' means sustainable, inner delight, goodness and reflection and awareness and the constancy of that fullness of you as an individual. You do exist but because of that eternal mysterious life in you, your existence is not just limited to your miserable ups and downs, body, mind and intellect. It's far, far more than that.

REAL LIFE

$$ يَـٰٓأَيُّهَا ٱلَّذِينَ ءَامَنُوا۟ ٱسْتَجِيبُوا۟ لِلَّهِ وَلِلرَّسُولِ إِذَا دَعَاكُمْ لِمَا يُحْيِيكُمْ $$

O believers, respond to God and His Messenger when he calls you
to that which will give you life. (8:24)

You see this puzzle? What is it that gives you life? The *ayah* addresses us who are supposed to be alive. He says, 'O those of you who have trust and faith in that, you will come to know that which is the only truth and source and essence of knowledge. Follow that until you come to know that there is another life.' There are many, many such *ayahs* in the Qur'an but in different facets, one of which will also come later.

Real life is Eternal Life and you and I and he and she have a spark of that in us. If we do not dwell upon that spark, ride on its wings, to realize that the spark carries the same characteristics of the eternal life, then you haven't done it. You will then always remain between certainty, uncertainty, frustration, anger and occasional happiness and goodness and so on. And then you will also fall into the many traps that the Qur'an describes such as,

$$ أَلْهَىٰكُمُ ٱلتَّكَاثُرُ ۝ $$

Competition in (worldly) increase diverts you. (102:1)

'Our numbers are increasing', 'this *tarīqa* has more people'—what does that mean? What do you mean by 'more'? More of what? Where are you when you declare *Allahu Akbar* (God is Greater)? When the Absolute is referred to, all relative issues disappear?

Isabelle outgrew the spiritual state of the Sufis in Toronto and Shaykh Salim recommended that she visit Istanbul and the Grand Shaykh Aminullah. After much physical, mental and spiritual preparation, she was on her way with two other Sufi ladies towards Istanbul. It took them a week to settle down after the numerous mishaps, stomach bugs, bed bugs and other adjustments. And then, the three ladies from Canada plunged into the arduous life of the tekye.

There are 9 different names for *tekye* (Sufi cloister). *Tekye* means where you rest your back. The North African names differ, such as *zāwiya* which means a corner, so hopefully you get cornered and leave your presumptions, assumptions, your personality and your profile behind. So they were in the life of the *tekye*.

After two weeks they were enjoying the hospitality and the epiphanies of day-to-day life. You know how it is, you have savings, you have money, so every 10 minutes you have an epiphany. God's Hand comes to you and you say you don't know what happened, miracle upon miracle and so on. There will always be Shaykh Salims who will add these to their repertoires. Enormous miracles! They don't know that before the breath, after the breath, in between the breath is the miracle of miracles. So that's why we are chasing pebbles.

STATES & STATIONS

Isabel was beginning to become more secure in her spiritual journey and more convinced that the purpose of life is to refer to the light within the heart at all times. Several times during the end of dhikr, she nearly passed out and was revived by Turkish rose water and sugary Turkish delight. One evening after dhikr, Shaykh Aminullah asked her about her stay in the tekye, and she gave a glowing account of how happy she was. He invited her for coffee the next morning. She trembled with joy and anticipation. Her eyes and heart were focused upon the Shaykh as she sipped the thick coffee. She was in ecstasy and her heart overflowed. The Shaykh asked her about her stay. 'This place is heavenly and I feel I am already in paradise'. The Shaykh laughed and quietly murmured, 'I hope your mood becomes a mode for what we want is constancy, not the comings and goings.'

وَمَا مِنْ غَآئِبَةٍ فِي ٱلسَّمَآءِ وَٱلْأَرْضِ إِلَّا فِي كِتَٰبٍ مُّبِينٍ ٧٥

And nothing is hidden in heaven or on earth except that it is in a manifest book.
(27:75)

They who believe and were pious—to them glad tidings in this present world, and in the hereafter. (10:63-64). So if your present day-to-day little bits of pleasure or good feelings or generosity, if they do not extend to its source which is in your heart, which is the sacred light of your *rūh* or your spirit, then you are not truly progressing in any sustainable, real way. You will only accumulate yet more pleasure, which will always lead to its cancelling side, displeasure.

The Shaykh continued, 'Paradise appears as glimpses to begin with and so does Allah's light until you realize that this is the only true purpose of life. Happiness on earth is short-lived and is always tinged with sorrow and fear and the human quest is to return to the eternal garden. If you say that Adam was exiled from paradise then the only drive for his offspring is to return'. Isabel sighed deeply with an expression acknowledging all of this and her own weakness. The Shaykh nodded sympathetically, 'I pray that you will be whisked away on the flying carpet of your faith and that you realize that whatever you loved and wanted is already within you.'

He touched her shoulder gently and said, 'In this world we are like kids playing with pebbles, sharing, caring, buying, selling, giving, taking and all other human activities, until the experience of the presence of the sacred treasure in your heart becomes constant. Once you know that the biggest mine of diamonds is within you, you won't care anymore for the inferior gemstones. Celebrating joy is good but better than that is beyond all your experiences and pleasure or joys. Earthly dualities remain our battlefield until we experience life through the perfect lens of unity. The world of suffering can be the springboard to the ever-present divine offering. Human intentions and actions can be sublime or ridiculous and when sacred presence is realized, we will experience infinite blissful moments. The purpose of life is through dedicated intention and attention to experience and celebrate sacred oneness that envelops and permeates all. Don't ever be distracted by anything else until you are able to celebrate this truth.'

THE PLACE OF NO PLACE & NO TIME

ٱدْخُلُواْ ٱلْجَنَّةَ لَا خَوْفٌ عَلَيْكُمْ وَلَآ أَنتُمْ تَحْزَنُونَ

Enter the garden, there is no fear upon you nor will you grieve. (7:49)

وَأَمَّا مَنْ خَافَ مَقَامَ رَبِّهِۦ وَنَهَى ٱلنَّفْسَ عَنِ ٱلْهَوَىٰ ۝ فَإِنَّ ٱلْجَنَّةَ
هِىَ ٱلْمَأْوَىٰ ۝

Those who feared standing before their Lord and curbed the self from its whims,
the garden shall be their abode. (79:40-41)

You see, the garden implies beyond space and time, beyond where we have been caught in this world. Otherwise, it is a pleasure which will always be tinged and tainted. That is why, you see, whenever there is worldly celebration, there is sadness that increases as the time comes closer to the end of the party. It is ending and everybody will disperse. That gatheredness which gave us a slight hint of the original one-ness or singularity before the Big Bang or whatever, is now going to disappear. Unless these small, little worldly pleasures lead you to the zone in you of indescribable, total, utter joy of that which people term as unison—but there is no such thing. There is only One.

TRUTH CANNOT BE MEASURED

These are all figures of speech: 'I want to get closer!' That is why I run away from those who are desperately seeking the path. They come to you saying, 'Shaykh, am I closer to God now or not?' Run away from these people because their God has a measuring rod. How far is it? How near is it? So it is another realm, it is metaphysical. Do not deny the physical—it has measures, its ups, its downs, but it is all emanating from the meta-physical, beyond the physical. And this knowledge has been going on for thousands of years.

As she was fastening her seatbelt on the return journey to Toronto, Isabel thought that she was now entering a new stage of her life and was longing to communicate with her long dead uncle, Ignacio. She also felt much compassion and understanding for Zeki and the rest of humanity. Upon her return, Shaykh Salim realized the transformation of Isabel and asked her if she could begin teaching and play her role in promoting Sufism and spirituality. She smiled to herself and agreed to look into his request, but deep down she was so content with Allah's prefect ways that she was still basking in the joy of witnessing His perfections. There was no personal drive to do anything good or bad. She felt truly gripped totally by the divine presence and was in ecstatic celebration, timelessly and in time.

SEAMLESS CONNECTION

A week later she had a dream of Shaykh Aminullah who asked her to sit with him after his breakfast and share his coffee again. She was nervous at first. He touched her shoulder and looked straight into her anxious eyes and said: 'Now you taste the truth, now your taste of truth has become regular, you must pay more attention to the worldly plays and dramas, don't be afraid that they will afflict you. You may occasionally burn a finger or two, but it is necessary for completion of your journey. A time will come when you'll see the seamless connection between earth and heavens.'

Novice Sufis often talk about the outer and the inner and the higher and the lower.

$$\text{وَهُوَ مَعَكُمْ أَيْنَ مَا كُنتُمْ}$$

And He is with you wherever you may be. (57:4)

$$\text{وَتِلْكَ ٱلْأَمْثَٰلُ نَضْرِبُهَا لِلنَّاسِ وَمَا يَعْقِلُهَآ إِلَّا ٱلْعَٰلِمُونَ ۝}$$

And We present these parables for humankind; but no one grasps them except the wise. (29:43)

Listen to all wisdom but remain in your secret heart's cave of utter one-ness. See all dualities through the light of unity and acknowledge all, for all emanate from the sacred one-ness. Do not deny any and celebrate the eternal light that has brought about the flash of your life. Play your role in the time, play your role to the tune of the sacred music maker. That is completion of your journey. Salām, salām, salām (peace).

Lā ilāha illā'llah!

وَتَوَكَّلْ عَلَى ٱللَّهِ ۚ وَكَفَىٰ بِٱللَّهِ وَكِيلًا ٣

Put your trust in Allah and Allah suffices as trustee. (33:3)

سَيَهْدِيهِمْ وَيُصْلِحُ بَالَهُمْ ٥ وَيُدْخِلُهُمُ ٱلْجَنَّةَ عَرَّفَهَا لَهُمْ ٦

He shall guide them and set their affairs in order and admit them into the garden, which He made known to them. (47:5-6)

CHAPTER TWELVE

The Universal Message of the Qur'an

Given in 2013

- A Mercy for Mankind
- Reading the Qur'an Through the Qur'an
- Oneness: The Essence of Qur'anic Unveiling
- Book of Patterns
- Book of Allegory
- Book of Cosmology
- Book of the Field
- Book of Humanity
- The Book of the Garden

A MERCY FOR MANKIND

I want to share with you a series of snapshots which attempt to cover the whole package of this amazing gift of the Qur'an, which, like many other gifts, have been showered from the unseen upon the various elemental, celestial bodies and then the terrestrial sphere over billions of years.

For thousands of years humans have attempted to go beyond the limitations of human consciousness, personal consciousness, thought, and mind. They have grappled with the questions of what is it all about? Where is God? Who is God? What is death? Who am I? Who are you? Why do we quarrel? Why do we smile? Why do we upset each other? And so on and so forth. How do the two—duality—come from the One—unity— and return to the One?

The Qur'an is the culmination of thousands of years of such human endeavour. We all know there is an outward evolutionary path. Things began with one cell and have progressed and evolved to a very complex situation. There is a lot of randomness within it if you look within a short timeframe. But there is also a very clear direction of time and rise of consciousness.

Each one of us is also a mini or micro universe. You begin in the womb where you are protected in an aqueous state, as had been part of the universe, and then you are ejected with a cry and suddenly you find yourself dependent on air. Then you realize you are made of earth, water, fire and air and then you try to cope. God is your mother and then soon the father begins to prove himself to be God. If you are a boy, by the age of two or three, you begin to compete with Him because you want the exclusivity of attention. And if you are lucky enough, they whisper in your ear that 'you are my favourite' so that you don't have to begin life with that broken, desperate need for affirmation.

READING THE QUR'AN THROUGH THE QUR'AN

The Qur'an gives us the whole story. I have selected 50 *āyāt* which put these snapshots together and if you manage to absorb them all at the same time, then they flow at the appropriate rate for you to see a 'script'. You and I are the players in that script, so the only problem is that we occasionally get stuck in one part of that script. We suddenly become this victim, we become this role where we become religious or pious or special or dejected or rejected or failed. These are all tiny little scripts on the stage the Qur'an gives us. The script gives us a stage, opening up for us the whole panorama.

So the approach has to be *Al-Qur'an Bi'l-Qur'an* (the Qur'an through the Qur'an). It reveals itself, just like you and I reveal ourselves. I am now revealing myself in the sense that I have been blessed with time and energy and some Arabic. Then I see this amazing incredible gift of gifts that has drenched whatever we have in terms of humanity, in terms of our values on this earth. But like all other gifts, you have to unwrap it, you have to appreciate it, you have to love it, you have to absorb it, you have to *be* it. Only then does it reveal itself. You too, only reveal yourself when you are utterly and openly and honestly engaged. Otherwise, you become this pompous fellow who boasts about having done this or that, or how many times you have been to Hajj. That also has a role but are you content? Are you ready to die joyfully? This is the ultimate test. Are you as content in your heart when you are successful and people look up to you, respect you as when you are totally dejected and rejected? If you are not the same, then who are you? What have you been doing? Who is the author? Why haven't you adored the author of that script? The author is One. In truth, there is only One.

ONENESS: THE ESSENCE OF QUR'ANIC UNVEILING

The advantage of this last of the major revelations of the Qur'an is simplicity. It is not that other prophets were lesser. The Qur'an declares:

لَا نُفَرِّقُ بَيْنَ أَحَدٍ مِّن رُّسُلِهِ

We make no distinction between any of his messengers. (2:285)

But their times were different, their cultures were different, the way they presented the message was different. Also their outer do's and don'ts and laws were different as was appropriate to that time. Here we have the ultimate culmination. All prophets say there is only One—there isn't you *and* God. *Lā ilāha illā'llah*: there is only One. From that One comes all others. From one integrated seamless whole Attributes manifest among us as the so-called virtues we seek to embody—humility, self-awareness, accountability, reflectiveness, and so on.

I have divided this chapter into 6 sections or 'books'.

BOOK OF PATTERNS

إِنَّ هَٰذَا ٱلْقُرْءَانَ يَهْدِى لِلَّتِى هِىَ أَقْوَمُ وَيُبَشِّرُ ٱلْمُؤْمِنِينَ ٱلَّذِينَ يَعْمَلُونَ ٱلصَّٰلِحَٰتِ أَنَّ لَهُمْ أَجْرًا كَبِيرًا ۝

Indeed, this Qur'an guides to that which is most suitable and gives good tidings to the believers who do righteous deeds that they will have a great reward. (17:9)

The most important thing to bear in mind is that we all need guidance. We want to be guided. We want to do the right thing at the right time. We don't want to fail. We don't want to make stupid mistakes. We don't want to be ill irrevocably. We don't want any of these things. We are programmed wanting goodness and excellence.

The beginning of this part of looking for guidance, accepting guidance, following guidance, is to have faith and trust (*īmān*). It will come to you. Goodness is already there but when I look at my past habits and my complaints and whatever negative faculties I have I get stuck at that. The Light (*Nūr*) is already there but we are used to the images of habits, to the veils and shadows. We should stop it. That is why day is followed by night to give us the respite of sleep. So that you move into another level of consciousness and are given another chance.

The Compassionate, taught the Qur'an (55:1-2)

The first thing was the creation of these patterns, the Qur'an, the inscription of reality, of countless infinite patterns, seen and unseen. This is the *'ilm ul-Qur'an* (knowledge of the Qur'an). Qur'an is the accumulation, the gatheredness of all of these.

The Goal is Supreme Consciousness

$$خَلَقَ ٱلْإِنسَـٰنَ ۝$$

He created man (55:3)

Then we are reminded that all of these higher consciousnesses, lower consciousnesses, all of the cosmic sounds, are there to aim for the perfect absolute, all enveloping, mysterious, Supreme Consciousness, God Consciousness. We cannot expect that from a frog. It has its instincts, its own soul and its soul takes it up to a certain level, no more. That is why domestic animals look up to their owners for getting that additional energy. They absorb something further, something higher. Lesser creatures have a soul that is limited. The ant's soul is limited but they also have, as we know ,a lot of characteristics which we consider to be of high value, such as altruism. And that, according to evolutionary biologists, is for the species' survival, which is fine because of the Oneness you see again.

Guidance only for the Committed

تِلْكَ ءَايَـٰتُ ٱلْكِتَـٰبِ ٱلْحَكِيمِ ۝ هُدًى وَرَحْمَةً لِّلْمُحْسِنِينَ ۝

These are verses of the wise Book,
As guidance and mercy for the doers of good. (31:2-3)

It is only guidance for those who are committed. You can't get all the benefits of the club unless you enter, until you are committed to be a member and with the membership comes certain regulations. You may have to take your shoes off outside or pay your $50,000 or whatever other regulations you have. Then you have entered.

قُلْ يَـٰٓأَيُّهَا ٱلنَّاسُ قَدْ جَآءَكُمُ ٱلْحَقُّ مِن رَّبِّكُمْ فَمَنِ ٱهْتَدَىٰ فَإِنَّمَا يَهْتَدِى لِنَفْسِهِۦ وَمَن ضَلَّ فَإِنَّمَا يَضِلُّ عَلَيْهَا وَمَآ أَنَا۠ عَلَيْكُم بِوَكِيلٍ ۝

Say, O mankind, the truth has come to you from your Lord, so whoever is guided is only guided for [the benefit of] his soul, and whoever goes astray only goes astray [in violation] against it. And I am not over you a manager. (10:108)

Look at the immediate responsibility. If you are guided it is for your sake. And if you are lost, you are lost, then tough luck—but it doesn't mean others may not help, nor that you don't ask for help.

Courage & Change

Allah says:

إِنَّ ٱللَّهَ يَغْفِرُ ٱلذُّنُوبَ جَمِيعًا إِنَّهُۥ هُوَ ٱلْغَفُورُ ٱلرَّحِيمُ ۝

Indeed, Allah forgives all sins. Indeed, it is He who is the Forgiving, the Merciful. (39:53)

You can immediately change if you are sufficiently courageous. You change everything. In the *shari'a* of Islam—as you know *shari'a* (outer law) and *haqiqa* (inner truth) are totally linked—you mustn't play around with dead bones. But look at us: most of the time we are even proud of the dead bones. Look at the house with the photographs on the mantelpiece, especially that of the wedding day. It's a tragedy. It's a reminder of a tragedy. 'The one day he really looked at me. Every day after that is not the same. I wear better dresses but he doesn't look at me.' So if you have lost you are lost. But once you are aware of the situation you can change it.

BOOK OF ALLEGORY

وَتِلْكَ ٱلْأَمْثَلُ نَضْرِبُهَا لِلنَّاسِ لَعَلَّهُمْ يَتَفَكَّرُونَ

And these examples We present to the people that perhaps they will give thought. (59:21)

The Qur'an is full of symbols, metaphors, and parables *(amthāl)*. These teach-ings and stories require a key to unlock them, a faculty called the *'aql* or intellect.

وَمَا يَعْقِلُهَآ إِلَّا ٱلْعَٰلِمُونَ

And none will understand except those of intellect. (29:43)

Intellect

'Aql (intellect) is to contain or fathom something. And nobody 'gets it' except those who have intellect. Many readings of the Qur'an are redundant: you read the Qur'an, you recite the Qur'an, but it's like talking about meals or about the dish from which you have not yet taken the nourishment from it. Why? Because your intellect is not ready to absorb it, to accept that it is about you. You are the principal actor but you always think of others—what do they say.

I have a few mechanisms to test this. Whenever somebody says 'unfortunately', I immediately know I have to run away because they are in an unfortunate situation. I want to be fortunate. I don't want to be unfortunate. And there are many others. Whenever people complain about 'other' Muslims or other Christians or the other people, run away. Because they are looking for what is worth looking for but assuming it is more special in one place rather than the other. They are not using their intellect and powers of discrimination.

Illusion of Sacred Space

And this takes us to the illusion of sacred space. Do you mean to say that the *nūr* (light) of Allah is not universal? The sacred space means a place where people have left behind more of their own baggage, their own stupidities, and their own quarrels. But go to many of these sacred places and stay there for a bit of time. You will find the people who are supposed to be the guardians have more quarrels and are worse and more vicious.

The whole of life is sacred! Your *rūh* is sacred and you are alive because of your *rūh*. But we do need designated sacred places. We do need sacred times to remind children of spirituality while growing up, until they themselves can realize that:

$$\text{فَأَيْنَمَا تُوَلُّواْ فَثَمَّ وَجْهُ اللَّهِ}$$

so wherever you turn there is the Face of Allah. (2:115)

Wherever you turn, it is already there. But it is like childhood, like going through layer after layer of healthy, natural evolutionary, spiritual evolutionary veils.

Do not negate the World

$$\text{وَمَن كَانَ فِي هَٰذِهِۦٓ أَعْمَىٰ فَهُوَ فِي ٱلْءَاخِرَةِ أَعْمَىٰ وَأَضَلُّ سَبِيلًا}$$

And whoever is blind in this [life] will be blind in the Hereafter

and in a worse way. (17:72)

First I wish to remind you not to denounce the world. This idea of renunciation had different meanings in the olden days. Don't renounce anything. But the *ayah* says and 'if you are blind in the world of duality, in the world of rationality, if you don't see it, you cannot read it, then you will be more blind in the next life'. So do not denounce it. All that it means is, in your attitude, do not put the love of *dunyā* (material world) in your heart because you will be pained by it. You will be hurt by it. You will have expectations that no one can meet. Because your true expectations are that of the *rūh* and the *rūh's* (soul/spirit) boundaries are endless. The *rūh* knows its Creator and its Creator is the most generous, the most powerful, the most wealthy, etc... All of the attributes of Allah are within you, so how can anybody else fulfil those attributes? They help you, in a worldly sense of solace, comfort and ease and illness and also spiritually when sometimes we are weakened, we have doubts.

Situations change and so you need a bit of a mirroring and solace. It's helpful to think that never mind we will get there, but that which we are looking for is already there—hopefully. If we remember that then we are a little more illumined.

BOOK OF COSMOLOGY

The next part that I wanted to share with you is how existence occurred and how creation came about.

هُوَ ٱلَّذِى خَلَقَ ٱلسَّمَوَتِ وَٱلْأَرْضَ فِى سِتَّةِ أَيَّامٍ ثُمَّ ٱسْتَوَىٰ عَلَى ٱلْعَرْشِ يَعْلَمُ مَا يَلِجُ فِى ٱلْأَرْضِ وَمَا يَخْرُجُ مِنْهَا وَمَا يَنزِلُ مِنَ ٱلسَّمَآءِ وَمَا يَعْرُجُ فِيهَا وَهُوَ مَعَكُمْ أَيْنَ مَا كُنتُمْ وَٱللَّهُ بِمَا تَعْمَلُونَ بَصِيرٌ ﴿٤﴾

It is He who created the heavens and earth in six days and then established Himself above the Throne. He knows what penetrates into the earth and what emerges from it and what descends from the heaven and what ascends therein; and He is with you wherever you are. And Allah, of what you do, is Seeing.

(57:4)

There are at least 20 *āyāt* reflecting this beginning of the *kun-fayakun* ('Be!' and it is) of the Big Bang, or whatever you like to imagine is the start of visible or tangible or sensory-based separation or dispersion in creation.

We also had this '*kun*' during biblical times and even before the Prophet Ibrahim (AS). There are stages and phases in this creation. These people somehow had a better feel of the broader aspects of astrophysics, that there were different stages in the occurrence of this amazing phenomenon of our universe. As we all know there may be countless other universes, multiverses even, but let's try at least to make sense out of what is in front of us, and then our imagination or our higher consciousness could lead us to a full acceptance of that which is infinity or that which is constantly at its boundary and yet within bounds.

Science has contributed a lot to our understanding of all these things and I find a great pleasure and joy all the time in coming across the latest understandings. For me it was a big breakthrough when a few years ago it was established fully that space and time are inseparable. There is no such thing as their separation. You cannot make any sense out of anything except by reference to the Qur'an. The Qur'an is magnificent. Begin with a mental background and intellectual understanding and then you find the spiritual resonance of it.

And then we have this idea of Allah at the earliest part of His creation:

$$ثُمَّ ٱسْتَوَىٰ إِلَى ٱلسَّمَآءِ وَهِيَ دُخَانٌ$$

Then He directed Himself to the heaven while it was smoke. (41:11)

It is an amazing ayah: '… and it was all smoke.' As you know from its great heat it was mainly smoke to begin with.

$$وَمِن كُلِّ شَيْءٍ خَلَقْنَا زَوْجَيْنِ لَعَلَّكُمْ تَذَكَّرُونَ ۝$$

And all things We have created by pairs, that ye may reflect. (51:49)

We have tended to ignore the key parts of the *ayah*. The key word here is *tadhakkarūn* (reflect/remember). And from everything that we can discern in existence there are twos—visible or invisible, meaning or form, good/bad, up/down, dark/light, hard/soft, and so on. From everything, it says, we have created pairs so as to remember. Remember what? The origin is One. Oneness is in it and to Oneness it reverts. What a liberation! There is only One. A One that has no two. Twos and threes and the countless emanate from that mysterious *Lahūt* (Divine Nature), and from it comes *Jabarūt (Divine Omnipotence), then the Malakūt* (Realm of Divine Dominion) and and the *Mulk* (Realm of Creation)— so that is how it cascades.

On Trust

$$إِنَّ فِي ٱلسَّمَٰوَٰتِ وَٱلْأَرْضِ لَآيَٰتٍ لِّلْمُؤْمِنِينَ ۝$$

In the heavens and the earth are proofs for the believers. (45:3)

Witnessing the signs and making sense of them is only for those who have faith and trust that they will come to see the truth. Only then are there signs for them. Otherwise it is meaningless. They are all the time in a hurry from this to that, and then the cell phone rings, and the child cries, and the husband threatens that he is running away with the secretary, or whatever. It is endless. How you are defending or offending becomes a battle of survival.

Individual Survival in Society

For twenty thousand years or so, human beings survived because of families, clans and groups. Even 100 years ago most people would find that if you were rejected by your grandfather, or great-grandfather or whatever, your chance of physical survival would have been very low. So we had to pay attention. But it became a highly patriarchal society, with the balance of power and decision making in the hands of men, which often led to women being oppressed. And even until now many people still want to have a compound where three or four brothers and their families live together. It is often a recipe for disaster because jealousy comes in, other factors, and also the distribution of responsibilities: who is paying for what. When it comes to money, know for sure that it is going to bring about destruction. Every one of us knows that. Every one of us has had countless experiences with that. Unless there is trust and faith, we will not see the signs because we are too busy, too occupied.

BOOK OF THE FIELD

Then we have these great *āyāt* affirming that everything is oriented towards that mysterious, spiritual and electromagnetic field.

وَإِن مِّن شَيْءٍ إِلَّا عِندَنَا خَزَآئِنُهُۥ وَمَا نُنَزِّلُهُۥٓ إِلَّا بِقَدَرٍ مَّعْلُومٍ ۝

And there is not a thing but with Us are the stores thereof. And we send it not down save in appointed measure. (15:21)

Khazā'ina, the plural of *Khazīna* (store/coffer), is the source. Everything has an essence or source from which the blueprints have come about. All that appears to us or comes to us is a measure, only a small amount, of a greater scheme. We have only a few years of life. Our so-called humanity, civilizations, and religions are only 10,000 years at most. It is all short-lived.

And during the occasional epiphanies which you have, your heart opens. It's only a spark. Why doesn't that continue? Why didn't you have that inner spiritual high continuously? It is because of the lower side of us, the survival side, the animal side brings in its darkness. The 'me' and the 'you'.

This is where the curse is and this is where virtue begins. The so-called you is essentially the same as me. You want happiness, you want contentment, you want certainty that *innā'llaha ma'anā* (Certainly, Allah is with us). Everyone wants that.

Wanting to Belong

Wherever you go you want to belong. You already belong to the soul, however. The soul is *min amri Rabbi* (By the command of my Lord). It is already done. That is why the Prophet (S) had this magnificent impact of the highest voltage teaching. The pen of destiny has dried out—*jaff al-qalam*. This does not mean you do not have any freedom. You have *limited* freedom. You have freedom to lift this and put it down, but no freedom to decide that tomorrow at 5 o'clock you'll be as happy as you were a minute ago, for example. You have no control because there are many other factors and forces that come into that formulation that can spoil it. You are feeling very well but you had great expectations of a certain person whom you had held in high regard for all these years who had been kind and generous but suddenly they came and gave you a kick. You'll be very upset. You invested wrongly in human emotions.

And on that issue the Qur'an also reminds us:

$$لَوۡ أَنفَقۡتَ مَا فِى ٱلۡأَرۡضِ جَمِيعًا مَّآ أَلَّفۡتَ بَيۡنَ قُلُوبِهِمۡ وَلَـٰكِنَّ ٱللَّهَ أَلَّفَ بَيۡنَهُمۡ$$

If you had spent all that is in the earth, you could not have brought their hearts
together; but Allah brought them together. (8:63)

You can never be sure of people's hearts. You can help them towards better conduct. You can also be generous, kind, compassionate and all of that, but you can never be sure how their hearts will turn. Because the heart connects with the soul and the soul is *min amri Rabbi*——you never know. You have been kind to people and others and so on and suddenly they turn away from you. Congratulations! You are free from that now. Say 'thank you very much, I was connected and I did what I could and now you have relieved me. Celebrate.

Life on Earth

$$وَٱللَّهُ أَنزَلَ مِنَ ٱلسَّمَآءِ مَآءً فَأَحۡيَا بِهِ ٱلۡأَرۡضَ بَعۡدَ مَوۡتِهَآ$$

And it is God who sends down out of heaven water,
and therewith revives the earth after it is dead. (16:65)

After the earth cooled down——the Qur'an gives us a number of wonderful clues to that process——it had to be sufficient for this consciousness, life consciousness, to occur. So it happened, maybe 600 or 700 million years ago, that one cell that began to oscillate and vibrate and then the first thing it did was perpetuate itself. The *ayah* which says everything in existence glorifies Allah indicates how it did it. It wanted to replicate/continue——to be everywhere.

We are lying to each other. The entire United Nations declaring that we are all one people is not true. We are one *rūh*, yes, but we are perpetuating injustices to others in the name of civilization or country, or something——in the name of the Olympics! They started 400 odd years BC, and were vicious. During the Olympic games people were crushed——it was described as 'war without bullets'. And here we are, these wonderful people, very nice and civilized. But it is all commercial, moneymaking business.

Water is key in the Qur'an. Whenever there are *āyāt* that deal with life, growth, or higher consciousness, water comes into it for it means many things. It means the physical water——H_2O. It means that mysterious entity essential for life. And it is also this mysterious entity that snuffs life out when the floods come. I often wonder whether a flood is more dangerous than a fire, or is it wind, or is it something else? Really we don't know. From whence life comes it also leaves. It is Allah who brings life from the dead and brings the dead out of the living.

Return in Every Moment

وَيَسْـَٔلُونَكَ عَنِ ٱلرُّوحِ قُلِ ٱلرُّوحُ مِنْ أَمْرِ رَبِّي وَمَآ أُوتِيتُم مِّنَ ٱلْعِلْمِ إِلَّا قَلِيلًا ۝

And they ask you about the soul. Say: The soul is one of the commands of my Lord. (17:85)

They ask you about what this *rūh* is, for it is mysterious.

هُوَ يُحْيِۦ وَيُمِيتُ وَإِلَيْهِ تُرْجَعُونَ ۝

He gives life and causes death, and to Him you will be returned. (10:56)

This business of return is perpetually invoked in the Qur'an. You return to Allah. And whenever the *āyāt* are about afflictions and difficulties, it always ends up with:

لَعَلَّهُمْ يَرْجِعُونَ

so as you return. (3:72)

Return to what? To your origin. Who is your origin? It's your *rūh*. Who is your *rūh*? It is a spark from that unfathomable universal overflowing Light.

Ease and Difficulty

$$إِنَّ ٱللَّهَ فَالِقُ ٱلْحَبِّ وَٱلنَّوَىٰ$$

It is Allah Who causes the seed-grain and the date-stone to split and sprout.
(6:95)

This is a prescription. Not one of us, no matter who you are, will be spared from the *Rahma* (Mercy) of Allah, of being constantly given situations of having to choose between difficulty and ease, good and bad. What is 'good'? Good is what is going to liberate you. Good deeds. There are few hundred verses of *'amal sālih* (good actions) in the Qur'an. They are all to do with the little you can do.

The Prophet (S) says if there is an orphan and you have nothing to give, at least give them a little rub on the head, or on the back. Be gentle when somebody is in need.

$$وَأَمَّا ٱلسَّآئِلَ فَلَا تَنْهَرْ ۝$$

And as for the petitioner, do not repel. (93:10)

But if you can do more, it is even better. The more you do the better. Until such time you find that it is all to do with your attitude. It is not so much by quantity, but by your intention.

BOOK OF HUMANITY

This is what concerns us most. For humanity the key issue, the focal issue, is the *nafs*. And there are enough *āyāt* on that. What an amazing thing this *nafs* is. It is a shadow or the presence or the outer manifestation of the *rūh*.

It is the *dunyā* part of the *rūh*.

$$وَنَفۡسٍ وَمَا سَوَّىٰهَا ۝$$

And the soul and He who proportioned it. (91:7)

How did this arise? Again, we have this wonderful *mithāl* (example), or unveiling, of the creation of Adam in the garden:

$$وَإِذۡ قَالَ رَبُّكَ لِلۡمَلَـٰٓئِكَةِ إِنِّي جَاعِلٌ فِي ٱلۡأَرۡضِ خَلِيفَةً$$

And when thy Lord said to the angels, 'I am setting in the earth a steward'.
(2:30)

Khalīfa (steward) is from the root word of *khalaf*—behind. That means the *khalīfa* is behind you. Allah has no physical presence or physicality due to that light. But you and I have a physical manifestation of a *rūh* which is the direct, if you like, connection with the eternal cosmic light. So we are the *khalīfa*, the stewards. We are vicegerents. We are responsible for what we do. So with that comes great honour. That is why we have to honour each other because within us lies this sacred precinct.

Then, for those who follow this route,

$$لَهُمُ ٱلۡبُشۡرَىٰ فِي ٱلۡحَيَوٰةِ ٱلدُّنۡيَا وَفِي ٱلۡأَخِرَةِ$$

For them are good tidings in the worldly life and in the Hereafter. (10:64)

For those who really know that they have sacred presence, that you are a carrier of something which is beyond description in its glory, in its beauty and it is all of the *asmā' ul-husnā* (Divine Names or Attributes). So you have immense caution, immense respect for that. Therefore, for you there is the good news that the garden has been created for you, not you looking for the garden. The state of the garden is in your heart, in your soul.

Adam was created in the Garden, in paradise. That's why we are looking for gardens all the time. The two most popular hobbies in the world for the last 20 years are gardening and fishing. Catching something free. Now the fish, even if somebody gives it to you, you decline because you want to catch it yourself. There are fruits available here but there are some on the tree and you find that even children would like to pick it themselves. You like to be dependent on the unseen. Parents who invite their children to come work with them prefer to go down the road to earn pocket money elsewhere. Why? Because they want to be independent of anything that is discernible. We want to be independent of anything that is materially definable. Independent, that is, until we realise we are totally dependent. On what? On all of these things—on air, water, your body, ultimately, on the Mercy of Allah. We are totally dependent. If we realise our utter dependency then we are Allah's guest. Then we are Allah's friend.

أَلَآ إِنَّ أَوْلِيَآءَ ٱللَّهِ لَا خَوْفٌ عَلَيْهِمْ وَلَا هُمْ يَحْزَنُونَ ۝

Now surely the friends of Allah, they shall have no fear nor shall they grieve.
(10:62)

You have no fear. You are now Allah's guest. Allah is there. But people don't know this.

You will find people who do and they are different. So turn your attitude towards being a guest here and you will find goodness upon good-ness even when you are stopped and deprived. You may find it very good for you. Maybe one day you go without food. It is practise for Ramadan. One day nobody wants you. Wonderful. Sit under a tree and sing——how brilliant! Test the situation where you have no credit cards on you. And nobody wants you and nobody knows you. You know some celebrities pay fortunes in order to end up on a desert island where nobody knows them? Enjoy the anonymity. Look into the meaning behind the situation and you will be inwardly awakened to a perpetual intoxication while maintaining outer sobriety. Do not mix the two up.

مَرَجَ ٱلۡبَحۡرَيۡنِ يَلۡتَقِيَانِ ۝

He has made the two oceans meet each other. (55:19)

The two oceans meet. One of them does not overcome the other. Outwardly you are sober because you have reason, *'aql,* intellect, compassion and accountability. Inwardly you have a *rūh* (soul/spirit). If you do not put the two together, then humpty dumpty has not been put together. Your job, my job, her job, his job, is none other than practising a clearer mind, a sharper mind, and practising unison between the mind and the heart——the heart meaning the soul. The heart is a metaphorical faculty that contains the *rūh* the spirit or the soul. These are words indicating realities——do not fall into the trap of literalism.

The Qur'an is the most difficult book and the most wonderful, because it uses many terms interchangeably. In the last few decades we have been trained to pigeon-hole everything. What is the <u>exact</u> meaning? Referring to the word *nafs* in the Qur'an, it sometimes means *rūh* (soul/ spirit), sometimes it means the 'lower self' as the Sufis call it, the ego. Some other time it means *Insān* (mankind). Don't be fixated. It is a description, a universal unveiling depending on context.

Read your Map

I wish to try to share with you the story of humanity. Our business here is reflected in the following verse:

قُلۡ هَلۡ يَسۡتَوِى ٱلَّذِينَ يَعۡلَمُونَ وَٱلَّذِينَ لَا يَعۡلَمُونَ

Say: 'Are those equal, those who know and those who do not know?' (39:9)

Do you know your map? Do you know the basic blueprint of what you are made of? That you are a self and a soul and contain all attributes, vices and virtues? Have you mastered your ego and has the light of soul taken over your waking consciousness? With this mapping comes knowledge, a cause to celebrate, and enlightenment. Whatever goodness comes to you is from the unseen. Whatever discord, unhappiness, misery is from you not doing the right thing in the right time in the right place.

The Goodness of Affliction

مَّآ أَصَابَكَ مِنْ حَسَنَةٍ فَمِنَ ٱللَّهِ وَمَآ أَصَابَكَ مِن سَيِّئَةٍ فَمِن
نَّفْسِكَ وَأَرْسَلْنَاكَ لِلنَّاسِ رَسُولًا وَكَفَىٰ بِٱللَّهِ شَهِيدًا ۝

Whatever good happens to you is from God, and whatever bad happens to you is from your own self. We sent you to humanity as a messenger, and God is Witness enough. (4:79)

We will all be afflicted by goodness. What is 'goodness'? You suddenly want something or you won a contract, made a lot of money. Now immediately those cousins you've never heard of or the mosque committee come for collection. You wonder what shall you do now? So often you find businessmen deny their success——'not really, I am not really so well off'. Until of course it comes out to the whole world what you are.

So whatever goodness comes to you is an affliction. Whatever badness comes to you it is good for you because it touches your heart. So be careful. Be careful because then it goes into your head, and then the ego grows.

There are many other *āyāt* on that such as 'Know that your wealth and your offspring are a *fitna* (test).' *Fitna* is a test to show who you are. Again, if you go to the origin of the Arabic word, the word *fitna* began when they wanted to know if gold was pure gold or not. It used to be called *dīnārun maftūn* (Dinar of tested purity) Because as you know all currency devalues. From the beginning, from 800 – 900 BC when they began in Libya and elsewhere with coinage—people would clip coins so they gradually reduced and became less and less. *Maftūn* indicates how much gold there is, how 'real' a coin is because the tendency is to dilute it.

So the trials and tests are there to show you who you are. We are like that because we want to be saved. We want to be left in the best of states. The best of states is constant. That constancy belongs to your *rūh*, not to your mind. The mind is to be challenged all the time and it *will* be challenged all the time. If you do not take on a project that is to do with charity or for a higher cause or for knowledge, the roof will come down on you.

Changing Times

In the old social systems, people who attained certain wisdom had of course married much earlier in life. By the time they were in their 40's they'd gone out and discovered what we are sharing now: that you are not who you think you are. So they came back but did not return to the same house. They stayed in the same village where they were given a little hut. Their families came to them and others and they became the gurus or the teachers. But look nowadays at the poor fellow! By the time he is in his 60's, he is often not that popular. Children laugh and snigger because he does not know how to operate the computer. If he lives into his 70's he is totally rejected.

Old people become decrepit. They can't sing because they don't see the music, they don't hear the music. I grew up in an environment where old people were sought-after. As kids we also used to love to be with the great aunts etc., because the lifestyle was so different. They would always be available, they would tell stories and often had some sweets or things to give the children. But you can't go back to it. Now people ask: where is the rest of your family? Lives have changed. We have been atomised. Consumerism has done it to us. Because of its instant power, and the ability to help us do things immediately, we cannot go on the rampage against consumerism. That is why so-called spiritual seekers become business people. They become very clever. They claim if they have more money, they will build more mosques. And you go to the mosques to find them empty or the Imam is screaming. It is like this, and yet we have to always be aware of the blueprint that you are both heavenly and earthly.

Soul Consciousness

The soul is really beyond basic animal consciousness, basic restricted consciousness, or conditioned consciousness. As a human being I am a conditioned consciousness. I have the past, a history, I have a culture, I have a genetic heritage, colouring, hair, this and that. But I know that as a conditioned consciousness I exist because of the Supreme Consciousness whose light is in me. The more I refer to it the more I am loyal. Why do we like loyal people? It is because if you are loyal to your heart, if you are loyal to your spirit, if you are loyal to Jesus in you, or the light of Muhammed in you, whatever name you like to give it, if you are loyal to that then your calibration is more constant. Then you do not have to constantly apologise and go back and forth—although it is wonderful to apologise for any occasion because it humbles the ego, the lower self, because you are not only that. That only exists to remind you of that which I call lasting happiness. For the soul is ever happy.

Intentions and Actions

$$ٱذْكُرُواْ ٱللَّهَ ذِكْرًا كَثِيرًا$$

Remember Allah with much remembrance. (33:41)

This is a prescription.

$$كُلُّ نَفْسٍ ذَآئِقَةُ ٱلْمَوْتِ$$

Everyone shall taste death. (3:185)

You are owned by what you have earned. You are what you intended and what you have done; and if you don't see it and know it now you will know it at death. All you will have is that——pure light covered by what you intended and what you had done. That is why if it was murky you will regret it because you cannot soar into the other realm of consciousness.

Contentment and Return

$$\text{يَـٰٓأَيَّتُهَا ٱلنَّفْسُ ٱلْمُطْمَئِنَّةُ ۝ ٱرْجِعِىٓ إِلَىٰ رَبِّكِ رَاضِيَةً مَّرْضِيَّةً ۝}$$

But as for you, O tranquil soul. Return to your Lord, pleased and accepted.
(89:27-28)

O self that is now certain that there is a path, a map, a purpose in this life, a return to that other closer energy of *Rubūbīya*, Lordship, content that you are doing what you can. Every instant is then fresh. You are aware, you are accountable, you are living it. Therefore, you are already entering into eternal life. The moment is self-continuous forever. You are already experiencing an aspect of eternity, the edge of eternity.

So *rādiya* means content that you're aware and present and *mardīya* means you know everything else is present with you. If not, apologise and move on. Do not leave a lot of baggage behind. Don't leave a lot of bad karma behind. Especially if the other person whom you have wronged decides to die. That is a terrible thing for you. Catch them before they die. Otherwise, how can you make up for it?

The Need for Like-Minded Company

Allah says:

$$\text{كَتَبَ عَلَىٰ نَفْسِهِ ٱلرَّحْمَةَ}$$

He has inscribed upon Himself mercy. (6:12)

The whole thing is based on the original energy of goodness and *rahma*.

قُلْ إِن كُنتُمْ تُحِبُّونَ ٱللَّهَ فَٱتَّبِعُونِي يُحْبِبْكُمُ ٱللَّهُ وَيَغْفِرْ لَكُمْ ذُنُوبَكُمْ

If you love Allah, then follow me, Allah will love you and forgive your faults.

(3:31)

The word love is very important. In the Qur'an it comes in different ways. If you truly love Allah, then follow His Prophet. Allah will love you. 'Follow me' meaning what? Hang your ideas on me, your aspirations, and connect with somebody who is ahead of you. For your health you go to a physician who is better qualified than you. For your mind you go to somebody who hopefully knows how the mind works—though how can there be psychology without sociology, as you are both, an individual and a community. So for spiritual awakening, for awakening to the higher consciousness, you also need to be with people who have gone ahead of you. Not because they are greater or lesser but you need that specific tuning. If you want to study anything, you go to where the masters are. You have to find them. So it says if you love Allah, follow me. Allah will love you. Allah already has created out of love. Love is the glue that keeps diverse entities close together.

THE BOOK OF THE GARDEN

وَعَدَ ٱللَّهُ ٱلَّذِينَ ءَامَنُوا۟ مِنكُمْ وَعَمِلُوا۟ ٱلصَّٰلِحَٰتِ لَيَسْتَخْلِفَنَّهُمْ فِى ٱلْأَرْضِ كَمَا ٱسْتَخْلَفَ ٱلَّذِينَ مِن قَبْلِهِمْ وَلَيُمَكِّنَنَّ لَهُمْ دِينَهُمُ ٱلَّذِى ٱرْتَضَىٰ لَهُمْ وَلَيُبَدِّلَنَّهُم مِّنۢ بَعْدِ خَوْفِهِمْ أَمْنًا

Allah has promised to those of you who believe and do good that He will most certainly make them rulers in the earth as He made rulers those before them, and that He will most certainly establish for them their religion which He has chosen for them, and that He will most certainly, after their fear, give them security. (24:55)

Allah has promised if you have faith, trust and perseverance, grooming your lower self, leaving it more behind, being more and more the higher self, your *rūh*, ready to leave this world any minute with no anchor, without anger, content without reason for contentment, just being. If you have that then the garden is at your feet.

جَنَّـٰتٍ تَجْرِى مِن تَحْتِهَا ٱلْأَنْهَـٰرُ

...gardens beneath which rivers flow. (66:8)

There are no less than a dozen *āyāt* that relate to how you cannot see how these fruit trees and vegetation in paradise are fed. It is unseen. All of it is unseen. It's all little photons that come in, start a process and nutrition begins.

وَرِضْوَٰنٌ مِّنَ ٱللَّهِ

...and contentment from Allah. (3:15)

And the ultimate joy that overflows is greater that all of these. There are again many parables and examples. There are some magnificent *āyāt* in the Qur'an which I consider part of the gnostic Qur'an, such as 'And those who are in the ultimate garden, they cry':

رَبَّنَآ أَتْمِمْ لَنَا نُورَنَا

Our Lord, perfect for us our light. (66:8)

Oh Allah, 'Complete our light', meaning they no longer seek more gardens, for they have already discovered the garden here. You have already had the best of relationships, you have disappeared into your nothingness in your prostration, in your meditation, in your reflection. You know that you are a tiny little speck of a magnificent cosmic consciousness. You know that. You have tested it. You have seen it. You want only that now. You don't want more gardens. It's already past, you've been through that childhood.

$$\text{هَـٰذَا ٱلَّذِى رُزِقْنَا مِن قَبْلُ}$$

This is what was given to us before. (2:25)

We have already tasted all of this. We have already seen it on this earth. You have already tried your best to create a *Janna* state. *Janna* is a state of heart.

$$\text{لَا يَسْمَعُونَ فِيهَا لَغْوًا وَلَا تَأْثِيمًا ﴿٢٥﴾}$$

There, they hear no vain speaking nor recrimination. (56:25)

No agitation. Before creation, there was no agitation. One of Allah's names is *As-Salām*. There is only peace. But here now we talk of *Salām, Salām* (peace) and we kill each other. Because we do not have the map. Without the map, you won't be able to drive along the appropriate highways. And the ultimate highway is the constant referencing with your spiritual GPS. There is only One, none other than that, so watch out!

Humanity is Your Family

Don't waste your time. Don't waste energy and don't be a nuisance to others by wheeling in the effigy of your piety. There is nothing more ugly than spiritual superiority. That is why we have come to an age where the great masters and teachers among Sufis are now moving into another phase. Everybody has to be responsible for their *khalīfa*-dom in them. Each one of us must hold ourselves to account: What are you doing? Why are you wasting this? Is it the right time? What about the other people that are poorer? The whole of humanity is your family. This is the advantage of the Qur'an. Until the advent of the Qur'an it was not very clear, that all of humanity is the same. It is only 20 years ago that we discovered physiologically, biologically, genetically that it is really true: we are all from the same genetic origin. Yet this amazing Qur'an was revealed 1,400 years ago. Inwardly, we are the same, we are of a *rūh* aspiring to be with its ultimate ocean of all the souls, the *arwāh*. in which potentially everybody is the same. But on earth every day is different. Tomorrow is not the same as today. No two fingerprints are the same. Outwardly our colour, our shape, our attitudes, our minds are different. Inwardly, we are exactly the same. We all want happiness, joy, contentment, and certainty. Certainty about what?

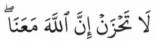

Be not sad (or afraid), surely Allah is with us. (9:40)

Huzn implies fear and despair. Fear is for what is lost and cannot be retrieved. Do not ever have any concern or fear. You know Allah is with you, Allah is within you. Allah's *nūr* is there but you are looking somewhere else. That is the issue.

CHAPTER THIRTEEN

Illumination – The Purpose of Human Life

Given in 2014

- Gratitude
- The Battle of Dualities—the Thrill of One
- The Illusion of Normality
- A Brief History of Religion
- From the Horizontal to the Vertical
- From Religiosity to Spirituality
- Consciousness
- Illumination
- Connectedness and Continuity
- Purpose
- Prescriptions

وَإِن تَعُدُّواْ نِعْمَةَ ٱللَّهِ لَا تُحْصُوهَا

And should you count the favours of Allah, you could not enumerate
them. (16:18)

Every time we think it is better and better so he has been the string. He has
been an anchor, a reference, a constancy.

GRATITUDE

Gratitude, gratitude, gratitude!!!

لَئِن شَكَرْتُمْ لَأَزِيدَنَّكُمْ

When you are in gratitude, I increase you. (14:7)

The more you are in a state of contentment and gratitude, the more you are
accessing higher zones of consciousness, the more you have insights, until
you are no longer curious about insights. Outer sight will lead to insight.
Outer senses will lead to the inner senses. Outer action will lead to inner
intention and then you go beyond wonderment. You go past all of that.

THE BATTLE OF DUALITIES—THE THRILL OF ONE

Initially you seek thrills, joy, whatever name you like to give it, until there is
nothing other than that thrill. Initially in your life you are in a fog. All of the
battles and quarrels are because of dualities battling each other, strangling
each other. Dualities cannot remain together because there is only One. So
the countless dualities of up and down, he and she, good and bad—the
endless tragedies—are the norm of the *dunya* (world). Because the truth
behind all of these dualities is One. There is none other than that. Therefore,
if you refer to the One, then you find all these dualities are simply there to
stop you wandering even further. Otherwise, it all amounts to a miserable

274

biography. This is the way it is.

THE ILLUSION OF NORMALITY

People nowadays are addicted to their cell phones. What does this mean? It represents connectedness. He wants to be connected. He may miss the opportunity. He may miss the job. He doesn't know that he is going to miss somebody who has just died in the hospital. A third of the time people are in miserable weddings, another third in hospitals and a third in burials. What sort of life is that? I won't exchange it with anyone of you. This is where it ends up. No space, no time left, for bliss, for beingness.

Everyone is in a misty fog. You are hoping to see the light behind it. A time may come if you are fortunate enough, if you have worked enough, if you have abandoned enough, if you have let your ego die enough, then you will see light. In the background you will still see a bit of mist. So it is the reverse of what you and most people consider to be normal. It's actually very abnormal, not normal.

The norm is that your heart is illumined while the shadows are in the backdrop. They won't afflict you. You realise they are shadows. But these shadows manifest in the mind and assert transient reality.

Let us turn to some thoughts on seven concepts with you before some prescriptions.

A BRIEF HISTORY OF RELIGION

Along the timeline or scale of human history, 'religion' is basically a very recent occurrence. It is human nature to want to explore and discover. To 'dis-cover' is to remove the cover. Go beyond. So from babyhood we are crawling and putting all kinds of whatever in our mouths, mud and everything, and the poor mothers run around trying to avoid a health disaster.

Discovery, knowledge, exploring, expanding, are drives within us.

We all want to discover what is behind the façade. This is what religion is. It is to find out what is behind death, what comes after this? What is the other side of the ocean? What is beyond the stars? What is the beginning or the end?

Thousands of years ago, maybe 150,000 to 200,000 years, the frontal lobe of the human brain grew and something happened to this being in terms of consciousness, possibly with the increase of proteins in the diet. The metaphorical being, Adam, was born. Whatever happened over a few thousand years this species prevailed. By about 30,000 years ago, homo sapiens more or less developed in parallel with other hominids and replaced the other species that were cousins. And now after these 30-40,000 years, especially after the emergence from the rift valley, what we have is this so-called common humanity. In our gene pool there may be a few traces from the Neanderthal people—they say it's about 3 percent Neanderthal genes. But it doesn't matter. We are all truly made of the same template.

Religion was what came after, when we started asking 'What is real? Who is God?' Names were given. Then about 12-15,000 years ago the physical, literal congregations for worship began to take assemble, especially the equivalent of what we term pilgrimage or Hajj. In the North West of Asia and many other locations, people would congregate at a certain time of the year and go through certain ritual motions because everything was vibrating, everything was oscillating. And then by 6-7,000 years ago came the advent of prophethood. Previously there had been thousands of shamans, many who were seers whose inner senses were more developed and predominant.

Then you have these dramas of the flood. Most nations with a recorded history or early history had a flood. We had the flood of Noah, for example, and Gilgamesh before and so on. These beings arose who combined supreme consciousness, God consciousness, with human consciousness and while they belonged to a tribe slowly they expanded. Their teachings began to exhibit a certain universality, rather than just limited to their own group.

So the rise of religion occurred very recently in human history.

And it developed with thousands of these beings complementing each other. Since the languages and cultures were different, you find certain differences in the outer expressions. The inner message is almost all the same. There is a light or something equivalent to that energy within every human being, and it is sacred and it is divine, but you and I and he and she also exhibit all the animal inheritance of evolution. Within us is contained in our understanding all of these things.

Take the inheritance of altruism, for example. The altruism of an ant is similarly inherent. When there is a flood, they were here. When there is quite a lot of rain right next to you some ants would come up in order to be a bridge and die for the others to cross over them. It is the preservation of the species that drives them. It isn't a matter of selflessness, as if suddenly an ant decided, 'I'm going to be a heroine or a hero and I'm selfless.' It is inherent. It is in us. That is worshipping *Al-Bāqī* (the Eternal), so anything that occurs wants to continue.

This also applies to your thoughts. Watch out for your thoughts! Anything that occurs will want to continue. It is like telling somebody not to think and yet they start thinking. If someone tells you 'Don't think of a button', when you have never thought of a button, but once somebody tells you not to think of a button, you cannot help thinking of it.

Though the history of religion is very recent it has emerged from a long social tradition, which was essentially horizontally networked: it was formed of families, clans, neighbours, and local communities. And then we had kings and priests in league with each other. It was perfected around six thousand years ago with agricultural settlements and then the Pharaohs in Egypt made it into a totalizing doctrine that all knowledges were the preserve of the priests and the priests were accountable to the Pharaohs. Essentially it was about survival and a prime tool was the nilometer (used to measure water levels and sediment in the Nile River), measuring water levels to work out whether it was going to be a good year in terms of agriculture so that taxation could be adjusted.

The same thing was repeated over and over: priests and kings or rulers were in league. The rulers stayed in their palaces with their luxuries and the priests harangued and frightened people about hell or promising them paradise if you gave them a talisman, as long as they paid for it of course.

FROM THE HORIZONTAL TO VERTICAL

This luxury is over! This is what I wanted to share with you. The luxury of 'horizontal connectedness' has almost come to an end. It is now you and your bank account, you and your car key, you and your password, and you and your own self. Whatever that may be.

After a thousand years, the horizontal connectedness has suddenly shifted to being a vertical one. There is no one that does not have a special issue on their hands, a special drama. Whether it is the health of an aunt or a wayward child or a lost cousin or wallet you have left somewhere. Whatever the issue, no one is spared.

This is Allah's *Rahma*. If you do not see Allah's hand behind it then you are fantasising. There is none other than One Doer, none other than One Governor. Because horizontally we have gone more and more astray, having become more and more structured, more and more in competition with each other as to whose religion is more important, who has more mosques and so on. The Muslims in the last 40-50 years have built no less than 40-50 enormous monumental mosques, some of them in very beautiful architectural styles, mostly by international architects—a lot of French and Italians and others. But most of them are also empty. Most of them are tourist sites. Go and see. Go to the big mosques in Morocco and the others. They visit because they are thirsty. They want to wake up. They want to get out of the prison of this illusion that 'I am this entity' so they think this is a place of sacredness. I will certainly discover God there. What sort of a funny God it is that He is more in one place than another? How strange.

وَهُوَ مَعَكُمْ أَيْنَ مَا كُنتُمْ

And He is with you wherever you may be. (57:4)

But most do not think, listen, contemplate or understand.

This is how it is. It is an evolutionary process. It has taken many thousands of years and in the last hundred odd years the population has quadrupled and instead of being half a billion we are now over 7 billion. But in that is also a good motivation for us to find new resources, new ways of minimising waste. There is goodness in every situation, in every affliction.

إِنَّ مَعَ ٱلْعُسْرِ يُسْرًا ٦

Verily, with every difficulty there is relief. (94:6)

FROM RELIGIOSITY TO SPIRITUALITY

Now we have the word 'spiritual'. This is an extreme case. 'Spiritual' implies against or in parallel with the material; in other words it is physics/metaphysics. It is Makka/Madina. Makka is only light, there is nothing. Go inside the Ka'ba and see.

Another way to understand spiritual/material is earthly/heavenly, or conditioned consciousness/pure consciousness. We could list several hundred of these parallel complementary dualities. You have the material—it exists in space and time. You and I and every one of us is an *insān* (being) caught in space and time.

The spiritual side, however, is not subject to space and time: it is pure consciousness, Supreme Consciousness. Earthly is relative, spiritual is absolute, if you like. Bear in mind each of these terms has in it a certain dimension balancing itself against the other aspect of the same thing—vices and virtues. Both vice and virtue are of the same origin. If you do not see the vice of your *nafs*, of your ego, wanting to assert itself, you are nowhere near the door of all the virtues of your *rūh*. The two go together.

279

CONSCIOUSNESS

In terms of human consciousness, it evolves over many years from birth to death. One begins at around 3-5 years-old, as patterns of referencing in the mind develop. With teenagers they begin to experience through acion how interaction with the outer world can take place to heighten or improve consciousness. As an adult you are at the edge of higher levels of consciousness, which lead to pure Divine Consciousness.

Many people I've met in their 40's are still three or four years old. They are 'growing' because the ego is growing. Nothing wrong with that when you are a child. But by the time you are in your mid-30s, if the ego has not been crashed, or thrashed every now and then, maturity may not happen. If you are in your 60's or 70's and still want to be in control, you still have not yet caught a glimpse as to who is truly in control.

Everything is controlled within its perfect ways. You and I are given a tiny little leeway to exercise something. So the question arises: do you have any power or is it all decreed? Is it all fated or do you have any influence? It is both. You have a little power—to lift this or stop that. But no power to be sure that in the next two hours I am going to be around, healthy or happy. We cannot tell. There are millions of other factors that will come in.

We have been given a complete story of this issue, of the extent to which we have freedom of action and to what extent we don't. Repeatedly, we have been given the similar and different facets in the Qur'an. For example, Sura Āl-Imran, ayah 154 (3:154).

ثُمَّ أَنزَلَ عَلَيْكُم مِّنْ بَعْدِ ٱلْغَمِّ أَمَنَةً نُّعَاسًا يَغْشَىٰ طَآئِفَةً مِّنكُمْ وَطَآئِفَةٌ قَدْ أَهَمَّتْهُمْ أَنفُسُهُمْ يَظُنُّونَ بِٱللَّهِ غَيْرَ ٱلْحَقِّ ظَنَّ ٱلْجَٰهِلِيَّةِ يَقُولُونَ هَل لَّنَا مِنَ ٱلْأَمْرِ مِن شَىْءٍ قُلْ إِنَّ ٱلْأَمْرَ كُلَّهُۥ لِلَّهِ يُخْفُونَ فِىٓ أَنفُسِهِم مَّا لَا يُبْدُونَ لَكَ يَقُولُونَ لَوْ كَانَ لَنَا مِنَ ٱلْأَمْرِ شَىْءٌ مَّا قُتِلْنَا هَٰهُنَا قُل لَّوْ كُنتُمْ فِى بُيُوتِكُمْ لَبَرَزَ ٱلَّذِينَ كُتِبَ عَلَيْهِمُ

ٱلۡقَتۡلُ إِلَىٰ مَضَاجِعِهِمۡۖ وَلِيَبۡتَلِىَ ٱللَّهُ مَا فِى صُدُورِكُمۡ وَلِيُمَحِّصَ مَا فِى قُلُوبِكُمۡۗ وَٱللَّهُ عَلِيمٌۢ بِذَاتِ ٱلصُّدُورِ ﴿١٥٤﴾

Then after the setback, He sent down security upon you. Slumber overcame
some of you, while others cared only for themselves, thinking of God, thoughts
that were untrue—thoughts of ignorance—saying, "Is anything up to us?"
Say, "Everything is up to God." They conceal within themselves what they do
not reveal to you. And they say, "If it was up to us, none of us would have been
killed here." Say, "Even if you had stayed in your homes,
those destined to be killed would have marched into their death beds."
God thus tests what is in your minds, and purifies what is in your hearts.
God knows what the hearts contain.

And there are no less than 40 other occasions in the Qur'an which touch upon this. You have been given some opportunity but that is about it. And that opportunity leads to the next and so on and so on until such time you find yourself, as we do now, in the current situation in the so-called Muslim world. They are in a valley whose topography they cannot even understand.

From Outer Authority to Inner Authority

How did we land up in this situation? One step at a time, you've slipped, slipped again, and then you are finished. That is why you need a reference point. You need outer *and* inner references. Outer references for a child are parents, family, and relatives, and later on, colleagues, friends, and others. Later on comes one's own methods of realignment, such as prostration (*sajda*) and disappearance into one's own *rūh*.

Later in life if you do not access your own inner authority then you are missing your wholesomeness. Initially you see authority as outer to begin with—the parent, the teacher, the policeman, the judge—and later on, as an intelligent person, you reject it, even though you may hide that rejection.

You may not announce your rebellion but you are secretly rebelling because you want to discover your *inner* authority. This is Allah's design. You are hooked by that design and stamped with it.

$$\text{أَلَسْتُ بِرَبِّكُمْ}$$

Am I not your Lord? (7:172)

You are completely enslaved by that Absolute Perfection. So you will not accept anything less. So that is what 'spiritual' means. We are *all* spiritual.

You are a spirit caught in the body which is alien. This is why while you are in exile here, no matter how much health, wealth, love, affection, goodness you have, it is not enough, because it is still within space and time. Your reality is non-spatial, non-temporal—your soul, your *rūh*, your essence. Call it any name you want. Get out of this trapping of names. You need to have names as a kid. But once you have grown up, you understand that there are the three phases: first it is all sensory. I prefer this chocolate, that toy. Soon the next phase develops which is conceptual and mental. Doing good, making a difference, fulfilling your needs. The third is transcendence, where you are no longer in the field of duality or plurality. You have left that behind—for a while, which means the power of life in you is without shadow.

Death before Dying

The prophet said, 'Die before you die.' What does this mean? We like to quote well-known traditions and give them certain, if you like, sanctity but do not live them. It means let your inner ego profile die. Be humble. Then you'll be alive.

Once you become arrogant then it is finished—'*izzat*' (pride) they call it, you see why. In Pakistan it's all '*izzat*'. We are a proud people! Proud of what? If it is *rūh* (soul/spirit) it has no pride. *Rūh* is totally utterly content in bliss. It is your *nafs* that occasionally becomes proud and occasionally gets squashed. You are vacillating. Half an hour ago I was very well because everybody pampered me and they thought I was great, but now nobody looks at me, I am depressed. Everybody has become bipolar!

ILLUMINATION

Another issue here is 'illumination'. They are no less than 60 or 70 terms used nowadays to represent this. Whether it's illumination, enlightenment, awakening, or realisation, all it means is a very simple thing: that you have flipped from conditioned consciousness into the zone of pure consciousness or higher consciousness.

There is no such thing as claiming: 'I am now a realised being, so everybody has to be on their knees.' When you or a group of people acknowledge that somebody is awakened or illumined it only means that they have flipped to a higher field of consciousness. However, Supreme Consciousness is universal—call it God consciousness, pure consciousness, or universal consciousness.

It's like a venn diagram. There is a large circle, Supreme Consciousness, and several smaller ones. The first of them is conditioned consciousness—You and I. Part of it derives its energy from Supreme Consciousness. In other words, when we are in prostration or have observed 2-3 days of meditation, we are semi-human. When we emerge someone might say, 'Oh there is light on your face.' The second smaller circle is when one strand emerges from conditioned consciousness and supreme consciousness. In some ancient cultures they would signal days in which they were completely disturbed, such as not putting on a tikka mark if they have had a death or emotional shock. This signals that their consciousness has been compromised. We are humanity but within us is the light and the life of divinity. They are just touching each other. That is the state of the novice.

And a third circle is just developing a bit more until 'enlightenment', which is that this so-called 'You' consciousness, your individual consciousness, is within this sphere of supreme consciousness. And that is what is called illumined. It is not the end, it is the beginning of full awakening.

You have a life. Life is consciousness of consciousness that I am conscious that I can move my hand, I am alive, I like to sleep, I am hungry, I am ill, or I have heard something that is agreeable or disagreeable. Life is that awareness of awareness in an individual sense. If this individual life of mine does not lead me to supreme consciousness, so that I know Life is forever, I have squandered it. Very simple.

Life is Capital

You are losing your only true capital, which is life itself. That is why:

$$وَٱلْعَصْرِ ۝ إِنَّ ٱلْإِنسَٰنَ لَفِى خُسْرٍ ۝$$

By time, verily Man is in loss. (103:1-2)

At all times you are in the process of losing your capital. All your capital is the knowledge that you have nothing. But you are already within that zone from where everything descended. You are included, not excluded. So, if your life does not lead you to knowledge, not just understanding, but knowing it and experiencing it, then it doesn't matter.

$$أَلَآ إِنَّ أَوْلِيَآءَ ٱللَّهِ لَا خَوْفٌ عَلَيْهِمْ وَلَا هُمْ يَحْزَنُونَ ۝$$

Now surely the friends of Allah, they shall have no fear nor shall they grieve
(10:62)

So you have no fear anymore. Fear is self-preservation. When you know there is no self, there is only *rūh*, there is no need for preservation. Nor will you grieve, because that implies regret or remorse.

Here we have a key issue: You are a conditioned consciousness aiming to fall within God consciousness, supreme consciousness, eternal consciousness. Once you are established in that, the process is filtered through infinite layers and levels of that.

The Prophet (S) says there are 70,000 layers of light between your light, the invisible light, and Allah. You move on and on. Once you fall into supreme consciousness, then you are the humblest, you are in total gratitude because now you have nothing in your hands but you are in the Hand of Him Who has brought everything. You are Allah's guest.

When we go on Hajj we recite 'labbayk, Allahumma labbayk'. Oh Allah I am hear for you, at your service! Yet for most of us it is a lie. Over 1,300 years ago when they asked Imam 'Ali, 'Was it a big Hajj?', he replied, 'No. This year there was a lot of noise. but there were only three who made *hajj*—myself, my camel and one man from Yemen.'

The Qur'an reminds us in repeated ways:

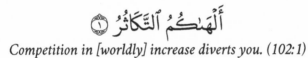

Competition in [worldly] increase diverts you. (102:1)

So many of us are dead people. They are themselves *maqābir* (tombs). You are in a cemetery. They are all dead but on two legs. It is the generosity of nature. Allah (SWT) says if I am going to hold you accountable for your stupidity, there'll be no life left. He is sparing them in case. Why is it you want longevity? To live longer? Do you want to punish people more? They have suffered all these years, another 10 years 20 years, now they are old, the eyes have gone, the senses have gone, no more romance, they are all crippled.

CONNECTEDNESS AND CONTINUITY

Why do we want more? Because we want continuity. Why do you love habits? Because it is a matter of continuity: they give you the illusion that things won't change.

There are two most fundamental forces in life: one is connectedness—connect, connect, connect! We have a lot of friends. Or we think we do—on Facebook you have several thousand! You know it's a lie. You know at the

285

end of the party everybody is miserable because there is a dark shadow: you know it will end—unless that connectedness is based on the supreme Connector, the Source of all glues, which is sacred Love. What is Love other than universal glue? And there are thousands of different types of glues. But the ultimate connector is Allah.

How to get to that? You need to climb the ladder. Love others, share, care, help. Why is it that in all religious, and spiritual, all esoteric paths, there is an emphasis on serving? To reduce your ego and open your heart, which is the home of your soul, so it becomes transparent. The light of your soul begins to shine. But if your ego is in the way, if your heart is full of pus and lust and fear and anxiety, it won't work. Who are you kidding?

There is a technology, an inner technology. We go for course after course to learn a language, to learn courses of all other applications but not the spiritual app. Every other app is on but not the spiritual one.

PURPOSE

Then there is the word 'purpose'. Purpose is the outcome. What is it you want? You want to have the best relationship with people. You want to be the ultimate voice, the ultimate sound in truth. Who is speaking? To what extent is it your miserable ego, your *nafs*? And to what extent is it the true voice of *Haqq*. Admit it from your heart. There is a huge difference if it is from your heart, for then it has *baraka* (blessing).

وَمَا رَمَيْتَ إِذْ رَمَيْتَ وَلَـٰكِنَّ ٱللَّهَ رَمَىٰ

And you threw not when you did throw but Allah threw. (8:17)

There are no less than 40 ayahs on this topic.

قُلْ هَلْ يَسْتَوِى ٱلَّذِينَ يَعْلَمُونَ وَٱلَّذِينَ لَا يَعْلَمُونَ

Say: 'Are those equal, those who know and those who do not know?' (39:9)

What a difference! It is not the same if you are really *yadullah* (hand of Allah).

We have a lot of that culture but not enough lived and not experienced enough. Once you have experienced that it is not you who is doing, then whatever you are trying to do you will wait. You don't want to be the doer as the so-called 'you'. You wanted to be 'potentised' by the One and Only Source. Then it works.

Purpose is ultimate, the pursuit, the end. What we want is happiness and joy and that is the nature of your *rūh*. You cannot attain happiness. You cannot attain knowledge. You cannot attain deity, clarity, and spirituality. You can get out of the shadows. Get out of misery through 'no'. Your job is to say no! The 'Yes' is already there.

Toxic *Dhikr* of the Self

Lā ilāha illā'llah shines. So just take away what isn't. This is *takhliya* (emptying out). People on the spiritual path do not spend enough time emptying out. They come in and have a nice spiritual gathering and it's very uplifting. But actually it is the worst because you have not taken the weeds out before you have sweetened the ground; you have put on more fertiliser so all the weeds will come out stronger. It is worse if you don't do *takhliya*, empty out, before you engage with *tahliya* (sweetening). There are hundreds of such examples in our traditions. One of the most frequent things Shams of Tabriz said: 'you know I am your friend if you feel I have been the hardest upon you. If you think I have been like your enemy that means I love you and why I love you because I see me in you and I want you to be liberated from the so called you'. But then it becomes another Sufi talk, another Rumi talk. It doesn't work.

You cannot sweeten something that's bitter. That's why *dhikr* (invocation) for most people doesn't work. It can actually make things worse. Because they have not emptied out, they are suddenly putting a lot of nutrients into a ground that is toxic.

Being Human

The other word is 'human'. We are both. We are humanity and we are divinity, which is sacred. We are self and soul. And we are the most evolved in creation in terms of souls. So our souls know all of the other thousands of *arwāh* (souls). The *rūh* (soul/spirit) of the rosebush is not the same as that of the apricot tree.

PRESCRIPTIONS

I want to end up very briefly with giving you prescriptions. I have given you a good description of space, time, levels of consciousness, and the 2 C's: everything in life is based on these two forces which continue, continue forever because your *rūh* is forever and the other is to connect, connect, connect. These are the two forces. Everything returns to those two forces.

Know You are a Self-Soul

Most of your children, teenagers especially, are rebellious because that horizontal way of life is over. Now it is vertical. They cannot accept the horizontal because it does not give them that instant connectedness. They want to connect now and it can only be with the highest. This is good news! In 2-3 generations the basic model of the family will change. Society, community and nations will change. It will be much more based on vertical movements with some horizontal.

In the past our links and networks, in terms of awakening, had been horizontal and more parochial, but with little verticality. If there were instances of occasional verticality, somebody who had awakened, we preferred them dead. That is why a dead saint is always better than a living one because you can make money out of the tomb. Go to the sub-continent and see. He doesn't answer back, he doesn't eat, he also doesn't become ill—really much better. A dead saint or Imam is far more useful than a living one.

The prescription is: please realise that you are, we *all* are, oscillating and vibrating between supreme consciousness and personal consciousness, which is based on my past, my mind, fears, anxiety and presence—so you are a 'self-soul'.

Phases of Consciousness

In the beginning, every one of us are like children, we are novices. Every time you do *Allahu Akbar* in your *Salāt*, if it is not fresh as though you have not said it before, renew your *wudū'*. You have not sealed yourself. It must be fresh, ever now, scintillating.

The next level is the middle 'muddle'. After 10, 15, 20 years you are entering into that higher level of ego, identity and personality. Here is where you really need to begin to practise self-discipline and self-awareness. The parents have done their biological duty and the upbringing is done. The influence of your biological history begins to be challenged as you question the authority of your parents and the past. The inner drive to grow and expand nudges you towards resentment of their authority as you seek your own. You are exploring your own connectedness vertically. This middle phase is an exercise in achieving balance.

The last phase of the 'awakened state' or 'higher consciousness' is mostly when you really need a guide. Early on you can muddle through and you can change. But later on it is like people on a skiing slope. Initially as you learn to ski you fall repeatedly. The snow is still soft and your neighbours show you that if you want to stop you need to lean forwards, not back—as such it is quite counterintuitive. Earlier on a guide is helpful but not essential. At the intermediate level you also don't need one as long as you follow reason, but when you are about to truly wake up, it is then that you need to watch out. The danger is spiritual materialism and self-important pietism. The turban gets bigger and the religious paraphernalia also get bigger.

Earlier on, to have an ego like a gangster is fine, but later on, after a few epiphanies, people start wondering how come the gangster is quoting *āyāt*, spouting *hadīth*, one after the other—as if he has gone to Bukhara with

Bukhari (the famous compiler and editor of hadīth). Suddenly he seems awakened. And yet, an air of hypocrisy hangs around him. This is why many millions of young people, especially of eastern background but brought up in the west, do not accept this situation. I see in this the best of news. But we also need to provide them with a map, which I have been trying to share with you. A new and better kind of guidance for the modern era.

In summary every living entity is a combination of a mysterious divine spirit or soul, which provides life and is eternal and boundless in nature, and a physical identity which connects the divine attributes of the soul with all earthly, transient realities and shadows. With intelligence and faith you will realize how descripitons will provide seeds of prescriptions. IF you dwell on either, they are two facets of the same reality. One descrfibes in the other leads of responsibility and drive. From the inert to the dynamic and moving. All emanates from the unseen, and that is how *ghayb* and *shahada* are connected,

In the words of Ibn Mashish:

Plunge me in the oceans of Oneness,
pull me back from the mires of tawhīd.
And drown me in the source of the ocean of Unity
so that I neither see nor hear nor am conscious nor feel except through it.

GLOSSARY OF TERMS

'Abd Allah	Servant of God, worshiper.
'Abd al-waqt	Slave of the moment; inhabiting the present with full awareness, intentionality, and presence.
Ahadīya	Oneness.
Akhlāq	Character, moral behaviour.
'Ālim	Person of knowledge; scholar.
'Amalan sālihan	Good deeds, virtuous actions.
Amīr	Leader.
Asmā' ul-husnā	Most Beautiful Names or Divine Attributes.
Āya	Sign; verse in Qur'an; pl. *āyāt*.
'Azza wa jalla	Possessor of Complete Glory and Majesty.
Banī	Children of, as in Banī Adam, children of Adam.
Baraka	Blessing.
Barzakh	Interspace barrier, isthmus between seen and unseen; *barzakhīya* is a neologism.
Bātin	Inner, hidden, unseen.
Bismillah	In the name of Allah
Da'wa	Invitation to faith and practise; calling.
Dhawāt	Essences; pl. of *dhāt*.
Dhāt	Essence.
Dhawq	Taste, direct experience.
Dīn	Pathway of Islam; life-transaction.
Dīnār maftūn	Tested Dinar in terms of purity.
Du'ā'	Supplication, calling on Allah.
Dunyā	This world, the material world.
fana' fi'l-Shaykh	Annihilation in the shaykh: a technique specific to certain Sufi *tarīqas* in which the image of one's spiritual master is visually held in the mind's eye in meditation.
Farq	Differentiated.
Fī sabīli 'llah	In the way of God, for the sake of God.
Fitra	Original pattern of human nature.
Fitna	Trial, affliction, test.
Fu'ād	Heart, inner heart that does not lie.
Fuqarā'	Poor, in need of God, ascetics on the path.
Furqān	Differentiation, criterion, discrimination, discernment.
Ghafara	To cover in forgiveness. *Al-Ghafūr*, the Divine Name of Forgiving.
Ghayb	The Unseen hidden world.
Ghufrān	Forgiveness.

Hadīth qudsī	Sacred or divine tradition; revealed by God to the Prophet Muhammad (S).
Hāfidha	Faculty of recollection, memory.
Hakīm	Wise person, sage; doctor.
Halāl	Permissible.
Haqīqa	Reality.
Haqq	Truth.
Harām	Forbidden.
Hiss al-mushtarik	Combining sense which integrates all other inner senses.
Hudhūr	Presence.
Huzn	Despair, sadness, combined with fear.
'ibāda	Worship, devotion.
Idhn	Permission.
Iftār	Fast-breaking.
Ihsān	Excellence, virtue, goodness.
Ikhlās	Sincerity, purity, unity.
Ilhām	Intuition, inspiration.
'ilm	Knowledge, science.
Īmān	Faith, belief.
Imtiyāz	Standing out, distinguish.
Inqilāb	Revolution, turning; see *qalb*.
Insān	Humankind, man.
'Ishq	Longing, love, passion, yearning.
Jabarūt	The realm of Divine Omnipotence.
Jaff al-qalam	The pen (i.e. ink) has dried. A phrase indicating Divine decree.
Jalāl	Majesty.
Jam'	Gathered, gatheredness.
Jamāl	Beauty.
Janna	The Garden, Paradise.
Jihad	Struggle, utmost effort.
Khalīfa	Representative, steward, vice-gerent; who stands in the place of.
Khaneqah	Sufi hall or centre.
Khayāl	Inner faculty of imagination. Not creative imagination, but that by which the experience of reality is rendered real in shape and form and duration.
Khayr	Goodness.
Khazā'ina	Stores, coffers of wealth; pl. of *Khazina*.
Khumul	Obscurity, being unknown; lethargy.
Kufr	Denial of reality.
Kun	'Be!'; the command to come into existence.
Lāhūt	The realm of Divine Nature.
Lā jadala fi'd-dīn	There is no argument in religion.
Lutf	Subtlety, grace, gentleness.
Madhhab	School of law.

Madrasa	School; religious school or seminary.
Maftūn	Tested, tried, proven.
Malakūt	Divine Dominion & angelic realm.
Maqām	Station, in contrast to states.
Mardīya	Pleasing; from *radīya*, to please.
Mash'ar	Centre of pilgrimage.
Miḥrāb	Prayer niche; lit. the place of battle with self.
Min amri rabbī	From the command of my Lord.
Miskīn	Destitute, impoverished, needy.
Mithāl	Metaphor, simile; pl. *amthāl*.
Mīzān	Balance; the balanced tension in which the entire creation is held; justice.
Mulk	Created Realm; this world.
Mu'min	Believer.
Murīd	Student, follower; lit. desirer.
Mutafakkira	faculty of contemplation and reflection.
Muwaḥḥid	unified or unifying; from *tawḥīd*, unity.
Nafas	Breath.
Nafl	Supererogatory, of act of worship beyond the obligatory.
Nafs	Ego self, lower end of spirit.
Nafs al-mutma'inna	The self that is certain.
Nifāq	Hypocrisy; *nafaq* is a tunnel with two entrances.
Nifāq ul-khafī	Hidden or subtle hypocrisies.
Ni'ma	Blessing.
Nūr	Light.
Nūr al-anwār	Light of lights.
qadā'	Decree, fulfilment of completion.
Qalb	Heart; see *inqilab*.
Qibla	Direction of prayer, orientation of worship.
Qudra	Power, ability.
Rabbānīya	Divinity, Lordship.
Rādīya	Content, pleased.
Rahma	Mercy, grace, compassion.
Rak'a	Cycle of prayer, bowing.
Rātib	Litany.
Rīyāh	Scents, breezes; related to *rūh*.
Rūh	Soul spirit.
Sahāba	Companion, friend.
Sajda	Prostration, also known as *sujūd*.
Salāt	Prayer.
Shāhid	Witnesser.
Sharī'a	Outer revealed laws of the path; lit. the road or way.
Shaytān	Satan; that entity or energy that causes one to diverge from the path. *Shayātīn*, pl.

Shirk	Association, ascribing partners in power to God; essentially breaking the unity underling existence.
Sibghat Allah	The colour of Allah, taking on the 'colours' of Allah symbolically, reflecting His Attributes.
Shahāda	The visible or seen world.
Sīra	Life story.
Siyāsa	Politics, the where-to and how-for of interaction with others; judicious policy.
Sulūk	Wayfaring; the etiquette of journeying.
Sunna	Custom or tradition, way; often synonymous with custom of the Prophet Muhammad (S)
Tajrīd	Isolation, seclusion for inner orientation.
Takāthur	Abundance, plenty.
Taqwā	Awareness of God in all states and moments; fearful awareness, god-consciousness.
Tarbiya	Upbringing, grooming; discipline.
Tarīqa	Way, Sufi path, complementary to *sharī'a* and essential to realising *haqīqa*.
Tawakkul	Trust and reliance on Allah.
Tawhīd	Unity, Oneness.
Tawhīd al-af'āl	Unity of Action.
Ummatan wasata	Middle Nation; people of the middle way, poised between the seen and unseen.
Urs	Wedding; union
Wahba	Bestowal of gift.
Wahdānīya	Oneness.
Wāhid	One, singular; integrated.
Wāhima	Evaluative faculty; attribution of meaning & subjective value to objects or experiences.
Wahm	Illusion, fanciful conjecture. *See wāhima.*
Walī	Friend of Allah; awakened being.
Waslān	Arrival.
Wazīfa	Daily practise of a prescribed form.
Wudū'	Ritual ablution in preparation for prayer.
Yawm al-qiyāma	The Day of Resurrection, of final account.
Zāhir	The manifest, outer, seen.
Zuhd	Doing without, hence asceticism.
Zujāja	Glass, glass lamp.

DIVINE NAMES

Al-Ākhir	The Last
Al-ʿAlīm	The All-Knowing
Al-Awwal	The First
Al-ʿAẓīm	The Mighty
Al-Bāqī	The Everlasting
Al-Bātin	The Hidden
Al-Ghafūr	The Forgiving, Clement
Al-Ghanī	The Rich
Al-Hayy	The Alive, Ever-Alive
Al-Karīm	The Generous
Al-Qawī	The Strong
Ar-Razzāq	The Provider
As-Sabūr	The Patient
As-Salām	The Peace
As-Samad	The Independent, Self-sustaining
Al-Wāsiʿ	The Vast

Milton Keynes UK
Ingram Content Group UK Ltd.
UKHW010728110124
435856UK00005B/228